NARRATIVE, EMOTION, AND INSIGHT

Studies of the Greater Philadelphia Philosophy Consortium

Michael Krausz, editor

Already published:

Joseph Margolis, Michael Krausz, and Richard Burian, eds.,
Rationality, Relativism and the Human Sciences
(Martinus Nijhoff Publishers, 1986)

John Caputo and Mark Yount, eds.,
Foucault and the Critique of Institutions
(Penn State Press, 1993)

Joseph Margolis and Jacques Catudal, eds.,
*The Quarrel Between Invariance and Flux: A Guide for
Philosophers and Other Players*
(Penn State Press, 2001)

Michael Krausz, ed.,
Is There a Single Right Interpretation?
(Penn State Press, 2002)

Paul Thom,
The Musician as Interpreter
(Penn State Press, 2009)

Edited by
Noël Carroll
and
John Gibson

NARRATIVE, EMOTION, AND INSIGHT

The Pennsylvania State University Press
University Park, Pennsylvania

Library of Congress Cataloging-in-Publication Data

Narrative, emotion, and insight / edited by Noël Carroll and John Gibson.
    p.   cm.—(Studies of the Greater Philadelphia Philosophy Consortium)
Includes bibliographical references and index.
Summary: "A collection of essays, written for this volume by leaders in the field, that
study the emotional and cognitive significance of narrative and its implications for
aesthetics and the philosophy of art"—Provided by publisher.
ISBN 978-0-271-04857-4 (cloth : alk. paper)
ISBN 978-0-271-04858-1 (pbk : alk. paper)
1. Discourse analysis, Narrative—Psychological aspects.
2. Narration (Rhetoric).
3. Emotions in literature.
4. Literature—Philosophy.
5. Description (Rhetoric) in art.
6. Intuition in literature.
7. Language and languages—Philosophy.
I. Carroll, Noël, 1947– .
II. Gibson, John, 1969– .

P302.7.N3666   2011
808'.0014—dc22
2010051381

Contents

    Susan L. Feagin   154

9   Imagination, Fiction, and Documentary
    Derek Matravers   173

    List of Contributors   185
    Index   187

Acknowledgments

We would like to thank Michael Krausz, Patrick Alexander, and Kathryn Yahner for their help, editorial and otherwise, in bringing this book to publication. We would also like to thank Gerald Vision, Marc Moreau, Margaret Moore, the Free Library of Philadelphia, and the Greater Philadelphia Philosophy Consortium for making possible the conversation out of which the book grew. Finally, we owe a great word of thanks to Ronald Moore, who offered uniformly perceptive comments and helpful suggestions on the final draft of the volume.

Introduction

John Gibson

The idea for this book grew out of a conference held at the Free Library of Philadelphia on October 17, 2006. The conference, generously funded by the Greater Philadelphia Philosophy Consortium, was titled Fiction, Emotion, and Insight. John Gibson organized it, Peter Goldie gave the keynote, and Noël Carroll, Susan Feagin, and Richard Eldridge each contributed papers. Though only one of the papers in the present volume can claim that conference as an ancestor (Eldridge's), the discussion we started that day concludes in the following pages. It was an auspicious beginning. Noël Carroll was the last speaker of the day, and before he was able to finish presenting his paper, two men in suits entered the auditorium and began hurrying the audience away, denying us every conference's birthright: a closing discussion of the day's papers. The men in suits, it seemed, needed to do a security sweep to prepare the auditorium for that evening's event: a senator from Illinois was in Philadelphia to give a speech. While the senator spoke in the expropriated auditorium, we philosophers took shelter in a cozy South Philly restaurant (the storied Snockey's, for those in the know), where we had the discussion that should have taken place at the library. Despite the drama, it was by all counts a very good day. The senator eventually got the White House, and we eventually got a book.

The conference participants were asked to prepare papers exploring what they took to be promising new approaches to two of the showcase debates in contemporary aesthetics: debates concerning how works of fiction can be sources of knowledge (hence the inclusion of "insight" in the title) and debates concerning the nature of emotional responses to fiction (hence the inclusion of "emotion" in the title). It turned out to be a good thing that the participants uniformly ignored part of the question put to them. All of them ended up saying little about fiction and opted instead to concentrate on narrative. We were immediately struck by how much this seemed to blow life into these debates, if not always by showing how to solve the old problems, then certainly by opening up fresh and fascinating topics of discussion. We were onto something, we thought, and so we decided that the conversation should migrate from the auditorium to a collection of original, new essays.

With this in mind, the question we put to the contributors to this volume was the following: "Discussions of the nature of emotional responses to art and of the cognitive value of art tend to concentrate almost exclusively on the problem of *fiction:* how can we emote over or learn from objects we know do not exist? How will aestheticians be able to say something new about these questions if they instead frame the matter in terms of having *narratives*—rather than, or in addition to, fictional characters and events—as the objects of emotional and cognitive attention?" We did not want to have nine essays all on exactly the same topic, so we asked contributors to use this question as a point of departure, encouraging them to follow whatever line of thought it prompted, as long as it led them back to at least two of the three terms of the title: narrative, emotion, and insight. The hope was to produce a book that as a whole would demonstrate how this approach opens up new possibilities for addressing fundamental issues concerning the emotional, ethical, educative, and cognitive value of art. Since analytic aesthetics has for some time paid significantly less attention to the "worldly" significance of art in favor of discussions of the nature of fiction and the imagination, we thought a volume such as this would be poised to play a role in the shift toward discussions of the cultural relevance of art that is becoming increasingly central to current work in contemporary analytic aesthetics.

We were delighted, then, when we began to receive the chapters and saw what this approach had produced. The first thing we noticed was that the discussion moves seamlessly between all the major arts—music, theater, film, poetry, and the novel—and so placing emphasis on narrative does not by any means restrict one to a consideration of just the literary arts. The second thing we noticed was the extent to which this approach puts aesthetics in touch with other areas of philosophy. One of the successes of the huge amount of work analytic aesthetics has put into the study of fiction is that it has given aestheticians a stake in important debates in metaphysics, epistemology, and the philosophy of language. We were very pleased to see that deemphasizing (though not ignoring) the role of fiction in art in favor of a discussion of narrative preserved these points of contact while at the same time forging new links to cutting-edge work in ethics, the philosophy of self, and moral psychology. The impression we had, and one we hope readers will share, was of a collection of nine essays that maintain a sense of unity and common purpose while exploring a rich diversity of art forms and philosophical issues.

One thing we found especially interesting is that thinking about literature from the standpoint of narrative rather than fiction makes the passage from art to life not only easy but natural. In a sense this was to be expected. To think about the importance of narrative is to consider the nature and significance of *stories,* and we tell stories not only when we write literary works but also when we attempt to make sense of ourselves and our lives. Stories are, in this respect, a currency of communication common to art and life. And it is easy to see why this should be so. According to most common definitions of a narrative, a narrative just is the recounting of a story: narratives are, in more technical parlance, "representations" or "presentations"—depending on one's preferred vocabulary—of stories. But the way a story is told matters immensely. To tell a story a certain way is to invest it with a kind of significance, with a *point.* If framing one's thinking about literature in terms of the problem of fiction emphasizes what is "unreal" in literature, framing it in it terms of narrative highlights the endless points of contact between the two: the vast array of ways we use stories to forge a precise sense of the meaning and import of those experiences, practices, and pursuits that we find in both fictional worlds and in ours.

At this point the philosophical debate on the nature of narrative can become rather technical, as can those on the nature of emotion and knowledge, all of which are discussed in the following chapters. We've organized the chapters so that the basic philosophical concepts and terminology at play in the debates this volume explores are introduced and defined gradually. The opening essays offer an excellent foundation in the philosophy of narrative and related areas, and the reader who has little familiarity with the fields of philosophy this volume touches on would do well to read the chapters in order. Readers with a basic background should feel welcome to skip around. But on the whole the contributors have managed to avoid the sort of critical and theoretical jargon that can make philosophy inaccessible, and so any educated reader who is curious about the role of stories in literature and life will find herself at home here.

We open with Peter Goldie's rich and wide-ranging "Life, Fiction, and Narrative." The issue Goldie explores is one that has long interested philosophers: what gives a life coherence and, ultimately, meaning? An answer philosophers increasingly give to this question is that it is a matter of possessing a narrative of a certain sort: the ability to see our lives as a kind of story, a story, one hopes, not only in which we have a starring role but of which we are also in part *authors*. Goldie's interest in this chapter is to assess the considerable skepticism this idea has met. The specific worry Goldie considers is that when we conceive of a human life in narrative terms, we are prone to "fictionalizing tendencies," as he puts it. The sort of cohesion, closure, and meaning that narrative makes possible in literary works is, according to this worry, dangerously distorting when removed from a literary context and applied to real life. In his characteristically sophisticated style, Goldie acknowledges the dangers of these fictionalizing tendencies, and he sets himself the task of showing us what is nonetheless reasonable and indeed helpful about thinking of our lives in narrative terms. Goldie concludes with a brief but important conjecture about the source of these fictionalizing tendencies: they arise from our need, psychological at root, to find meaning in a world without much of a point. If Goldie is right, this marks perhaps the most basic difference between our lives and the lives of fictional characters: in the end they, but not we, exist for a reason, even if we are all, at some level, creatures of narrative. This makes it clear that one must proceed with caution when looking to literature to make sense of life.

Berys Gaut's subtle "Telling Stories: Narration, Emotion, and Insight in *Memento*" looks at a narrative strategy that has become increasingly influential in contemporary film and literature: backwards narration. Through a detailed analysis of the film *Memento*, Gaut argues that the ways in which backwards narration reverses normal temporal sequencing highlight unique possibilities for both cognitive and emotional engagement with stories. A striking aspect of Gaut's essay is his argument that *Memento* not only presents claims about reality, it also partially *confirms* these claims. This is an original and provocative move: even those sympathetic to the idea that art bears cognitive value often think that the one thing art never does is provide any sort of confirmation for the claims it apparently makes about reality. Gaut develops his argument by exploring in detail how *Memento* implicitly makes three claims about the nature of memory, and how the very narrative structure of the film—the way in which it weaves its particular story—can be seen as attempting to establish the truth of these claims.

Noël Carroll's "Philosophical Insight, Emotion, and Popular Fiction: The Case of *Sunset Boulevard*" continues with the theme of the epistemological significance of narrative art. Like Gaut, Carroll believes that films can put forward veritable claims about reality, but, contrary to Gaut, he sees the relevant act of confirmation as occurring in the minds of the members of the audience and not in films themselves. For Carroll, films like *Sunset Boulevard* do not merely prompt philosophical thought; they can be seen as actually *doing philosophy*. And they do philosophy by in effect functioning as philosophical thought experiments, leading viewers to draw a conclusion about some state of affairs by prompting and guiding philosophical reflection on the fictional scenarios of the film. Carroll's account of this shows that narrative art often enlists both the mind and the passions in the service of philosophizing, and thus that the form of insight it can offer is exceptionally rich, neither narrowly emotional nor cognitive but a melding of both.

The next four essays examine the various roles narrative can play in making possible certain forms of self-understanding. In "Thick Narratives" John Gibson explores a resemblance certain kinds of narrative bear to "thick concepts," as philosophers, following Bernard Williams, call them. Like thick concepts (concepts such as *courageous, vile,* etc.), these "thick" narratives are descriptively rich, so much so that they are able to convey a very precise sense of the *character* of the object of narration, whether that object is a self or a society. In literary works these thick narratives are often used to explore the ethical structure of our cultural practices and the kinds of experiences, relationships, and, ultimately, lives these practices make possible. This, Gibson argues, reveals a novel way to defend the idea that literary works bear significant ethical value.

Amy Mullin's "Narrative, Emotions, and Autonomy" considers how our encounters with literary narratives can help us to achieve a kind of personal autonomy. The brand of insight literary narratives offer is, for Mullin, bound up with a kind of sentimental education in which we acquire an insight into the nature of our emotions and thus into what we basically value and find significant. Through a careful reading of various novels, Mullin documents how this enables us to see what it is we really care about and then to be capable of cultivating relationships in accordance with this knowledge, resulting, in this respect, in a kind of freedom. Like Goldie, Mullin is careful to point out that as a resource in the search for autonomy, literary narratives also present certain dangers, and hers is ultimately a sensible position that is mindful of the worries philosophers express about narrative conceptions of selfhood and agency.

Richard Eldridge's "Narrative Rehearsal, Expression, and Goethe's 'Wandrers Nachtlied II'" explores the way in which narrative art can help us respond to and overcome many of the uncertainties and anxieties of modern life. He develops a notion of "narrative rehearsal" according to which narrative arts foster the development of reflective capacities that make available to us new possibilities of feeling and thinking. Like Mullin, Eldridge is especially interested in how art plays a role in our search for autonomy, by helping us to achieve awareness of who we really are and then to become self-determining in accordance with this awareness. To illustrate how art makes this possible, Eldridge offers a probing and nuanced reading of Goethe's "Wandrers Nachtlied II" (Wayfarer's Night Song II). The poem, Eldridge argues, leads the reader through a process of "working through" not only its content but also the emotions and moods it provokes, and this process in turn brings about a kind of clarification of the self, of what we love, value, and desire. Goethe's poem, and art more generally, "achieves a kind of fullness of both attention to life and expression of that attention" (Eldridge, 126).

In "Rubber Ring: Why Do We Listen to Sad Songs," Aaron Smuts turns from the literary arts to music. Smuts's concern here is especially with *sad* songs, those that typically feature narratives about lost love, separation, missed opportunity, regret, hardship, and all other manner of heartache. Many of us are drawn to sad songs in moments of emotional distress. The problem Smuts identifies is that sad songs do not always make us feel better; on the contrary, they often make us feel much worse. So the philosophical question becomes, why do we listen to sad songs? Smuts makes the surprising and fascinating claim that we seek out sad songs partly to *intensify* distress. We do this, he argues, because it helps us to reflect on situations of profound personal significance. According to Smuts, this is hardly irrational or paradoxical, contrary to what some philosophers have said about the apparent delight we take in painful art. "It is perfectly human. We need to feel in order to understand what we care about" (Smuts, 149). Like Mullin and Eldridge in their accounts of literature, Smuts makes a case for the importance of certain forms of narrative art for prodding us to clarify what we really care about.

The discussion turns to drama in Susan Feagin's "Discovery Plots in Tragedy." If tragedy is painful, it is often because of the kind of truth it delivers, those terrible truths that reveal to us, as they did to Oedipus, something about the contingency and uncertainty of life. Feagin's interest is to explore in detail this form of insight tragic stories offer. She develops an original account of what she terms "discovery plots" and their role in certain tragedies. Discovery plots are those in which the protagonist acquires knowledge of some fact—often a tragic fact—about herself, thereby occasioning a kind of self-discovery that will become "the fulcrum of the plot, the central event around which the plot revolves, and not just another element in the unfolding of the action" (Feagin, 156). One of the most interesting implications of Feagin's careful treatment of discovery plots is that it helps us to see the extent to which the tragic form has survived in contemporary theater, contrary to the idea that in the culture of late modernity a genuine work of tragedy is impossible. Through a subtle reading of Wajdi Mouawad's 2005 play *Scorched*, Feagin shows that discovery plots remain the engine of some of the most powerful works of contemporary theater.

The volume concludes with Derek Matravers's elegantly argued "Imagination, Fiction, and Documentary." Matravers here exposes as mistaken one of the central reasons philosophers provide for believing that our emotional responses to fiction are different in kind from our responses to "real" characters and events. The commonly proffered reason is that emotional responses to narrative fictions lack the motivational element often thought to be essential to genuine emotions. For example, when we see someone in harm's way in "real life," we act, *we do something,* at least if we are genuinely moved by that person's plight. Yet when viewing the same sort of thing on, say, the silver screen, we remain in our seats, perhaps gasping, but if we are sane we do not attempt to intervene. This severed link between emotion and action has led many philosophers to think that there is something exceptional and odd about our emotional responses to narrative fiction. Matravers's response to this assumption is gracefully simple, but its implications are far-reaching. The absence of motivation, Matravers argues, has little to do with the fact that we are witnessing a fiction and everything to do with the fact that we are regarding a *representation.* Were the representation of something real, say of a war in some corner of the world, we would not suddenly find ourselves driven to act. Regardless of whether the content is fictional or nonfictional, we would look odd, indeed crazed, if we tried to interact, in the required sense, with a *representation:* a portrait, a film, or a novel. Matravers develops his argument with a sophisticated set of distinctions and observations that, if correct, will require a rethinking of precisely what is so paradoxical in the so-called "paradox of fiction."

Life, Fiction, and Narrative

Peter Goldie

Many of us (at least many of us in the West today) often think about our lives, or about part of our lives, through narrative thinking. This kind of thinking, involving the narrative sense of self, is often said to be malign, or at least deeply problematic, on the grounds that our lives are not appropriate to narration. This is said to be so even if we accept that narrative thinking, in particular narrative thinking about the past, can be both true and objective, in spite of being perspectival. And it is also said to be so even if we put to one side the use of narrative thinking to weave Walter Mitty–like fantasies and daydreams, in order to avoid facing up to what is commonplace and tawdry about us and our lives; we might well do that too, but if we do, then they are simply that—fantasies and daydreams.

The concern, rather, is with narratives of our lives of the kind which we ourselves believe to be true, so that, if we relate them, we invite our audience to believe (rather than to make-believe) what we are saying. What is malign about these narratives, it is said, is that they tend to be dangerously close to fictional narratives, and in particular to fictional narratives of the kind one finds in literature.[1]

I will begin by saying, very briefly, what narrative and narrative thinking are. I will then go on to discuss four ways in which narratives of our lives tend to be dangerously close to fictional narratives—what I will call *fictionalizing tendencies*. I will discuss how each of these fictionalizing tendencies manifests itself as part of our psychology (although no doubt more empirical work is needed here). And I will also discuss what is, so to speak, the other side of the coin in certain well-known philosophical accounts of the role of narratives in our lives: these too tend, in one way or another, to assimilate real-life narratives to literary narratives. Inevitably, my discussion will not draw too sharp a distinction between these two sides of the one coin.

The thrust of my argument will be to acknowledge that these four fictionalizing tendencies are dangerous. However, I will at this point diverge from some other philosophers who point out these dangers, and who then go on to criticize the role of narrative in our lives and to criticize the philosophers who are its proponents.[2] I deny that the fictionalizing tendencies vitiate entirely this role of narrative, which has, I believe, a central place in our thinking about our past, our present, and our future, expressed in the narrative sense of self. Nevertheless, acknowledging the dangers of the fictionalizing tendencies, coming to an understanding of what these tendencies are, and understanding the dangers that they involve will help us to avoid their excesses. An analogy might be helpful here to indicate the thrust of my argument. It might be said that we are often self-critical to excess, and that this is a bad thing. However, one can acknowledge these dangers of excess and then go on to insist that knowing about the dangers will help us to avoid them and to be self-critical as we should, in which case self-criticism can be a virtue, or at least an executive virtue.

Finally, in the last part of this chapter, I will consider whether these four fictionalizing tendencies have a common source in our psychology. Speculatively, and very provisionally, I will suggest that they have a source in our need for meaning in a bleak, impersonal, disenchanted world.

Narrative and Narrative Thinking

A narrative about people (the only kind of narrative with which I will be concerned) will have three characteristic features. These three features arise through the process of what Paul Ricoeur nicely calls "emplotment" in his subtle and complex reading of Aristotle's *Poetics*.[3]

First, a narrative has *coherence,* in the sense that it reveals causal and other connections to the audience in a way that a mere list or chronicle does not.[4] Emplotment, as Paul Ricoeur puts it, "extracts a configuration from a succession" (1983, 66). Secondly, a narrative is *meaningful,* in the sense that it enables the audience to understand how the actions of those who are internal to the narrative could have made sense to them at the time. And thirdly, a narrative has *emotional import:* it reveals the narrator's external evaluation of, and emotional response to, what happened, from the ironic distance that his external perspective allows.[5] People narratives will typically have this feature, but, as Noël Carroll has argued, not all such narratives need give rise to an emotional response: some narratives can be boring and affectless, in which case the appropriate emotional response is null.[6]

Narrative thinking is simply thinking through a narrative. So, in narrative thinking about people, the representation of the sequence of events, the episode, is a mental representation—a sequence of thoughts that can have coherence, meaningfulness, and emotional import. With this sense of representation in place, one can see immediately that a narrative need not be narrated in the sense of being written down, spoken, or otherwise represented in a publicly available medium. It can simply be thought through by a single person. So a thought-through narrative is publicly narratable but need not be publicly narrated.

It will be important for what follows that, on this account, emplotment is a matter of degree: a narrative can have these three characteristic features to a greater or a lesser extent. At the more minimal end, a narrative will be little more than a bare causal explanation, simply making sense of why something happened by appeal to prior events. For example, I might explain why I was late by reference to the unusually bad traffic. As we move up from the minimal end, we come to the places where the fictionalizing tendencies begin to surface. What are these tendencies?

The First Fictionalizing Tendency: We Plot out Our Lives

We often think of ourselves, in a way that is perfectly natural, as plotting the course of our lives. Through narrative thinking, we make plots and plans for the future, form hypothetical imperatives, and so on, often based on narrative thinking about our past. For example, I might think back on how I made myself late for the meeting yesterday by dawdling at home checking my e-mails, and as a result resolve that tomorrow I will not dawdle. Or I might think through in narrative form what it might be like to work in some different part of the world, and as a result look out for job opportunities there, and then take up one of the jobs as I planned to do.

So there is this connection between narrative and life: as the psychologist Jerome Bruner puts it, life "is constructed by human beings through active ratiocination, by the same kind of ratiocination through which we construct narratives" (2004, 692). And when we come to "act out" our plots and plans, there is a sense in which it is true to say that what we are "acting out" is an "enacted narrative." Alasdair MacIntyre, making more or less the same point as Bruner, says that narrative is "the basic and essential genre for the characterization of human action" (1981, 208). But the dangers readily creep in at just this point when, taking MacIntyre again, it is said that we are the *authors* of our lives: "What I have called a history is an enacted dramatic narrative in which the characters are also the authors" (215).

So what precisely is wrong here? First, there is an exaggeration. There is much in our lives that we do not plan and cannot plot out or control in an author-like way. For one thing, as MacIntyre himself acknowledges, we are, at best, "coauthors" with other people who constrain our lives, and it would be an illusion to think otherwise; "Only in fantasy do we live what story we please" (213). Moreover, many of our actions are constrained, not only by other agents, but by non-agential forces; this is a point to which I will return shortly.

Secondly, life is not a narrative: to elide or to identify the narrative and the life which is narrated is to lose the distinction between representation and what is represented.[7] And in this sense there is an equivocation of the notion of author when we pass from narrative (what, for example, is written) to life (what is written about) (Ricoeur 1992, 160).[8] We are not literally the authors, or even the coauthors, of our lives.

The Second Fictionalizing Tendency: Finding Agency in the World Where It Is Not

We have a tendency to find too much agency in the world. We have seen this already in the first tendency: to explain too much of what happens by appeal to our *own* agency. Greg Currie and Jon Jureidini have a very nice discussion of this second, wider phenomenon, in which they say that it is "a near universal feature of the cognitively normal population" (2004, 410). For example, we often look for a "meaning" for some natural event or accident, imputing it to an action by some other person or persons, or by some kind of nonhuman agency, such as gods, ghosts, and monsters (409). We explain what is sheer happenstance as the product of a conspiracy theory. We attribute symbolic "meaning" to things in nature, such as finding a four-leaf clover or seeing a solitary magpie. And when something goes wrong in our lives, especially when the same misfortune occurs several times, we see ourselves as being, as Freud put it, "pursued by a malignant fate"; "it was never meant to be," we sigh in despair (1984, 292).

Currie and Jureidini ask why this tendency is characteristically narrative in form. Their explanation, which I find persuasive, is that narratives, which are concerned with causal and other relations between particular events—being what R. G. Collingwood called "idiographic"—are especially suitable for representation of agency. Moreover, narratives are expressive of agency and mind; if an event is described in the narrative, then we assume that it is of significance, so what is related has a coherence that the real world does not (Currie and Jureidini 2004, 417–19); again, this is a point which I will come back to.

Now let me briefly say what is—quite obviously—wrong with this tendency, and then go on to say why it is a *fictionalizing* tendency. What is wrong with it is that it misrepresents the way the world is: it represents non-agential events as being actions, initiated and controlled by agents of some kind. As we have just seen, this manifests itself in part in conspiracy theories and the like, and in part in finding something agential in the mere forces of nature. Collingwood puts very well what is wrong with finding agency in mere nature, as part of his essential contrast between a natural process and what he calls a historical process; the former is a "process of events" and the later a "process of thoughts." He then continues:

> There is only one hypothesis on which natural processes could be regarded as ultimately historical in character: namely, that these processes are in reality processes of action determined by a thought which is their own inner side. This would imply that natural events are expressions of thoughts, whether the thoughts of God, or of angelic or demonic finite intelligences, or of minds somewhat like our own inhabiting the organic and inorganic bodies of nature as our minds inhabit our bodies. Setting aside mere flights of metaphysical fancy, such an hypothesis could claim our serious attention only if it led to a better understanding of the natural world. In fact, however, the scientist can reasonably say of it, "Je n'ai pas eu besoin de cette hypothèse," and the theologian will recoil from any suggestion that God's action in the natural world resembles the action of a finite human mind under the conditions of historical life. (1946, 217)

Why, then, do I call this tendency a *fictionalizing* tendency? The answer is that this tendency to attribute agency in ways that is not appropriate to real life is in fact *appropriate* to much fiction and literature. In other words, what is wrong in interpreting real life is right in interpreting fiction and literature. Children's stories are replete with ghosts, gods, monsters, and magic. Fairy tales and myths involve explanations of natural disasters (floods, plagues, and so on) as the intentional product of some nonhuman agent—as part of what Collingwood calls a historical process rather than a natural process. Conspiracy theories are the very stuff of spy novels and thrillers. The predictions of the witches in Shakespeare's *Macbeth* and of the gypsy in Verdi's *Masked Ball* have to be understood as being accurate predictions of what will happen. The mud and fog at the start of Dickens's *Bleak House* must be understood as symbolizing the chaos of the world of the novel (Lamarque 2007, 124), as must the fog that pervades Marcel Carné's film *Quai des brumes*. And Victorian novels are full of coincidences explained by the intervention of an active god. David Goldknopf, the literary scholar, having given several very nice examples of coincidences from Dickens, Brontë, and elsewhere, goes on to say this:

> In the cases cited, the author has deliberately *emphasized* the element of fortuitousness, and for the same reason: to liberate a crucial incident from the realistic network of causality. Far from evidencing sloppy plotting, the fortuitousness is as legitimate a part of the work's formal design as are the hovering angels in Renaissance religious paintings. In each instance the author has floated his characters away from the order of mundane connections to bring them under the direct control of an *au courant* God. The purpose of the coincidence, in short, is to make God a character in the novel. (1969, 44)

The Third Fictionalizing Tendency: Narrative Thread and the Desire for Closure

The third fictionalizing tendency follows on nicely from the second, and in particular from one of the properties of narrative that Currie and Jureidini point towards to explain the phenomenon of overattributing agency, namely the property of being expressive of agency.

First, there is the tendency to think of one's life as having an unbroken narrative thread which holds it together, so that what I have called the narrative sense of self is, as MacIntyre puts it, "a concept of a self whose unity resides in the unity of a narrative which links birth to life to death as narrative beginning to middle to end" (1981, 205).

This idea is deeply problematic—and remains so even when we have clearly distinguished the narrative of a life from the life that is narrated. To begin with, the narrative sense of self, as I conceive it, will be massively "gappy": from our childhood onwards, large tracts of our lives will be lost to us for all sorts of reasons, most notably of course through failures of autobiographical memory, perhaps just because of the passage of time, or perhaps because of some traumatic event which caused memory loss. So, under those circumstances, even if there were a unity of some kind, it is not narratable by the agent, or, quite possibly, by anyone else.[9]

Secondly, the difference between the unity of a real life and that of a fictional life is not just a contingent difference, for, as Bernard Williams has argued, "fictional characters have a special unity that no real life can have, that the end of them is present at their beginning. . . . their wholeness is already there, and ours is not" (2007, 7). This is true even of Sartre's Roquentin in *La Nausée:* because he is a character in a novel, Roquentin's life necessarily cannot represent the sheer contingency that Sartre wants; his wholeness is already there, including the contingencies.[10] And this special unity that fictional characters have could not apply to any real life, even the life of someone whose narrative is planned out from the beginning, as might be the life of a young prince who is the chosen heir to the throne in an ancient dynasty, for example.

And thirdly, the beginning and the end of our lives are a matter of happenstance. One's life can end just like that. In contrast, when we talk of the "beginning," "middle," and "end" of a narrative, these are *already* narratized notions: there is already something "fitting" about them in the narrative. Noël Carroll points out that for Aristotle's *Poetics,* these terms are "technical." Discussing the end of a tragedy, he says, "Aristotle is saying that the sort of narrative representation he is anatomizing concludes in the precisely appropriate place just as a piece of music with closure finishes on exactly the right note" (Carroll 2007, 3).

We might draw back from the idea of there being a narrative thread to a whole life, to a more restricted idea of there being a narrative thread to a *part* of a life, where that part is, so to speak, selected because of its narrative appropriateness. For example, we might think that there is a clear narrative thread to the events involved in someone's getting his "comeuppance": from a hubristic beginning, her nemesis was, somehow, just as it should be.

We can usefully relate this to Noël Carroll's (2007) insightful discussion of narrative closure, and what he calls erotetic narratives. An erotetic narrative is one that raises questions and provides answers, and that thus sustains narrative closure. In our engagement with erotetic narratives, we have a desire for all substantial questions to be answered, and accordingly, he says, there is something not right about a narrative that leaves a major question unanswered. The law of Chekhov's gun is familiar here: if the theater curtain goes up to reveal a gun on the wall of the room, then at some point during the play something must happen which involves the gun; otherwise the question "What is that gun doing here?" will fail to be answered.

As Carroll rightly argues, the desire for narrative closure is appropriate for those narratives that are created "for aesthetic consumption" (2007, 15). And Carroll's view is that this link, between narratives created for aesthetic consumption and the desire for narrative closure, is a normative link. For he finds confirmation of his thesis "in our ordinary critical responses to certain narratives": we feel a certain frustrating incompleteness because "answers to certain questions . . . which were implicitly promised were not delivered."[11] Carroll draws a contrast here with narratives of real life, saying that narrative closure "rarely figures in the stories folk tell their mates about their day at work" (2007, 15).

It is certainly no more generally true that a narrative of a day at work has narrative closure than that a narrative of a whole life does. Often a narrative of an incident in a day at work will raise more questions than it answers: for example, if I tell you the story of how my boss came into my office to ask to see me tomorrow about my promotion prospects, we will both be in suspense until tomorrow comes. But *sometimes* a narrative of part of one's life, told to a friend, is, and *ought to be,* erotetic. For example, if I begin by saying to you, "Let me tell you about an amazing escape I had last week," the narrative will fail to achieve its promised closure if I end the story with myself teetering on the brink of disaster.

What, then, is the dangerous fictionalizing tendency here? Before I answer that question, let me first draw a contrast between the desire for narrative closure and a related, but different kind of desire: the desire for emotional closure. This is a desire to emplot a narrative with coherence, meaningfulness, and the right emotional import, thus enabling one to have the appropriate emotional response to what happened. Satisfaction of this kind of desire is especially pressing when people need to come to terms with traumatic events in their lives.[12]

Now, to satisfy the desire for emotional closure, it is not necessary to satisfy the desire for narrative closure. For example, a couple who have lost their child in a sudden and mysterious illness might gain emotional closure through coming to terms with the loss and with their grief, coming to be able, as it is said these days, to "move on." But there might still be all sorts of unanswered questions: What was the illness? Why did it happen to this particular child? Could more have been done to save the child? It is often the case that part of what it is to find emotional closure is to come to terms with the fact that one will never know the answers to these kinds of questions.

It is just here, I think, that the dangerous fictionalizing tendency can begin to manifest itself: one hopes for, aspires to, narrative closure where this kind of closure is not to be found. One manifestation of this is the refusal to accept that narrative closure cannot be found, and thus one tends to become frustrated in psychologically damaging ways. For example, the grieving parents refuse to "let go," to "move on," insisting that they will not rest until they know the answers to all these questions. This is also a common phenomenon with people who lose in mysterious circumstances those whom they love, often abroad: the widow of the soldier will not let go until the body has been found, or until she knows whether the death was the result of friendly fire.

Alternatively, the quest for narrative closure can manifest itself in self-deception: wanting narrative closure, we turn life into fiction, where the law of Chekhov's gun holds. For example, the grieving parents might come to believe that the death of the child was in some sense "meant to be": visited on them by God, perhaps, because of something they had done wrong in the past, or in order to draw their marriage closer together. Of course, there are important issues here concerning what can be competing demands for truth and for psychological peace, but I will not deal with these here.

The simple fact about life is that "stuff happens." Life does not come with all the ends neatly tied together, and to seek a narrative which achieves this has the potential of being dangerously blocking to the possibility of emotional closure, or of being dangerously self-deceptive, and deceptive of others.[13]

The Fourth Fictionalizing Tendency: Genre and Character

In fiction, there is a close relation between genre and character. In a subtle discussion of what makes a narrative fictional, Anthony Savile asks whether it is "just a fortuitous matter that so much of the content of the fiction we know and love is imaginary" (1998, 137). He argues that it is not, and a central element of his reasoning concerns the relations between genre and character in literature. In literature, Savile argues, the genre determines certain facts about the characters in the fiction: "a choice of genre . . . obliges the characters to have such and such personalities, and that events of such and such a nature be taken to happen *whether the author explicitly tells his reader so or not.*" In literature, he says, "it is not open for a tragic hero to be a coward, and cowardly deeds are excluded not merely from the recounted action, but also from the hero's presumed past" (142).

This stands in stark contrast to our notion of character in real life. In real life, someone "cannot know that his brave friends will not flinch in unforeseen circumstances . . . *just because there is no fact of the matter*" (143). The fictionalizing tendency, then, is to impose genre on life in a dangerous way—in a way that leads to a distortion of the notion of character. We find traces of it in Jerome Bruner's account, in his *Acts of Meaning,* of the spontaneous autobiographies of his subjects. "It [the autobiography of his subjects] was constrained by the events of a life, to be sure, but it was also powerfully constrained by the demands of the story the teller was in the process of developing. . . . The larger overall narratives were told in easily recognizable genres—the tale of a victim, a *Bildungsroman,* antihero forms, *Wanderung* stories, and so on. . . . It soon became apparent not only that life imitated art but that it did so by choosing art's genres and its other devices of storytelling as its modes of expression" (1990, 120–21).

This tendency to bring about distortion of character in real life manifests itself in a variety of related ways which I can only briefly touch on here. The first distortion we have already had a glimpse of in Savile's remarks: this is the tendency to *flatten out* the character of a real-life person to a description which *requires* that someone think, feel, and act in a certain way: the real-life hero is sure never to go against his heroic "nature"; the ne'er-do-well is sure never to do well; and so on.[14] As a result of this, in real life we tend to expect too much of our heroes, and too little of our villains (give a dog a bad name). And this in turn leads to global attitudes of contempt and shame, and this "mistakenly equates persons with certain of their character traits or wrongly assumes that characters are monolithic."[15] For example, poor Lord Jim in Conrad's novel of that name expected too much of his resolutions to be courageous, and when he let himself down he saw himself as for all time utterly and irredeemably condemned to a life of hiding from the gaze of the world.[16] And finally, we can recall Freud's discussion of the tendency to blame a recurring event on fate: what he called fate compulsion (*Schicksalzwang*) or fate neurosis. Here the fate neurosis manifests itself in seeing one's fate as ineluctably bound up with one's own unchangeable, fixed character: one comes to think of oneself as a born loser, a victim, someone who, in the words of Marilyn Monroe's Sugar Kowalski in the film *Some Like It Hot,* "always gets the fuzzy end of the lollipop."[17]

We can now see just what is wrong here—and what is right—with what MacIntyre says about Becket, and with Bernard Williams's response. It is in the context of MacIntyre's claim that "I can only answer the question 'What am I to do?' if I can answer the prior question 'Of what story or stories do I find myself a part?'" (1981, 216). Earlier, MacIntyre has asked us to "consider the question of to what genre the life of Thomas Becket belongs, and he determines that the "true genre" of Becket's life is tragedy (213). To which Williams replies that, even if Becket's life is best described as a tragedy, "He certainly did not live it by asking, when considering what to do, how to carry on the tale of one locked in a tragic relation to his king" (2007, 6).[18] Williams's response shows clearly what is wrong with MacIntyre's view: we do not need to know what story or stories we are a part of before we can make any decisions about what to do. But what Freud's discussion of fate neurosis shows is that Williams is really pointing towards a normative claim: it is possible—but it is not wise—to see one's life as that of a loser, a victim, or of someone who is locked in a tragic relation with another, and fate compulsion will quite likely determine that this is just how things will turn out.

There is, however, another side to this coin: seeing oneself and one's character in a certain light can have important dynamic implications for character development and can be an important moral force for change for the better. Let me show what I mean with an example. I might give an autobiographical account of my dispute with my employers in terms of resisting and ultimately triumphing against their greater strength, and doing so on a matter of principle: of right against wrong. In my narrative I seek to reveal my steadfastness in the face of more powerful, but morally wrong, forces, and moreover, from my perspective as narrator, I also seek to reveal that I approve of courage and steadfastness and of the way in which they were made manifest in my actions, and I encourage you, the audience, to respond likewise. (This, of course, leaves it open to the audience to interpret my narrative in another way, as manifesting not courage and steadfastness against the forces of evil, but intransigent stubbornness in the face of reasonable authority.) Imagine, though, that, in spite of my best efforts, I had failed to hold out against the pressure exerted by my employers, and had finally let them have their way. I might then tell (or just think through) the story of my akratic pusillanimousness in a way that expresses my disapproval of how I behaved; I did not do as I know I ought to have done. Through the external perspective of narrator, I might also express the thought that I have changed: I am a different sort of person now, I think. In thinking this, I might not so much be revealing a change of character, but rather expressing a resolution to become different, just as the recently reformed smoker might say that he does not smoke, when really this is not precisely true. In narrating these events of my past life in this way, I show that I hope to have learned from my mistakes, and I set myself to be a different sort of person, in a process that might be far from complete; indeed, the process might hardly have begun. In this way, seeing oneself and one's character in a certain light can help one to stick to one's resolutions, and this can be for the good.

A Summary and a Speculation

So we have these four fictionalizing tendencies: we see ourselves as plotting out the course of our lives; we find agency in the world where it is not; we seek narrative closure where it cannot be found; and we transport notions of genre and character from fiction to real life. I accept that these tendencies are dangerous, and I have pointed out where the dangers lie. But there is nothing in these dangers, as I have set them out, that vitiates narrative thinking about our lives, which plays, I believe, a central role in the way we think about our past, our present, and our future (Goldie 2009). Nor do I think that those philosophical accounts that indulge these tendencies are simply to be written off as benighted; for they often very well reflect the other side of the coin—the psychological tendencies themselves. Knowing about these tendencies and their dangers can mitigate their effect in our narrative thinking.

Finally, I would like to suggest that there is something that unites these hypertrophies of narrativizing and that helps to explain why we are we subject to them.[19] First, we seek consolation in meaning because we cannot abide what Frank Kermode calls the "horror," the "loathsomeness," the "monstrous world" of contingency (1966, 136, 147, 143). We cannot accept the thought that sometimes stuff happens, stuff for which there is no rational explanation and for which no meaning can be found. Why should *this* child die of this sudden illness, why should it be *this* town which gets buried in the mudslide, why was it *me* who was so lucky to be the only survivor on that flight which was fatal to all the other passengers? Unbearable as it is, there are no answers to these questions. Asking, and not getting answers to, these kinds of questions is a permanent feature of our humanity.

But perhaps there is a second, more recent explanation of our narrativizing hypertrophies, one which is to be found in the advancement of the scientific age. What we are today confronted with is what Max Weber has called the "disenchantment of the world," which he traced to the development of the sciences in the Scientific Revolution. With the removal of numinous explanations by appeal to gods and monsters, we are left with the impersonal view of the sciences. Perhaps we simply cannot abide this bleakness, not this time of contingency, but of an impersonal worldview entirely bereft of all agency and meaning.

NOTES

Thanks to Derek Matravers, the editors, and others who have helpfully commented on earlier versions of this chapter.

1. I am using the notion of literature here in a wide sense, to include drama: film, theater, and opera, for example.

2. Examples of the critics of narrative and of what I am calling fictionalizing tendencies are Lamarque (2004, 2007), Williams (2007), Strawson (2004), and Vice (2003).

3. Ricoeur (1984). I discuss these features, and the notion of narrative thinking, in more detail in Goldie (2003, 2009).

4. For discussion of this contrast, see, for example, White (1980, 1984), Carroll (2001), Velleman (2003), and Williams (2002).

5. By "ironic distance" I mean here a kind of dramatic irony, in the sense that there is a difference in knowledge between the narrator's external perspective and the perspectives of those who are internal to the narrative, one of whom might be the narrator, as will be the case in autobiography. For discussion, see Scholes and Kellogg (1966) and Goldie (2007).

6. Carroll (2007), registering a disagreement here with Velleman (2003).

7. In the passages just cited, MacIntyre seems to be identifying history and narrative, to be identifying the events that are the subject matter of the narrative and the narrative itself. And yet, as he says elsewhere, in real life "stories are lived before they are told—except in the case of fiction" (1981, 197).

8. Vice (2003, 99–100) has similar criticisms of MacIntyre.

9. It will, however, remain true that one's diverse and gappy autobiographical memories will have a unity in the sense that they are all memories of this particular person which are, in principle, capable of being integrated. This is, as John Campbell has argued, a unity which "'requires the conception of time as linear" (Campbell, 1997, 108)

10. For discussion of Sartre along these lines, see Kermode (1966, 133–52).

11. Carroll rightly acknowledges that some narratives, such as *Last Year at Marienbad*, "may intentionally skirt closure in order to make a point" (2007, 6). The film *The Italian Job* might be another example. And then there are, of course, many narratives where a sequel is

promised and never comes; the film *Master and Commander: The Far Side of the World* comes to mind.

12. I discuss this in Goldie (2003, 2009).

13. Hayden White makes a similar contrast in relation to historical discourse: between one that narrates and one that narrativizes, where the latter seeks to satisfy a demand for closure that cannot be found in real events: "Insofar as historical stories can be completed, can be given narrative closure, can be shown to have had a *plot* all along, they give to reality the odor of the *ideal*. This is why the plot of a historical narrative is always an embarrassment and has to be presented as 'found' in the events rather than put there by narrative techniques" (1980, 24).

14. For the distinction between flat and round characters, see Forster (1962). For the way in which literature "links character identity to character description," see Lamarque (2007); he calls it the Character Identity Principle.

15. Mason (2003, 258), cited in Abramson (2010), who has a very clear discussion of the distinction between global and nonglobal attitudes of shame and contempt.

16. For discussion, see Doris (2002) and Goldie (2004).

17. Freud says that compulsion to repeat is found not only in neurotics but also in "normal people": "Thus we have come across people all of whose human relationships have the same outcome: . . . the man whose friendships all end in betrayal by his friend; . . . the lover each of whose love affairs with a woman passes through the same phases and reaches the same conclusion." In such cases, "we can discern in him an essential character trait which always remains the same and which is compelled to find expression in a repetition of the same experiences" (Freud 1984, 292–93).

18. For a similar criticism of MacIntyre and Bruner, see Vice (2003, 103–4).

19. No doubt there will be evolutionary explanations, but these need not compete with the kind of explanation I am putting forward.

REFERENCES

Abramson, Kate. 2010. "A Sentimentalist's Defense of Contempt, Shame, and Disdain." In *The Oxford Handbook of Philosophy of Emotion,* edited by Peter Goldie, 215–36. Oxford: Oxford University Press.

Bruner, Jerome. 1990. *Acts of Meaning.* Cambridge, Mass: Harvard University Press.

———. 2004. "Life as Narrative." *Social Research* 71:691–711. Originally published in *Social Research* 54 (1987): 1–17.

———. 1990. *Acts of Meaning.* Cambridge, Mass.: Harvard University Press.

Campbell, Jerome. 1997. "The Structure of Time in Autobiographical Memory." *European Journal of Philosophy* 5:105–18.

Carroll, Noël. 2001. "On the Narrative Connection." In *Beyond Aesthetics: Philosophical Essays,* 118–32. Cambridge: Cambridge University Press.

———. 2007. "Narrative Closure." *Philosophical Studies* 135:1–15.

Collingwood, R. G. 1946. *The Idea of History.* Oxford: Oxford University Press.

Currie, Gregory, and Jon Jureidini. 2004. "Narrative and Coherence." *Mind and Language* 19:409–27.

Doris, John. 2002. *Lack of Character: Personality and Moral Behaviour.* Cambridge: Cambridge University Press.

Forster, E. M. 1962. *Aspects of the Novel.* London: Pelican Books, 1962.

Freud, Sigmund. 1984. "Beyond the Pleasure Principle." 1920. In *On Metapsychology,* translated by James Strachey, 269–338. London: Penguin Books.

Goldie, Peter. 2003. "One's Remembered Past: Narrative Thinking, Emotion, and the External Perspective." *Philosophical Papers* 32:301–19.

———. 2004. *On Personality.* London: Routledge.

———. 2007. "Dramatic Irony and the External Perspective." In *Narrative and Understanding Persons,* edited by Daniel Hutto, 69–84. Royal Institute of Philosophy Supplement 60. Cambridge: Cambridge University Press.

———. 2009. "Narrative Thinking, Emotion, and Planning." *Journal of Aesthetics and Art Criticism* 67:97–105.

Goldknopf, David. 1969. "Coincidence in the Victorian Novel." *College English* 3:41–50.

Kermode, Frank. 1966. *The Sense of an Ending: Studies in the Theory of Fiction.* Oxford: Oxford University Press.

Lamarque, Peter. 2004. "On Not Expecting Too Much of Narrative." *Mind and Language* 19:393–408.

———. 2007. "On the Distance Between Literary Narratives and Real-Life Narratives." In *Narrative and Understanding Persons,* edited by Daniel Hutto, 117–32. Royal Institute of Philosophy Supplement 60. Cambridge: Cambridge University Press.

MacIntyre, Alasdair. 1981. *After Virtue: A Study in Moral Theory.* London: Duckworth.

Mason, Michelle. 2003. "Contempt as a Moral Attitude." *Ethics* 113:234–72.

Ricoeur, Paul. 1992. *Oneself as Another.* Translated by Kathleen Blamey. Chicago: University of Chicago Press.

Savile, Anthony. 1998. "Imagination and the Content of Fiction." *British Journal of Aesthetics* 38:136–49.

Scholes, Robert, and Robert Kellogg. 1966. *The Nature of Narrative.* New York: Oxford University Press.

Strawson, Galen. 2004. "Against Narrativity." *Ratio* 17:428–54.

Velleman, J. David. 2003. "Narrative Explanation." *Philosophical Review* 112: 1–25.

Vice, Samantha. 2003. "Literature and the Narrative Self." *Philosophy* 78: 93–109.

White, Hayden. 1980. "The Value of Narrativity in the Representation of Reality." *Critical Inquiry* 7:5–27.

———. 1984. "The Question of Narrativity in Contemporary Historical Theory." *History and Theory* 23:1–33.

Williams, Bernard. 2002. *Truth and Truthfulness: An Essay in Genealogy.* Princeton: Princeton University Press.

———. 2007. "Life as Narrative." *European Journal of Philosophy Online,* doi:10.1111/j.1468-0378.2007.00275.x: 1–10.

Telling Stories
Narration, Emotion, and Insight in *Memento*

Berys Gaut

The present volume addresses the role that narration plays in the emotional engagement of audiences with artworks and how this can foster various kinds of insights. One way to examine this issue is by philosophical analysis of the conceptual or other a priori interrelations between narration, emotion, and insight. A second way, complementary to the first, is by detailed attention to artworks to investigate how the process of narration can engage audiences' emotions and cognitive abilities and thereby convey insights into the world. Few artworks are more promising subjects for the latter kind of investigation than the film *Memento* (2000), one of the most narratively complex artworks ever produced, which moreover uses its narrative structure to engage viewers' emotions and to present some intriguing claims about the role of memory and interpretation in structuring our lives.

I begin with a brief overview of the film. I then show how the film's narration conditions cognitive and emotional responses by three methods. First, the film's narrational structure grounds multiple points of view on the major protagonists, and these points of view are both cognitive and emotional. Second, I show how the narrational structure sets up a complex cognitive challenge, one that surprisingly has a determinate resolution, and that this grounds a range of emotional responses. Third, I show how the film embodies a general vision about the role of memory and interpretation in structuring our relationship to the world, and how the film offers partial confirmation of that vision through its narrational method. The discussion of the film will illustrate some general philosophical distinctions and theses about how emotional engagement and cognitive insight can be provided by narrative artworks.

Remembering *Memento*

Memento is often cited as an example of backwards narration, categorized with the film *Irreversible* (2002) and Martin Amis's novel *Time's Arrow*. But *Memento*'s temporal structure is far more complex than that of either of these works. Most of the film, which is made up of color sequences, is indeed backwardly narrated: within each sequence, the action proceeds forward, but each sequence represents events that occur *before* the events that are shown in the immediately preceding sequence. The single exception to this backward sequencing but forward shooting is the opening sequence, which is shot in reverse time. Interleaved within the backward narration of the color sequences are black-and-white segments, which are presented in chronological order (they comprise in total about twenty four minutes of the one hour and fifty minute film). In addition, inserted in both the black-and-white and color sequences are micro shots, some lasting no more than a fraction of a second, which represent events that happened before the events in the main sequences. As we shall see, these micro shots are crucial to forming a correct interpretation of the film. The film is thus extraordinarily complex in its narrational structure and makes demands on the viewer's cognitive abilities that far surpass those made by almost all films.

The events presented by this narrational structure are bizarre. Leonard Shelby is a former insurance claims investigator who is intent on exacting revenge on the man, John G., who he believes raped and murdered his wife. During the rape, which he refers to as the "incident," Leonard was assaulted and as a result has suffered short-term memory loss (anterograde amnesia): he can no longer form new long-term memories and remembers only what has happened during the last ten to fifteen minutes or so. The film begins with the backwardly filmed shot of Leonard's murder of Teddy, who he believes is John G. It then moves to the first of the black-and-white sequences. In these Leonard provides voice-over narration and also explains his "condition," as he terms it, to someone on the phone whose identity we do not initially know. He constantly compares himself to Sammy Jankis, who also, he believes, suffered from anterograde amnesia, but whose insurance claim Leonard had disallowed. Sammy, says Leonard, had no system for coping with his condition, nor any reason to do so; Leonard, in contrast, does have a system—he takes photographs, writes notes on the photographs and on cards, and has the most important points tattooed on his body—and revenge on John G. is his reason for having this system. Sammy unintentionally killed his wife, explains Leonard: Sammy's wife could not believe that his condition was genuine, especially after Leonard told her that Sammy's condition was not physical, but psychological. So she tested Sammy by asking him repeatedly to give her insulin injections for her diabetes, to see if he could remember that he had injected her just a few minutes earlier. She went into a coma and died, and Leonard cannot help but feel guilty about this. Leonard uses Sammy's condition to explain to everyone his own state. Sammy, however, never responded to conditioning, but Leonard does: he can learn some things by this mechanism, bypassing the normal use of short-term memory.

Over the course of these black-and-white sequences, the unknown person on the phone feeds information to Leonard about his revenge quest: he claims that John G. was a drug dealer, and Leonard accordingly changes "Fact 5," which he is tattooing onto his body, from "access to drugs" to "drug dealer." The caller also slips under Leonard's door a photograph of a triumphant, bloodstained Leonard gesturing toward his chest. Toward the end of the black-and-white sequences, Leonard meets the caller: we recognize him as Teddy, the man murdered at the start.

The color sequences, interleaved among the black-and-white ones, culminate in Leonard's murder of the drug dealer, Jimmy Grantz. Teddy is finally revealed as a crooked cop who has manipulated Leonard to kill Jimmy by getting him falsely to believe that Jimmy is John G. Teddy's aim is to rob Jimmy of the two hundred thousand dollars he has brought in exchange for drugs that Teddy promised him. Consumed with anger at his wife's murder and unable to remember what he does, Leonard is the perfect murder instrument. The main color sequences also introduce Natalie, Jimmy's girlfriend, who manipulates Leonard to get him to beat up and warn off Dodd, one of Jimmy's associates, who believes that Natalie has the missing drug money. We are also introduced to Burt, the front desk clerk at the Discount Inn, where Leonard is staying, who manipulates Leonard by renting and charging him for two rooms simultaneously.

At the film's climax, after Teddy has admitted to Leonard that he conned him into believing that Jimmy was John G., there is a twist. Leonard, knowing that he will forget what Teddy has just told him, resolves to set up Teddy so that he, Leonard, will come to believe that Teddy is John G. He writes on his photograph of Teddy, "Don't believe his lies"; burns the photographs of the murdered Jimmy and the bloodstained photograph of himself; and writes on a card, "Tattoo: fact 6 car license SG13 7IU," the registration number of Teddy's car. We thus discover that Leonard has cold-bloodedly manipulated himself to murder a man who he knows, at the moment of his choice, is innocent of the murder of his wife. Further, Teddy claims to Leonard that Sammy was a faker who never had a wife, and that it was Leonard's wife who had diabetes. She survived the assault but did not believe his "condition," and Leonard killed her by injecting her with insulin, in the way that Leonard claims Sammy killed his wife. "So you lie to yourself to be happy. There's nothing wrong with that. We all do it," says Teddy. Teddy was the cop who investigated the rape and helped Leonard find and kill the real John G. more than a year ago: the bloodstained photograph was taken by Teddy after Leonard killed him. But Leonard has forgotten this: "You make up your own truth." Teddy also claims that Leonard has removed pages from his own police file and crossed out items so as to create a puzzle he could never solve. Leonard decides to set himself up to murder Teddy; when doing so, he echoes Teddy's thought: "Do I lie to myself to be happy? In your case, Teddy, yes I will."

The twist of the film is thus that Leonard has manipulated himself to kill Teddy. But whether Teddy's claims about Sammy and Leonard's wife are true is a major point of dispute in interpretations of film. I will argue later that they are correct, and that seeing this is essential to understanding the larger vision of the film.

Narration, Point of View, and Emotion

As even this basic summary of the film reveals, *Memento* is extraordinarily complex, and this complexity arises in large part from its method of narration. Narration in a broad sense is equivalent to storytelling. But in a narrower usage of the term that I will employ here, we can distinguish between the narrative and the narration in storytelling. The narrative is composed of the events that occur in the story; the narration is the way that those events are told or presented. Narrative is to do with *what* is presented, narration with *how* it is presented.[1] The two are distinct: one can imagine that the story events are presented in different ways: most evidently, the events may be presented by the film in a different temporal order from that in which they fictionally occurred, via flashbacks or flashforwards. Properties of the narration may differ from those of the narrative: for instance, narrational commentary, via the mode of presentation of the story events, is a property of the narration but not the narrative. And one can imagine two films with the same basic narrational structure (e.g., point-of-view shots in the same places in the shot order of the film) but telling different stories. Both narrative and narration matter for audience engagement, but it is easy to elide the distinction and in particular to miss the significance of the narrational aspect in cognitive and affective engagement.

One of the many advantages of discussing *Memento* is that it clearly demonstrates how narration is crucial for audience engagement. Though the film presents the story events in scrambled temporal order, there is a cut of the film, in a hidden menu on the DVD, which restructures the film in chronological order: the narrative of the actual and chronological cuts is the same; the narration is different.[2] It is striking how different the artistic properties of the two versions are. Most obviously, the twist about Leonard's self-manipulation that occurs at the end of the actual film occurs less than a third of the way through the chronological cut, so that the suspense, surprise, and radical reinterpretation required of events are largely lost. Much of the film's humor and disconcerting quality also disappears. In the actual film, Leonard discovers to his surprise a gun in Dodd's bedside cabinet and in the next color shot we learn that Leonard had put it there himself and then forgot about it. When the film is shown chronologically, there is no surprise for viewers and the humor shifts its grounding from being participatory in Leonard's condition to our feeling superior to him. In another scene we see Natalie return to her house, face streaming with blood, explaining that Dodd did this to her and persuading Leonard to exact revenge. In the actual film the next color shot shows the earlier scene, where Natalie enrages Leonard into striking her by slandering his wife and telling him that she is going to manipulate him and he will forget it. In the chronological cut the latter scene is shown first, so that the surprise and much of the pathos are lost. And, importantly, the actual film forces on us a radical reinterpretation of what has happened, from seeing Natalie as a victim to understanding her as a classic film noir femme fatale; the chronological cut requires no such reinterpretation of the two scenes. In shifting our understanding of the action, the film also thereby shifts our emotional responses to it: the dependence of emotions on cognitions is elegantly demonstrated. The chronological cut hardly ever requires reinterpretation of events by the viewer and therefore does not highlight this general connection between emotion and cognition.

The most striking feature of the narration, though, is that it first forces us into Leonard's perspective and then forces us out of it. The backward narration of the main color sequences recreates Leonard's epistemic situation for us by showing us earlier events only after we have seen later ones: Leonard cannot remember what he has done and we have not yet seen what he has done; so we are in the same epistemic situation as he is. I have argued elsewhere that identification with characters is a coherent and useful concept, and comes in multiple varieties. One general kind of identification, imaginative identification, involves imagining being in someone's situation and has different aspects: it can be categorized in terms of imagining what a character is seeing (perceptual identification), imagining feeling what a character is feeling (affective identification), imagining believing what a character believes (epistemic identification), and so on (Gaut 1999; 2010, chap. 6). Nolan found in backward narration a brilliant solution to creating epistemic identification with a character whose cognitive capacities are radically impaired. By requiring epistemic identification with Leonard, the narration thereby also encourages us to imagine what he is feeling (affective identification). And it also encourages us to empathize with him (to feel *with* him—actually to feel what he is feeling) and to sympathize with him (to feel *for* him—to feel concern for him, which may be different from what he is feeling for himself). As Nolan puts it in an interview (2001) with Elvis Mitchell, included on the DVD, "We really tried to put the audience into the head of the protagonist and make them experience some of his confusion and uncertainty and paranoia."

Having thus forced various types of identification with Leonard on us, the very same mechanism of backward narration gradually distances us from him. For, though we see later events before earlier ones, which creates an epistemic identification with him, unlike Leonard we have fully functioning memories, so we retain the information with which we are presented. So we gradually accumulate more information than Leonard has across the film and discover at the end what he almost immediately forgets, that he has manipulated himself to murder a man innocent of his wife's death. The epistemic privilege we enjoy over Leonard thus eventually produces a radically distinct cognitive perspective from his own, and this grounds a completely different evaluation and emotional assessment of him. The man towards whom we felt a large degree of sympathy as avenger of his wife's murder turns out to be a ruthless assassin who has employed his memory incapacity deliberately to manipulate himself into killing someone he knows to be innocent of his wife's murder. Our emotions are guided by our cognition, and our cognition is in turn guided by the epistemic perspectives with which we are provided by the film's narrational structure.

The shift of our cognitive and therefore emotional perspective guided by the narration is not confined to our view of Leonard. Natalie, as noted, seems initially to be Jimmy's innocent girlfriend, who begs Leonard to save her from Dodd's murderous intentions; but we discover in the next scene that she has manipulated Leonard to try to intimidate or kill someone who has not yet threatened her. (There is also some reason to believe that she comes to realize that Teddy is involved in the murder of Jimmy, and sets up Leonard to murder him.) Burt, the affable front desk clerk, manipulates Leonard into renting two rooms from the hotel; and, if Teddy is telling the truth, he is in league with Jimmy and has been feeding him information about Leonard. The change in cognitive and emotional perspective can go in either direction: whereas all the other characters become more sinister as we discover the truth about them, Teddy becomes somewhat more sympathetic as we reconfigure in our minds what has happened. He initially appears to be the rapist and killer of Leonard's wife, who is shot by Leonard in revenge. By the end of the film, though he is shown to be an instigator of Jimmy's murder, he is also revealed to have been innocent of the murder of Leonard's wife and to be sympathetic to Leonard's plight.

So the narration of the film prescribes and in some respects forces us to take up changing perspectives on the characters over the course of the film; it thereby changes our understanding of their characteristics and motivations, and by so doing it also alters our evaluations of them and our emotional responses to them. These shifts in perspective are an important reason why the film is as complex and interesting as it is. And, as we have seen, it is the narration, not only the narrative, that is crucial in grounding these features of the film, since the chronological cut of the film, with the same narrative but different narration, lacks many of the features that force reinterpretation and emotional reassessment of the characters. Narration matters to emotional engagement and cognitive insight.

Cognitive Complexity and Challenge

There is a second way in which *Memento*'s narration is significant in conditioning viewers' cognitive and emotional responses to the film. The film's narrative, that is, what the story events are, is extraordinarily hard to grasp. The narrational structure is so complex that the film's writer-director, Christopher Nolan, admits in his director's commentary on the DVD to often not knowing what will come next when he is watching the film, despite having seen it, he claims, "thousands of times." Yet watching the chronological cut reveals a straightforward sequence of events in respect of the three days and two nights in which the main action occurs (that is, setting aside the micro shot flashbacks to Leonard's pre-"incident" life). So the complexity of the film is in part a function of its temporally scrambled narration. Each color sequence ends with a brief segment that exactly or very nearly repeats what happened at the beginning of the immediately pre-ceding color sequence, so as to cue the viewer that the color sequence shown later represents events that happened before the sequence shown earlier. In the actual film, because of the complexity of the narrational strategy, this is vital to guiding the viewer to reconstruct the fictional events in their correct temporal order. In the chronological cut, however, we see strange, annoy-ing, and apparently unmotivated repetitions of events we have seen just a moment before.

This narrational complexity is the main explanation for the considerable cognitive challenge posed by the film: working out what is going on at even the simple level of the story events, setting aside their significance, is daunt-ingly difficult. But not only is trying to meet this cognitive challenge hugely satisfying, the endeavor to do so also grounds a rich array of emotions and feelings: initial bewilderment at what is going on; frustration at not being able to work out what is happening; pleasure and even elation when one starts to figure things out; then a perhaps rather obsessive desire to work out in more detail what has happened; and a reiteration of all the above states as one plumbs to a greater depth not just the story events but also what motivates the characters and more generally the significance of what happens.

After one obtains some grip on the basic narrative sequence, the main cognitive challenge one is posed is whether Teddy's claims at the end of the film are correct. Teddy maintains that Sammy Jankis was a faker who was exposed by Leonard; that Leonard's wife survived the attack; that Leonard killed her in a way that he believes Sammy killed his own wife; that Leonard has already killed the real John G.; and that Leonard is making up his own version of events to satisfy his need to engage in "a romantic quest" to structure his life. Whether these claims are true matters a great deal to the interpretation of the film. For if they are, not only is Leonard someone who has manipulated himself to kill Teddy, but his entire revenge quest is based on a delusional belief: not John G., but Leonard himself is his wife's killer. On this interpretation the film's vision is a far darker one than it would be were Teddy lying: Leonard is engaged on a delusive quest that essentially involves a complex act of self-deception facilitated, but not excused, by his cognitive impairment. And the natural conclusion to draw is that Leonard, in order to hold his temporally fractured consciousness together, will engage in an unending cycle of murdering people, each of whom he will convince himself is John G. Leonard would not be the still somewhat sympathetic victim of a vicious assault, but a deranged serial killer. And Teddy, I am going to argue, is telling the truth: the darker vision is indeed the one that the film conveys. I will discuss the evidence for this in some detail, since it illustrates how complex narrational strategy can be in creating a cognitive challenge.

Let me introduce some terminology concerning narrative propositions, propositions about what happens in the story.[3] I will call a narrative proposition *open* in some work when it is not fictional in the work that the proposition is true, and it is not fictional in the work that it is false: that is, it is indeterminate whether it is fictionally true or false. A narrative proposition is *closed* when it is not open: that is, either it is fictional in the work that it is true, or it is fictional in the work that it is false. For instance, the proposition that Leonard killed his wife by injecting her repeatedly with insulin is open if it is neither fictional in *Memento* that he did this nor fictional that he did not. And the proposition is closed if either it is fictional in the film that he killed his wife in this way or fictional that he did not. I will deem *works of fiction* open when they contain a large number of salient open narrative propositions and deem them closed when they contain very few or no salient open narrative propositions. The notion of salience should be understood in terms of whether the fictional truth of the narrative proposition matters for the correct interpretation of the work.

Is *Memento* an open work in respect of Teddy's claims about Leonard's wife and Sammy? There are reasonable grounds to think that it is. For instance, Teddy is an accomplished liar and intent on deceiving Leonard—in Emma's tattoo parlor he switches effortlessly to trying to persuade Leonard that he is not a cop but a snitch. Why should we think that anything he says is true? Andrew Kania, a careful interpreter of the film, holds that "the movie is ultimately ambiguous about some of these central questions, such as whether the tale Leonard recounts of Sammy Jankis is really about himself."[4] Nevertheless, there are good grounds for thinking that it is determinate in the fiction that Leonard killed his wife, and the narrational structure plays an important role in making it extremely hard for the viewer to work this out.

The key is to consider the relationships between micro shots peppered throughout the film. Consider first the four brief shots (the longest lasts four seconds), starting at about 105 minutes and 16 seconds, which occur when Leonard is driving his car towards the tattoo parlor after having killed Jimmy.[5] They show Leonard in bed with his wife; she is cuddled up to him, stroking his chest, with the words "I've done it" tattooed over his heart. The style is the same as that of the other apparent flashbacks to his earlier life. But this cannot be a memory. Leonard earlier in the film had told Natalie that maybe he is reserving the empty space over his heart for a tattoo to remind him when he has avenged his wife. But his wife is here shown alive next to that tattoo, and we can also see part of his main tattoo, "John G. raped and murdered my wife." Some apparent memories of Leonard's are fabrications.

Second, there are two micro shots, beginning at about 98 minutes and 30 seconds, which coincide with Teddy saying "the insulin" as he accuses Leonard of having killed his wife. The first shows a close-up of someone's hands flicking a syringe to remove the air, with someone in a white top in the background; the second reveals the person holding the syringe to be Leonard.

The third set comprises several shots. At about 99 minutes and 23 seconds we are shown Leonard injecting insulin into his wife's thigh, which occurs shortly after Teddy says, "It was your wife who had diabetes." Shortly thereafter, after Leonard says, "My wife wasn't diabetic," another shot shows Leonard instead pinching his wife's thigh. One of these two apparent flashbacks cannot be correct, and the obvious way to interpret the first of the pair is as representing a real memory of Leonard's injecting his wife and then Leonard's conscious rejection of that memory because he will not face the truth.

Finally, there is a black-and-white shot, occurring at about 86 minutes and 19 seconds, of Sammy in a home, with Leonard in voice-over explaining that you have to bluff recognition to get a pat on the head from the doctors. Someone passes in front of Sammy, occluding him, and for a fraction of a second, as our view is cleared, Sammy's face is replaced by Leonard's. Sammy is Leonard: what Leonard has said of Sammy is true of himself.

Or so at least the most straightforward interpretation of these micro shots holds. But this interpretation can be challenged. The first of the injection/pinching shots could be understood as being a false memory induced by Teddy's accusation and the second as the replacement of this false memory by a real memory of Leonard pinching his wife. This has some support, since exactly the same pinching sequence is shown as a flashback at about 52 minutes and 50 seconds, when Leonard throws on the fire his wife's hairbrush, which features in the flashback; and this flashback is not prompted by Teddy's accusations. And the Sammy/Leonard shot could be understood merely as reflecting the fact that Leonard has throughout been comparing himself to Sammy.[6]

However, this challenge can be answered. The truth of Teddy's accusation requires that Leonard's pre-"incident" memories about Sammy have been systematically distorted, and however we understand the Sammy/Leonard shot, it proves that this is true of at least one of those apparent memories. Leonard could not have magically merged into Sammy at the home. And if his pre-"incident" memories are distorted, with Leonard keeping up a constant pressure on his memory by incanting his story of Sammy to everyone he sees, then the apparent memory of pinching his wife while he burns her hairbrush would be part of this distorted sequence, required to hide the truth about his wife's diabetes from himself. Further, suppose that we were to accept that, though the Sammy/Leonard shot must be a distorted memory, it merely reflects Leonard's constant comparison of himself with Sammy. That view has some merit in the case of that particular shot, since after the death of his wife Leonard would likely have been confined to a home (as indeed the film's website says). But it will not work for another striking comparison that Leonard makes of himself with Sammy. Towards the end of the black-and-white sequences, Leonard becomes very agitated about his condition, saying to Teddy on the phone, "You feel angry, you don't know why. You feel guilty, you have no idea why. You could do anything and not have the faintest idea ten minutes later. Like Sammy. What if I'd done something like Sammy?" Towards the end of this speech, Leonard looks at his tattoo "remember Sammy Jankis," and his voice is staccato with stress. But his fear of having done something like Sammy is bizarre. For what Sammy has allegedly done, of course, is to kill his wife by injecting her repeatedly without realizing it. If Leonard's wife died in the assault that caused his amnesia, Leonard could not possibly have done what Sammy did. The only way to make sense of Leonard's fear is if at some level he realizes that he killed his wife.

Finally, consider another shot, which has escaped general notice. After Natalie first brings Leonard into her house and tells him to make himself at home, Leonard settles down on the sofa in front of her television. He looks at the words "remember Sammy Jankis" tattooed onto his left hand. And in a micro shot lasting less than a second, at about 78 minutes and 8 seconds, there is a flashback of a close-up of someone's hands flicking a syringe, with someone else in the background wearing a white top. Careful study of this micro shot reveals that it is exactly the same shot as that shown when Teddy is saying "the insulin"; but the latter micro shot is immediately followed by another micro shot, which reveals that the person flicking the syringe is Leonard. Now, crucially, the shot in Natalie's apartment is not prompted by any accusations of Teddy's about Leonard's having killed his wife: it is a spontaneous image, and we have no reason to deny that it is a memory. The micro shot shown when Teddy makes his accusation reveals the identities of the people in the earlier shot; but the earlier shot cannot be merely a product of Teddy's accusations. Nor can we try to show that Leonard did not kill his wife by claiming that the shot is to be understood merely as a comparison by Leonard of himself with Sammy, since the relevant point of comparison would have to be that Leonard's wife was diabetic. So there is very good reason to think that Leonard killed his wife and is repressing this fact through the production of apparent memories that are really delusions.[7]

One might still try to resist this conclusion.[8] Andrew Kania has raised an interesting objection: it makes no sense to think that Leonard is repressing memories of killing his wife, since the killing would have had to have occurred after he suffered anterograde amnesia, so he could not possibly have a memory of killing his wife, which needed to be repressed.[9] This may be an inconsistency in the film—a case where the narrative has it that Leonard remembers something that he could not have remembered. There is at least one inconsistency in the film: Leonard, sitting in his truck, decides to set himself up to murder Teddy. He writes down on a card "Fact 6." Repetition and habit can explain how he remembers to write something down to remind himself. What they cannot explain is how he knows it is fact 6. He does not look at his other tattoos to see how many "facts" he has recorded already. The film has just shown him doing something that he cannot do.

Though the inconsistency response is tenable, a better one is available. It is not in fact fictional in the film that Leonard cannot form new memories. On the contrary, he insists that he can do so, but not by the normal mechanisms. He says that he can form them through habit, repetition, and instinct. In a flashback we see Sammy being tested by a doctor, with Leonard watching. Sammy is asked to pick up any three of six metal objects arrayed before him, and the same ones are electrified each time. Despite repeated tests,

Sammy keeps picking up electrified objects. Leonard explains that Sammy was unable to learn through repetition, but Leonard can form new memories through conditioning. Notice another feature of Sammy's test: what is administered is painful. Something far more painful, even though occurring just once, could also produce a new memory, albeit not through the normal mechanism of fixing via short-term memory, but through an alternative mechanism that Leonard calls "instinct." This seems to be true of real-life cases: one cognitive psychologist reported a case where an anterograde amnesiac patient was shaken by the hand by a doctor who had a pin concealed in his palm; when offered the doctor's hand again, the patient refused to shake it, even though he had no conscious memory of having met the doctor before (Mottram 2002, 46). Both Christopher Nolan and his brother, Jonathan Nolan, on whose short story the film is based, read the medical literature and so would have been familiar with such cases.[10] And in his director's commentary, Christopher Nolan stresses at several points the varieties of types of memory and remarks that it is possible through habituation to form memories without being conscious of doing so. Nothing could be more painful to Leonard than the knowledge that he has killed his wife, and there was even a degree of repetition in his actions in killing her, since Sammy is shown to have injected his wife three times, and after the second time she clearly looks distressed. So Leonard may indeed have formed an unconscious memory of killing his wife, consistent with the film's basic claim about his memory condition.

This interpretation of the film's micro shots illustrates two important points about the relation of narration to emotion and cognition. First, spotting the crucial relation between the two syringe-flicking shots is extremely hard, because the shots are very short and more than twenty-one minutes apart. One could imagine another (now hypothetical, not actual) alternative version of the film where these shots are both of greater length and we are allowed to dwell on them. But given that the alternative version would be of the same story-events, the difficulty in the actual film stems from its narrational structure, rather than its narrative. (The point about the significance of Leonard's fear of having done something like Sammy depends, however, purely on features of the narrative.) So the narrational structure once again plays a crucial part in explaining the film's complexity and therefore its cognitive challenge. As Nolan has remarked, "the answers are all there in the film, but the terms of the storytelling deliberately prevent people from finding them" (quoted in Mottram 2002, 26). Narration, not just via scrambling temporal order but also by virtue of running shots for longer or shorter periods, affects aesthetically fundamental features of films, such as complexity. Narrational strategies can be very rich and complex.

Second, *Memento* is a closed film: its salient narrative propositions (those that matter for its correct interpretation) can be given a determinate resolution. Traditionally, open artworks have been regarded as aesthetically superior to closed ones. Classic European art-cinema films, such as Alain Resnais' *Last Year at Marienbad* and Michelangelo Antonioni's *L'Avventura,* are feted for their openness, their resistance to any resolution of what happens at the basic level of story events. As one examines them more attentively, one becomes aware that they are even more open than one at first supposed. They issue a cognitive challenge about what happens in them, but on close examination one is driven to conclude that this cognitive challenge cannot be met. This privileging of openness fits with an aesthetics that celebrates the free play of imagination that the open work grounds: there are very many ways in which one can legitimately imagine what happens in such films.

Certainly, the aesthetics of openness is legitimate and has its place. But there is another type of artwork, of which more popular genres such as the detective novel are exemplars, that is closed and has value for that reason. The cognitive challenge issued by such works can be answered: one can determine, if a detective novel is well constructed, who the killer is, even before reading the novel's resolution. And these works have their aesthetic value in part because their cognitive rewards are potentially greater than those for open works: in the case of the latter, a kind of cognitive lassitude can set in, since one discovers that one cannot determine what has happened. If one recognizes that a work is closed, so there is a determinate answer to the challenges that it poses, one will be driven to think harder about it, piece it together more carefully, dwell on it more attentively. There is a puzzle-solving aesthetic in such cases, an experience that is aesthetically rich not because of its capacity to ground multiple imaginings, but because of the cognitive demands it places on the viewer and the rewards it provides when these demands are met. *Memento* provides those kinds of rewards. And it is distinctive, though not unique, in being a work that appears to be an open work even after repeated encounters with it, but that on very close inspection turns out to be closed.

So when cognitive challenges are raised by an artwork, and where the narrational structure sets barriers to meeting those challenges, the work may, consistently with its narrational structure, be either open or closed. The nature of the emotional payoff varies somewhat between the two kinds of case. If open, the emotional rewards tend to be grounded on one's free imagining of possibilities; if closed, the emotional rewards tend to be grounded on identifying and solving problems. But it would be a mistake to think that if the difficulties presented by the narrational structure can be overcome and one discovers that the work is closed, it must be aesthetically inferior. *Memento* is at bottom a detective film, one located self-consciously in the long tradition of film noir, and it should be celebrated, not denigrated, for its having a determinate resolution, given how hard it makes the viewer work to discover what that resolution is.

Narration, Narrative, and Cognitive Claims

We have examined two ways in which narration can condition audiences' cognitive and emotional responses. The first is by providing a multiplicity of points of view on narrative events and characters and guiding or even forcing viewers to take up and then abandon some of these viewpoints, with the concomitant cognitive and emotional shifts towards characters and events. The second is by creating obstacles to determining what a work's narrative is (what the story events are); this grounds a cognitive challenge and the associated emotional and aesthetic rewards of imaginative exploration in the case of open works or puzzle solving in the case of closed ones. There is also a third way in which narration can condition cognitive and emotional responses. This is by providing partial confirmation of the cognitive claims about the *actual world* that are explicit or implicit in the narrative, and thereby also providing partial justification for the emotional responses grounded on those claims.

The narrative, the story events represented by a work, can present claims about the actual world, often by what characters say. *Memento* is rich in these sorts of claims. When they are eating lunch, Leonard gives Teddy a little lecture on the nature of memory, holding that even eyewitness testimony is unreliable: "memory can change the shape of a room, it can change the color of a car." Leonard says that memory is just an interpretation, not a record, of events. One of his tattoos reads, "Memory is treachery." The claim that memory is unreliable is naturally understood as applying to the real world too. Besides these unrestricted claims being advanced, often something is said about what Leonard's condition is like, and then it is remarked that his case is similar to real ones. There are of course a few real people who have Leonard's condition; in voice-over, recounting his dealings with Sammy, Leonard remarks that there is a real condition, short-term memory loss, which is rare but which the doctors assure him is legitimate. Also, though Leonard is keen to tell everyone about his "condition" and how it makes him different, he presents it as in certain ways a more extreme version of everyone else's. Explaining his tattoos to Natalie, he asks, "It's useful. You never write a phone number on your hand?" Other characters concur in finding basic similarities: as noted earlier, Teddy says to Leonard, "So you lie to yourself to be happy. . . . We all do it." Within this general framework of verbal generalization about Leonard's behavior, some of his actions are also to be understood as emblematic of actual behavior. Sitting in Leonard's Jaguar, Teddy challenges Leonard as to how he obtained his designer suit and car. As we later discover, both were stolen from the murdered Jimmy. Leonard cannot remember, but he invents a story that, since he used to work in insurance, he was well covered for his wife's death. Retorting to this piece of invention, Teddy asks, "So in your grief you wandered into a Jaguar dealership?" People standardly make up stories when they cannot remember something that is vital to their self-understanding. So embedded in the narrative are claims that are readily construed as assertions about what is the case in the actual world. I will focus on three of them.

The first concerns the unreliability of memory: some of what people think they remember is simply false or distorted, as Leonard notes in his lecture to Teddy. Nolan is explicit in his interview with Mitchell that he wants to get audiences to question their own memories by reflecting on the film, as did he and Guy Pearce (who plays Leonard) in making the film.

The second is that what we remember and apparently remember is partly to be explained by our aims, particularly our need to endow our situation and our lives with sense and structure: we tell ourselves stories to make our lives livable. At the end of the film, just before he stops at the tattoo parlor, Leonard remarks, "We all need memories to remind ourselves who we are. I'm no different." That is also the lesson of the Jaguar conversation, and it is the larger claim of the film. Leonard killed his own wife, I have argued, and his apparent memories about what Sammy did (memories that predate the "incident") are partly fabricated to hide his sense of guilt for killing her. And he at times self-consciously manipulates the props that serve him in place of memories, burning the Polaroids that show the murdered Jimmy and the bloodstained picture of himself. Leonard has structured his (apparent) memories around his overwhelming desire for revenge. That desire for revenge is in turn required as a way for him to knit together the shards of his experiences into a coherent whole. Talking to Teddy on the phone, he explains that, unlike Sammy, he has a system and a reason to make it work. While he says, "Yeah, I got a reason," he looks into the mirror, where his tattoo "John G. raped and murdered my wife" is displayed.[11]

The third claim is that memory is essential to understanding: one cannot work out what is happening by simple observation, however diligent, of a situation, since it is subject to multiple interpretations; only by understanding the context, including what has preceded the situation, can one determine which interpretation is correct.[12] Leonard is shown constantly having to interpret the situation in which he finds himself, whereas we would ordinarily suppose this to be a matter of mere observation, not realizing the role that memory plays in our understanding. The first black-and-white sequence starts with the question "So where are you?" as Leonard works out that he is in a motel room, but cannot tell how long he has been there. And the film ends with the question "Now, where was I?" At one point Leonard grabs a whiskey bottle in Dodd's motel room as a weapon; waiting for Dodd, he loses his memory of what he is doing, and, finding himself holding the bottle, wonders whether he has gone on a drinking spree: "I don't *feel* drunk." And memory is essential to understanding, since Leonard's attempts to overcome what he calls "the memory problem" are fraught with errors. He insists on talking to people face-to-face and seeing their eyes, rather than over the phone, but he is still manipulated by almost everyone. His records fail him at several points: the world is too complex to be reduced to a series of brief notes, and he cannot keep in mind the details of his voluminous police file. Notes he and others write are themselves subject to different interpretations: Natalie's note tells Leonard to "put him [Dodd] onto Teddy," by which she means him to tell Dodd that Teddy is the likely murderer of Jimmy, but Leonard interprets it so that he should phone Teddy. Leonard has six "facts" tattooed on his body; several are false or misleading, being the product of his own or others' manipulations. Fact 5, "Drug dealer," is a lie about John G. provided by Teddy. (Fact 3, about the murderer's first name, has "or James" added in a ballpoint pen tattoo to the professionally tattooed "John," the addition presumably being due to Teddy's misinformation too.) Fact 6 gives Teddy's license plate number, which in the context is taken to be John G.'s. Leonard has recognized problems with his system in the past: he has "Don't trust your weakness" and "Consider the source" tattooed on his body, but these warnings to himself go unheeded, since he does not remember that he has them. Ironically, his most successful use of his recording system exploits its weaknesses by using them to manipulate himself to kill Teddy.

The three claims just discussed are, partly because of the framework of verbal generalization in the narrative, to be understood also as claims about the real world. Whether fiction-based claims can count as genuine items of knowledge is a much-debated point between cognitivists and anticognitivists in aesthetics. This is because knowledge requires not only true claims but also some degree of confirmation. I have argued elsewhere not only that fictional works can advance true claims, but also that they can provide a degree of confirmation for these claims. This is for several reasons: fictional works can provide testimony; they may give us emotional experience to which we would not otherwise have access; we can try to experience the world in the light of their claims, to see if they hold up; and they can guide and discipline our imaginings, through which we can make discoveries and gain some confirmation about what it is valuable or what it is like to lead others' lives.[13] Several of these cognitive factors are in play in *Memento*. But there is also a more specific, unusual cognitive mechanism at work. This is that the method of narration acts as partial confirmation of the claims advanced in the narrative: I will call this *narrational confirmation.*

Consider the claim that memory is unreliable; Leonard says this in his little lecture to Teddy, so it is explicitly advanced in the narrative. The chronological cut of the film reveals a straightforward sequence of events, which is relatively easy to remember; but in the actual film, even after a very large number of viewings, remembering what is going to be shown next is extraordinarily difficult, and one is prone repeatedly to get it wrong. The two cuts differ, in respect of their storytelling features, only in their narration: so the actual film, through its narrational strategy, confirms the claim advanced in the narrative that memory is unreliable.

Second, the narrative claims that people's aims and in particular their need to make sense of their situation structures what they remember or appear to remember. The narration of the actual film confirms that too by rendering it salient in our experience: as viewers of the film we need to make sense of the film, but, given its complexities, we are prone to misremember what has occurred and the order in which it is shown so as to try to make sense of what is going on. As anyone who has seen the film repeatedly (and the present essay is the product of more than thirty viewings) can testify, later viewings reveal not only that one has forgotten significant details, but also that details that one thought were there are not in fact present, or occur in significantly different places in the film. Our memories and failures of memory are conditioned by our need to make sense of our situation, and that is true of our memories of film viewing too.

Third, the narrative claims that one can interpret situations in multiple ways and that memory is essential to grasping which interpretation is correct. The film's narration provides partial confirmation of that too. Recall the scene in which Natalie returns to her house, claiming that Dodd has beaten her: the next color scene reveals that Natalie had deliberately provoked Leonard to hit her and then, by removing all the pens, ensured that he could not write down what happened. What seems obviously true on first viewing—that Natalie is an innocent victim—is revealed as completely false, and the true situation can be grasped only if one knows the prior context. This forced reinterpretation is a function of the narration, since it is not a feature of the chronological cut. So we are made to experience the truth of the narrative claim: we not only grasp that Leonard cannot interpret the situation correctly because of his incapacity, but are also made to experience through the narrational strategy that *we* cannot grasp the situation correctly if are deprived of the information that memory would normally provide. And, when one watches the film again, the scene when Natalie returns home is experienced very differently in the light of one's memory of what she has done. As Nolan remarks, he wants to "show how the same situation can be viewed very differently, depending on what information you already know up to that point" (Mottram 2002, 36). More generally, the narration of *Memento* is so complex that it requires one to try out different interpretations of what is happening and determine which is correct by demanding exercises of memory—for instance, by grasping the relationships between the micro shots.

So the narration—the way of telling the story—provides partial confirmation in all three cases of the explicit or implicit claims advanced by the narrative. This is a kind of experiential confirmation: we are made to experience, through the way the story is told, the unreliability of memory; that memory and apparent memories are subject to our aims and our need to make sense of our lives; and that situations can be multiply interpreted and understanding of the context through memory is essential to grasping which interpretation is correct. Evidently, narrational confirmation has its limits: the unreliability of memory, for instance, is shown in reference to an extremely complex object, rather than the generally simpler situations we encounter in ordinary life. And only certain kinds of claims about the actual world can be given narrational confirmation. Nevertheless, narrational confirmation is a real phenomenon, and it is one whose existence is disclosed by detailed attention to *Memento*.

The three general claims advanced are not just important cognitively. If they are correct, they also ground a range of attitudes and emotional responses to life. If memory is unreliable, if it can be distorted by our need to tell stories that make sense of our lives, if we cannot simply observe a situation but need to interpret what is going on in the light of the overall context to grasp the truth, then a kind of epistemic and emotional caution is called for. We should be careful in our judgments and not respond immediately in emotionally strong fashion to events. We need to look, listen, try out different points of view that may not be at all obvious at first glance. Only then can we find out the truth, and that may be very hard to ascertain. The view is not a type of skepticism, subjectivism, relativism, or factual nihilism (the view that there are no facts). Rather, it is a plea for cognitive caution and rigor: we may have to dig very hard to find it, but there is in the end a truth to be uncovered; and our apprehension of this should condition our emotional responses to our own and others' lives.

Conclusion

I have argued, then, that *Memento* illustrates three ways in which narration can condition cognition and emotion. It can provide different points of view on the narrative events and characters, which ground different thoughts and therefore emotional responses to them; it can set cognitive challenges by creating obstacles to understanding what is happening in the work and can deliver the attendant emotional experiences; and it can provide partial confirmation of some general claims about the actual world advanced by the narrative and thereby ground emotional responses on these claims. By examining these three mechanisms in detail, we have seen how narration can position viewers both cognitively and emotionally, and how doing so can teach them things of some importance about the actual world.

The discussion of the film also illustrates a general methodological point about how to proceed in aesthetics. I began this essay by remarking on two complementary approaches to thinking about artworks: the way of a priori analysis of the relations between concepts applicable to artworks, such as narration, emotion, and cognition; and the way of detailed examination of individual artworks to see how their narration operates in respect of emotion and cognition. The second approach provides illustrative material for the first and a means to test out general theories. But in addition, we have discovered, it may be the best or only way to discover some possibilities about how artworks can operate. The possibility of narrational confirmation, for instance, is unlikely to occur to anyone thinking about narration in general at the a priori level. Only detailed attention to an artwork that employs narrational confirmation is likely to disclose its existence. And that is because sometimes the imaginings of a gifted filmmaker like Christopher Nolan are richer, deeper, and more interesting than are the thoughts of philosophers. Perhaps we should not be too surprised by that.

NOTES

I would like to thank David Davies and Andrew Kania for their helpful comments on this essay.

1. For a subtle discussion of the narration/narrative distinction that acknowledges its uses as well as complexities, see Wilson (1986, 139–44).

2. Of course, the actual film and the chronological cut share many narrational features: the point is that they differ in respect of their narrational features, not that the difference captures all narrational features of the film.

3. Note that I am restricting the notion of open and closed propositions to narrative propositions. A work may be completely narratively closed, i.e., it may be completely determinate what happens in the story, but still be open in respect of its other aspects, such as its themes.

4. Kania (2009a, 652). Kania thinks that this is true of the film considered in itself, but that the information on the associated website shows that Leonard did kill his wife.

5. The timings are all for the UK DVD, which uses the PAL format; timings for US DVDs, which use the NTSC system, may be a few minutes later.

6. For the last point and other grounds for doubting the correctness of Teddy's claims, see Kania (2009b).

7. There is also supporting evidence from outside the work: the film's website (which is now included on the DVD) was supervised by Nolan, and it is determinate there that Leonard's wife (named as "Catherine") survived the assault, which occurred on February 24, 1997, that she died in November 1997, and that Leonard was in a psychiatric institution after her death.

8. Martin-Jones (2006, 141–53) also offers an interpretation of *Memento*, according to which it is determinate that Leonard is deceiving himself in order to get away with murder. Martin-Jones makes several excellent points, though he seems to think that Leonard's memory is far more intact and his deception more self-conscious than I believe is the case; and he does not discuss the relation between two syringe-flicking shots, which I have argued is crucial to resolving the issue.

9. Kania (2009b). Kania also objects that the Sammy events occurred before the "incident," so Leonard should be reliable about Sammy. However, if Leonard is deceiving himself about his complicity in his wife's killing, he needs also to deceive himself about Sammy's story, so as to project the events and his sense of guilt onto Sammy. And the memories of even ordinary people are subject to self-deception.

10. Baxendale (2004) praises *Memento* as one of only three films that have portrayed amnesia relatively accurately. It is also interesting to note that Oliver Sacks (1985) discusses two cases of anterograde amnesia, and the patient discussed in chapter 2 is called "Jimmie G."

11. In this respect, Leonard is a member of the great gallery of obsessional figures that populate Nolan's films, from the young man who stalks people in *Following*, to the multiply

self-destructive magician Robert Angier in *The Prestige,* to the crime-obsessed Batman of *Batman Begins,* scarred by the childhood murder of his parents. What grounds their obsession is a fear of inadequacy, of emotional flatness, or of threatening chaos: the Joker, Batman's foe in *The Dark Knight,* describes himself as "an agent of chaos." The chaos that threatens Leonard, if he abandons his revenge-quest, is the destruction of his ability to function.

12. One might suppose that the claim about memory's being essential to understanding would, when taken with the other two claims (the unreliability of memory and its distortion by psychological needs), support an interpretation of the film as advocating epistemic skepticism, or even a denial of the existence of objective truth. But those views better fit an open artwork such as *Last Year at Marienbad;* in contrast, there are answers in *Memento,* if one looks hard enough for them. *Memento*'s point is that it may be extremely hard to uncover what the truth is, not that the task is impossible nor that there is no such thing as truth.

13. See Gaut (2007, chap. 7); in chapter 8 I argue that this cognitive capacity is under certain conditions an aesthetic merit in artworks.

REFERENCES

Baxendale, Sallie. 2004. "Memories Aren't Made of This: Amnesia at the Movies." *British Medical Journal* 329:1480–83.
Gaut, Berys. 1999. "Identification and Emotion in Narrative Film." In *Passionate Views: Film, Cognition, and Emotion,* edited by Carl Plantinga and Greg M. Smith, 200–216. Baltimore: Johns Hopkins University Press.
———. 2007. *Art, Emotion and Ethics.* Oxford: Oxford University Press.
———. 2010. *A Philosophy of Cinematic Art.* Cambridge: Cambridge University Press.
Kania, Andrew. 2009a. "*Memento.*" In *The Routledge Companion to Philosophy and Film,* edited by Paisley Livingston and Carl Plantinga, 650–60. Abingdon: Routledge.
———. 2009b. "What Is *Memento?* Ontology and Interpretation in Mainstream Film." In *Memento,* edited by Andrew Kania, 167–88. Abingdon: Routledge.
Martin-Jones, David. 2006. *Deleuze, Cinema and National Identity.* Edinburgh: Edinburgh University Press.
Mottram, James. 2002. *The Making of "Memento."* London: Faber and Faber.
Sacks, Oliver. 1985. *The Man Who Mistook His Wife for a Hat.* London: Duckworth.
Wilson, George. 1986. *Narration in Light.* Baltimore: Johns Hopkins University Press.

Philosophical Insight, Emotion, and Popular Fiction
The Case of *Sunset Boulevard*

Noël Carroll

Men more frequently require to be reminded than instructed.
—*Samuel Johnson*

Introduction

During the last decade, a veritable philosophical industry has arisen which posits an association between philosophy and mass culture. Three different publishers—Open Court, the University of Kentucky Press, and Wiley-Blackwell—sponsor series with the title Philosophy and _____, where the blank is filled in by some item of popular culture, like *Lord of the Rings,* or *Lost,* or even baseball. But often the blank is filled in by the name of some movie or movie director. Similarly, Routledge, a subsidiary of Taylor-Francis, has initiated a series called Philosophers on Film in which a single motion picture, such as *The Third Man,* is interrogated by a handful of philosophers.

The ties between the pertinent pop culture example and philosophy can be various. In some cases, philosophers use an episode of a TV series, such as *The Twilight Zone,* to illustrate some philosophical position, like the coherence theory of truth, or to raise a philosophical question; for instance: does death harm the deceased? Using popular culture in this way, of course, is of great pedagogical value, since it exploits the student's interest in the example as a device for seducing them to entertain, so to speak, philosophical issues that might otherwise try their patience. Call this the "spoonful of sugar" approach. However, in addition, some philosophers claim not only that popular culture can serve the Owl Minerva as a pedagogical tool, but that works of popular entertainment can *do* philosophy outright. That is, they hold that at least some popular fictions can produce philosophical knowledge.

Perhaps needless to say, the suggestion that any artifice of mass culture might afford philosophical insight has not been embraced by philosophers across the board. There are many skeptics. Some are broadly skeptical of the idea that *any* fiction, mass or otherwise, can deliver *any* sort of knowledge whatsoever, while others think that there is something about philosophical knowledge specifically that entails that popular fictions are incapable of providing it. In this essay, with reference to the movie *Sunset Boulevard,* I will argue that *some* popular narratives, including notably the aforesaid classic film by Billy Wilder, can promote philosophical insight, especially with respect to their intended audience, which is to say, the mass audience. That is, some mass fictions *do* philosophy in the arena of popular culture, where they encourage plain viewers, readers, and/or listeners to engage in what might be called popular philosophy.[1]

My case will be laid out in three parts. First I will introduce *Sunset Boulevard* and attempt to distill what I think is its philosophical content. In this section, I will also try show how the emotions, especially that of disgust, are enlisted to abet philosophical conviction. Then, in the ensuing section, I will consider objections to my conjecture that some popular narratives—in this case, *Sunset Boulevard*—can broker philosophical insight for their intended audience. That is, I will contend that the standard skeptical objections do not militate against the possibility of popular philosophy being propounded in popular narratives. Then this will be followed by a short summary.

Sunset Boulevard

PRODUCTION BACKGROUND

Sunset Boulevard premiered in 1950 at the Radio City Music Hall in New York. It was released by Paramount Pictures. It was directed by Billy Wilder, who had won the Academy Award in 1945 for the motion picture *Lost*

Weekend. Wilder was an important American film director by anyone's account. His masterpieces include, along with *Sunset Boulevard, Double Indemnity, Ace in the Hole, Stalag 17, Sabrina, The Seven Year Itch, Witness for the Prosecution, Some Like It Hot, The Apartment, The Fortune Cookie,* and *The Private Life of Sherlock Holmes,* among others. Wilder wrote *Sunset Boulevard* with his longtime collaborator Charles Brackett, although *Sunset Boulevard* was the last picture on which the two worked together. The film featured the silent film superstar Gloria Swanson as well as one of the major directors of that period, Erich von Stroheim, along with several other leading actors of the early twentieth century, including Buster Keaton. The iconic stature of these figures from yesteryear, as we'll see, is one of the major expressive strategies behind the articulation of the philosophical insight afforded by the film.

The film was a critical and a popular success. It garnered eleven Academy Award nominations, including Best Picture and Best Director, although it lost in most categories to *All About Eve*. Undoubtedly the face-off between these two films was somewhat ironic, since both are exposés of their respective milieus—Hollywood in the case of *Sunset Boulevard* and Broadway in the case of *All About Eve*. Nevertheless, Wilder and Brackett did not leave the award ceremonies empty-handed; they received the Oscar for best original screenplay.[2] For my money, *Sunset Boulevard* is clearly stronger than *All About Eve,* in part because it is superior in cinematic inventiveness. But, more importantly, *Sunset Boulevard* transcends being merely a show-business exposé. It is also a bracing example of popular philosophizing.

BRIEF SYNOPSIS

Sunset Boulevard begins with a shot of a curb with "Sunset Boulevard" stenciled across it. As police sirens blare, the camera pans upward and then begins to track down this famous Hollywood thoroughfare at a decidedly quickening pace. The credits start rolling by. In the background, we see police cars racing toward us and then veering into a driveway; and the voice-over narration begins.

The commentary is spoken by Joe Gillis, a Hollywood screenwriter, recently down on his luck, who is played by William Holden. Gillis is dead.[3] In one of the most memorable images in American cinema, we get a fisheye view from the bottom of the swimming pool of Gillis's body floating on the surface of the water.[4] Eventually the police will pull his body from the pool with garden tools; the overall impression of this imagery is of the body as meat.[5]

In Wilder's earlier film *Double Indemnity,* the story is narrated by a dying man, Walter Neff. In *Sunset Boulevard,* Wilder tops that, insofar as Gillis is a dead man—in effect, a ghost. This device, moreover, introduces us to the theme of morality that pervades the film.

In order to explain his untimely demise, Gillis returns us to a time roughly six months before his death. He was out of work. He had back rent due, and his car was about to be repossessed. In order to buy some time, Gillis lies to the repo men concerning the whereabouts of his vehicle. Desperate for money, Gillis approaches a producer with a project, he calls friends, and he buttonholes his agent on a golf course, but all to no avail. Stopped at a traffic light at an intersection, Gillis decides to give up his Hollywood ambitions and return to Ohio. But at that moment, the repo men, in an oncoming traffic lane, see him, and the chase is on. Gillis turns onto Sunset Boulevard with his creditors in hot pursuit. His tire blows out, and he veers into a driveway on the 10,000 block of Sunset Boulevard, thereby eluding his pursuers.

At first Gillis presumes that he has pulled into an abandoned estate. But it is not abandoned—it is owned by Norma Desmond, a former movie star of the highest echelon. As previously mentioned, she is played by Gloria Swanson, herself one of the reigning film queens of the silent era. From offscreen, she hails Gillis, mistaking him for the undertaker that she has summoned to bury her pet monkey. When the camera locates her, she is sitting behind a bamboo blind, her mirrored sunglasses highlighted; she looks like a creature in its lair.

Gillis goes into Norma's mansion and is sent upstairs by Norma's always lurking butler, Max (played by Erich von Stroheim). There the confusion over Gillis's identity unravels. However, before Gillis leaves, he recognizes Norma Desmond as a famous movie star of the silent cinema. She takes offense at his remark that she "used to be big" and replies, "I *am* big. It's the pictures that got small."

They are off to a bad start, but when Norma learns that Gillis is a screenwriter, she changes her tune. She quickly offers to hire him to help her edit a screenplay that she's been working on for years—a version of the story of Salomé which she hopes Cecil B. DeMille will direct and which, with her in the starring role, she is confident will relaunch her movie career. Of course, the idea is a preposterous, since it is established that Norma is well past her youth. Nevertheless, the Salomé project serves as a sign for the audience of the high degree of Norma's self-delusion and of her veritable denial of the mortal aging process.

Since Gillis has no better prospects and since his creditors are on his heels, he accepts the editing job. Ensconced in the lap of luxury, dressed (by Norma) in the finest attire, and lavished with food and drink, Gillis plows through Norma's script, which he confides to us is absolutely dreadful. But there is nothing else on his horizon. So Gillis takes the line of least resistance and soon is not only Norma's script doctor but her gigolo, lounging around the swimming pool she's had refitted for him and emptying the ashtrays of her guests, "the waxworks" (Buster Keaton, H. B. Warner, and Anna Q. Nilsson) while they play bridge with Norma.

Meanwhile, in a parallel development, a young studio script reader, Betty Schaefer (played by Nancy Olson), has resurrected one of Gillis's earlier movie proposals (or at least part of one) and has convinced Gillis to work with her in order to make a go of it. Despite the fact that Betty is engaged to one of Gillis's closest friends, Artie Green (played by a young and, for once, smiling Jack Webb), a romance seems about to bud. But in short order Betty learns of Gillis's affair with Norma, and Gillis, disgusted with himself, sends Betty back to Artie, vowing to leave Norma. But then Norma, in a jealous rage, stops him dead by putting a few bullets into his back. Gillis thus stumbles into her swimming pool, and we are back to where the story started.

The film concludes with the police ready to take Norma downtown, presumably to be booked. Norma is coaxed out her bedroom by her butler, Max, whom we earlier learnt was the famous silent film director Max von Mayerling (who, again, is played by von Stroheim, who was a major director during the silent era). Von Mayerling gets Norma to come down the stairs by pretending, with the help of some nearby newsreel cameramen, that shooting on her film *Salomé* is about to commence. The movie ends as Norma slithers toward the camera, as if to devour it, intoning one of the most frequently quoted lines from any film: "All right, Mr. DeMille, I'm ready for my close-up."

ANALYSIS

Sunset Boulevard belongs to the genre of what might be called the "Hollywood exposé." *The Bad and the Beautiful* falls into this category, as do various incarnations of *A Star is Born*. *Sunset Boulevard*, however, is arguably the finest example of this genre, not only for its virtually unflinching cynicism and corrosiveness, but also because of its imaginative cinematic and narrative design. Although Wilder is not usually regarded as a particularly visual director, it is through its imagery that *Sunset Boulevard* advances a great deal its criticism of Hollywood. In his youth, Wilder was a screenwriter in Berlin in the 1920s, and his grasp of German Expressionist symbolism is evident throughout *Sunset Boulevard.*

The Expressionist influence on *Sunset Boulevard* is perhaps most apparent in the horror-fiction iconography that pervades the film. One of Wilder's leading points is that Hollywood turns people into monsters, figuratively speaking. Norma Desmond, of course, is the leading example of this. That she is monstrous is literalized by Swanson in many ways.[6] She tightens the muscles in her hands in a fashion that makes them appear claw-like. Her strange, wire cigarette holder makes her hand appear gnarled, misshapen. She points her chin upward and clenches her teeth like a predator ready to clamp down upon its prey. Swanson also frequently growls her sentences. Her gaze is often steady, her eyes popped wide open and unblinking in a way that seems unnatural. And her turban suggests that she may share a haberdasher with the vampires from *Nosferatu* and *Bram Stoker's Dracula,*[7] where vampires themselves can be interpreted as horrific images of fantasies of immortality.

Moreover, the horror movie imagery of *Sunset Boulevard* extends into the architecture of the film. As the film script describes Norma Desmond's mansion, it is "mottled by the years, gloomy, forsaken, the little formal garden completely gone to seed" (Brackett, Wilder, and Marshman 1999, 23). Gillis compares the moldering building to Miss Havisham, one of Dickens's more Gothic creations. He thinks that it is an abandoned house, exactly the sort of place where monsters typically dwell. It is hard to resist the intimation that this is a haunted house, especially later when the wind blowing through the pipe organ emits the musical equivalent of a wheezing presence. Of course, the ghost is Norma.

That organ is played by Norma's butler, Max. His favorite piece of music appears to be Bach's *Toccata and Fugue in D Minor,* a favorite tune of mad scientists and opera phantoms in horror films (Staggs 2000, 142). Max himself has a limp, recalling the various crippled assistants of so many Doctors Frankenstein.

Wilder takes care to shoot the inside of the house in such a way as to emphasize not only its emptiness,[8] but also its largeness, a feature of so many of the castles and laboratories of horror films in the 1930s. Wilder shows us rats infesting the neglected swimming pool—rats being often-referenced correlates to the undead, notably vampires. And, of course, Norma is the kind of person we are apt to call metaphorically "a vampire," attempting to feed off of Gillis's youthfulness.

Gillis, somewhat ungraciously, labels Norma's friends, the former silent-film stars who are her bridge partners, "the waxworks," which was the title of a German horror film famous during Wilder's youth in Berlin. But perhaps the most extensive *hommage* to the horror film comes when Norma prepares for what she believes will be her return to the screen as Salomé. In anticipation, as Gillis puts it, "an army of beauty experts invaded her house on Sunset Boulevard. She went through a merciless series of treatments, massages, sweat cabinets, mud baths, ice compresses, electric devices" (Brackett, Wilder, and Marshman 1999, 98). These are rendered via a montage sequence which critics have remarked resembles nothing so much as an experiment by a mad scientist in a horror film, undoubtedly due to the profusion of electrical equipment in a number of the shots. It is, indeed, a kind of creation scene à la Dr. Frankenstein, and, as in the case of Frankenstein's experiment, it goes horribly awry. Norma emerges from this montage, not more beautiful, but rather grotesque, done up as she is in a chin rig that makes her face seem even more a frozen mask than before.

There are other horrific accents in the film. It rains quite a lot, as is often the case in the horror genre. There is the sardonically macabre dead monkey and then its burial in a child's casket, shot from a distance that makes it seem as though we are surreptitiously witnessing some unholy ritual from afar. And, of course, when Norma descends her staircase for her "close-up," she is demented, where insanity another recurring trope of horror fiction.

Through these various cinematic strategies and more, Wilder gives cinematic substance to his theme—that Hollywood transforms people into monsters. As Arthur Danto might put it, these stylistic choices embody the meaning of *Sunset Boulevard*. In this respect, *Sunset Boulevard* is arguably the most cinematically accomplished Hollywood exposé. By primarily visual means, Wilder is able to figure Norma as monstrous and to elicit the kind of feelings of disgust toward her that we typically muster for the creatures in horror films. However, *Sunset Boulevard* is more than a Hollywood exposé; it transcends that subgenre and transmutes itself into a compelling instance of popular philosophy.[9]

What is the leading philosophical theme of *Sunset Boulevard?* The denial of mortality. The film begins with the image of death—the ghostwriter, Gillis, about to tell us about the folly of an aging movie star.[10] It is hard to resist the notion that the story is set on Sunset Boulevard because Norma has reached the "sunset" years of her life; surely her stardom "set" years before. She is, so to speak, "fading," but Norma is in denial. She thinks that she can return to the screen once more, although we are abundantly reassured that this is impossible.

The theme of aging is written all over the mansion, with its abandoned tennis courts and swimming pools. Decay is everywhere. The antique car mounted on blocks—the Isotta-Fraschini—is an unmistakable objective correlative for Norma, whose career is going nowhere and is as obsolete as the beached automobile.

Photography, which Bazin maintained "embalmed time,"[11] is an important element in the articulation of the theme of aging and its denial. Everywhere in the house there are photographs of Norma at the height of her celebrity, underscoring the contrast between the young Norma and her present self, a disparity which Norma consistently represses. That Norma is a movie star enables Wilder to foreground the theme of aging by showing us moving pictures of the youthful Norma (Gloria Swanson in *Queen Kelly*) and then cutting to Norma watching herself over twenty years later. Of course, moviegoers who were familiar with Swanson from the silent era could not fail to be struck by how her dewy good looks had fossilized (an impression heightened by Swanson's extremely stylized acting). Photography, including motion picture photography, is a time capsule. And all of those time capsules lying around in *Sunset Boulevard* bear resounding testimony to the fact that Norma, her delusions notwithstanding, is long past her prime.

Norma's aging is remarked upon in the narrative by the constant emphasis on her faded glory: the younger security guard at Paramount fails to recognize her; the studio wants her car, not her; DeMille comments that thirty million fans have abandoned her; the phony fan mail; and so on. Similarly, the subplot involving Betty Schaefer serves as a pointed foil to the relationship between Norma Desmond and Gillis. Both women are writing a script with him; both love Gillis; but one is young (it is established that Betty Schaefer is all of twenty-two), whereas DeMille's assistant says of Norma that "she must be a million years old."

In *Sunset Boulevard,* Hollywood celebrity stands to youth as obscurity stands to aging. Norma's refusal to acknowledge that her movie career is over is part and parcel of her refusal to acknowledge the passing of time. It is this, Gillis suggests, that accounts for her reclusiveness. To encounter the outside world would force her to recognize change—change in the world and change in herself. It would compel her to give up her conviction that "stars are ageless."

Given the homology between stardom and nonstardom, on the one hand, and youth and aging, on the other, the earlier equation between stardom and monstrosity takes on an additional and deeper significance: what is monstrous and unnatural about Norma Desmond is her resistance to accepting her age, as that refusal is epitomized by her obsession with playing Salomé. It is not her actual age that is monstrous, but her struggle against acquiescing to it. As Gillis says to her, "Norma, grow up. There's nothing tragic about being fifty—unless you try to be twenty-five." And, of course, in her desire to be Salomé, Norma is trying to be fourteen! Norma would prefer to descend into madness literally, as she does at the end of the film, rather than admit her time of life.

It is this denial of aging that makes Norma a grotesquerie in Wilder's eyes. This is what is monstrous about her. And ultimately it is the denial of mortality in this respect and its existential costs that colligates and unifies the disparate elements—narrative, visual, aural, and dramatic—that constitute *Sunset Boulevard*.

The disgust that Wilder mandates that we direct at Norma is rooted in her refusal to act her age—in her delusion that time has stood still and that she remains as fresh and desirable as she was before the movies learnt to talk. And undoubtedly a certain visceral recoil toward Norma is also exacerbated by the socially inculcated tendency that many viewers have which leads them to regard the erotic liaison between a younger man and a much older woman as unnatural (and "creepy," for that very reason).[12]

There are moments when we are briefly encouraged to sympathize with Norma, such as the scene on the set of *Samson and Delilah*. For a few minutes, Norma seems unguarded and vulnerable. But more often than not, her defenses are up and she behaves high-handedly, selfishly, ruthlessly. She is arrogant, cruel, and, most of all, vain. And it is her extreme vanity that shapes her demeanor in such a way that it turns her from a caricature into a monster.

Norma's story is extreme. She believes she can play the teenager Salomé. Indeed, she seems certain that she has remained the teenager she was when she first became a star. Undoubtedly, much of the uneasiness or discomfort we feel in response to that last shot of the film is energized by the palpable difference we sense between Norma as she is and the teenage Salomé she imagines she is playing.

However, upon reflection, thoughtful viewers, particularly those of us who are past middle age, are also apt to recognize something of Norma, if not in themselves, then in certain of their acquaintances. For Norma's pathology is a recurring human trait writ large (as large as a major Hollywood motion picture production). It is the failure to acknowledge the aging process, and it is evident throughout our culture, in phenomena ranging from the so-called midlife crisis to our tendency to wear into old age the clothing of youth—e.g., faded blue jeans and athletic attire (jerseys, sweatpants, sneakers, and so on). How often does one hear or even say oneself, "I don't feel x," where x takes the value of some number of years past what we call middle age. Although some may come close to rivaling Norma in their obsession with appearing youthful—whole industries are now predicated upon abetting this illusion—most pull back from the abyss of madness that engulfs Norma.

Nevertheless, Norma is a symbol of something more generic and is exaggerated for that very reason. Maybe her name is "Norma" because it is only one letter short of "normal." That is, Norma exemplifies a normal human tendency—the denial of aging—albeit in a way that is immensely magnified and symbolized by means of the imagery of Hollywood stardom.

In *Sunset Boulevard,* the narrative arc of a Hollywood career—from strutting center stage to being ushered offstage—and the delusions this risks, functions as an analog to the trajectory of a human life and the consequent pathologies that the human condition may invite; few readily accept being a has-been in either register. Furthermore, particularly in our own time, the obsession with Hollywood-type celebrity may even be a causal ingredient that helps account for the compulsion many seem to experience nowadays to appear as youthful as possible and to disguise, if not utterly suppress, their actual age. Admittedly, the degree of self-deception to which Norma is victim is far greater than ordinary. Yet her story nevertheless manages to hold a mirror up to the rest of us—although it is more of the nature of the kind of funhouse mirror that enlarges everything it reflects.

Often the task of philosophy is simply to coin new ideas and concepts. But, sometimes its office is to remind us of matters we know but of which we are perhaps only vaguely and inarticulately aware, if at all, or even is something we know, but actively ignore or repress. According to Wittgenstein, a leading function of philosophy is to enable us to understand what is in plain sight, although perhaps unrecognized; Stanley Cavell finds movies exemplary in their capacity to dramatize what is in front of our eyes and thereby to rediscover the philosophical insights we already know, but may not acknowledge.[13]

Our mortality with respect to the inexorable process of aging is one of those features of human existence of which we easily lose sight, conveniently forgetting and even repressing our awareness of this phenomenon as, in the heat of life, we press forward with our projects. The philosophical insight on offer in *Sunset Boulevard* vividly recalls for viewers this very central fact of human life. And *Sunset Boulevard* does this by revealing the desire to be ageless—Norma's notion of stardom—to be monstrous and unnatural, a rediscovery made all the more arresting and unforgettable for being underwritten by visceral feelings of disgust and horror.[14]

How Can *Sunset Boulevard* Be Philosophical?

OBJECTIONS

On the basis of my analysis of *Sunset Boulevard,* I have just asserted that *some* (in the sense of at least one) narrative, fiction film can do philosophy. Of course, I believe that more than one narrative, fiction film has this capacity. But a single case is enough to defeat the skeptics.

Nevertheless, I predict that the skeptics will not be satisfied merely by an interpretation of the sort I have just offered. Nor should they be. They will undoubtedly raise a series of objections. Three of the most likely ones are (1) *Sunset Boulevard* is not an example of philosophy, properly so-called, because even if it advances a philosophical theme, it does not demonstrate it; (2) the theme of the denial of mortality that has been associated with *Sunset Boulevard* is too banal to be deemed genuine philosophy; and (3) what possible *philosophical* purpose does the creation of an artistic object as elaborate as *Sun*set Boulevard serve? Surely Wilder's energies are actually being spent on something other than doing philosophy. In what follows, I will try to allay these anxieties in turn.

The No-Argument Argument   Even if we grant that *Sunset Boulevard* advances a philosophical theme—say, the existential necessity of acknowledging our mortality—the skeptic will observe that we do not have anything that amounts to doing philosophy. A fortune cookie, stuffed with a suitably sage Confucian adage, might propose something that sounds philosophical, but, sans argumentation, we would not say that it was doing philosophy. Why not? Because doing philosophy is not simply a matter of expressing some or another philosophical theme. Doing philosophy, properly so-called, requires supporting that theme with argument. To assert baldly and blandly that every one of my actions has been causally determined by antecedent events does not count as philosophy, unless and until that assertion figures as the conclusion of an argument—whether deductive, inductive, or abductive, and, as well, one that is preferably original. The skeptic will not countenance as philosophizing anything, if we cannot answer the challenge "Where's the argument?" But there doesn't appear to be any argument warning against the denial of aging in *Sunset Boulevard*. So, the skeptic surmises, the movie doesn't amount to a philosophical contribution.

Of course, it is not clear that the skeptic's demand for argumentation as an essential characteristic of philosophizing is uncontroversial. Nietzsche's aphorisms and Wittgenstein's puzzles are usually accepted as philosophy, although they typically come unaccompanied by argument. But, for the moment, let us grant the skeptic his premise and see whether we can still make out the case for *Sunset Boulevard* as a vehicle of philosophical insight.

The skeptic maintains that philosophy requires argumentation, but notes that there is no argument in evidence in *Sunset Boulevard*. One way in which to meet the skeptic's challenge here is to suggest that the skeptic is looking for the pertinent argumentation in the wrong place. Don't look to the voice-over narration for the argument. Nor do any of the characters articulate it. The argument lies elsewhere. Where? In the minds of the audience. *Sunset Boulevard* provides the material that the reflective viewer can and—in the ideal case—does use to reach the relevant philosophical insight on her own.

In this regard, *Sunset Boulevard,* like a number of other fictional narratives, is maieutic. That is, it draws the conviction from the audience about the human condition that it endorses as a midwife draws the infant-child from her mother. Here Billy Wilder stands in the lineage of Socrates, who educed geometry from the slave-boy in the *Meno* by asking him a series of pointed questions. Likewise, *Sunset Boulevard* confronts us with an unavoidable question, namely, what drives Norma Desmond deeper and deeper into delusion? Moreover, the narrative supplies us with ample material that clearly heads us in one direction: the realization that madness is the cost that Norma must pay for repressing her recognition of the temporality of human life, her desire that life be like a film image, eternally changeless, embalmed.

It is not the case that the only structure of legitimate philosophical argumentation must take the form of a progression from premises to conclusions. Rhetorical questions, as well, can function argumentatively, eliciting abductive leaps from listeners by introducing a selection of data whose implications gel when a strategically crafted question is posed. In such instances, the reasoning required to reach the conclusion is rehearsed by the audience. But the rhetorical question is no less an argumentative design just because it delegates the relevant reasoning to the listener. Indeed, the reasoning may seem all the more compelling to the listener because she appears to have reached it on her own.

What I want to propose is that narrative fictions such as *Sunset Boulevard* may function cognitively in a way that parallels the rhetorical question insofar as they can dispose viewers to reason, under their own steam, to the philosophical theme the fictional narrative itself is meant to embody.

Of course, *Sunset Boulevard* is not literally a question. It is rather the celluloid equivalent of a thought experiment, in this case a fictional narrative, designed to guide the audience to a definite conclusion, namely that the denial of mortal aging is self-destructive, risking a species of delusional thinking that may verge upon madness. *Sunset Boulevard* presents the viewer with a story that the spectator, on the basis of her own extracinematic experience, accepts as probable and from which she infers the lesson—the cautionary advice that Gillis offers to Norma about acting her age—which the spectator assesses to be credible, again on the basis of her own life experiences.[15]

Moreover, with respect to narrative fictions like *Sunset Boulevard*, it is not the case that spectators must reach such conclusions while in the thick of engaging with the story. They may also arrive at it afterwards in what Peter Kivy has felicitously called the *reflective afterlife* of the narrative fiction—that is, during an interval after the fiction has been absorbed when one contemplates its portents on one's own or in the company of others, immersed in lively conversation (Kivy 1997).

By locating the relevant argumentation or reasoning in the minds of the audience, we are also able to evade what might be thought of as the skeptic's dilemma. That dilemma goes like this: either the requisite argumentation is explicitly in the fictional narrative or it is not; if it is not in the fictional narrative, then the fictional narrative cannot be said to be doing philosophy, since doing philosophy demands argumentation; but, on the other hand, if the argument is explicitly stated in the narrative—either by some character or some authorial agency—then it is not by means of the narrative *as such* (by narrative means alone) that philosophy is being propounded; rather, philosophy is merely being parroted by some character or narrative agency that just happens to inhabit the narrative; the narrative could proceed as effectively, the skeptic insinuates, without said discursive interludes.

This dilemma, however, is averted by relocating the argument in the minds of the audience (as primed by the narrative *qua* thought experiment), since by being in the minds of the audience, the requirement that there be argument or reasoning is fulfilled in a way that is not liable to the charge that someone—some character or some narrative agency—is functioning rather like a ventriloquist's dummy in the world of the fictional narrative. Rather the narrative as such has been structured in such a way as to propone or to call forth the relevant reasoning in alert audience members.

One objection to relocating the required reasoning in the audience is that if we treat the narrative fiction in this way—as an elaborate thought experiment channeling viewers toward philosophical conclusions much in the fashion of a rhetorical question—then the fictional narrative must explicitly let the audience know about the exact dialectical context into which the narrative is intended to fit. Thought experiments, like rhetorical questions, occur in certain contexts. If the narrative fiction is to function as a proper thought experiment, the narrative must make its role in the pertinent debate perspicuous as well as elucidate the way in which it secures its intended point. Yet this would appear to reintroduce the threat of a dilemma. Either the narrative fiction does not unfurl its argument, in which case it has failed to specify its place in the relevant debate, or it does lay out its argument explicitly (by means of a character or a narrative agency), in which case it is not doing philosophy by means of narrative as such.

On the one hand, I am not convinced that the context in which a thought experiment figures always needs to be made explicit in the way the skeptic stipulates. In certain situations, where the participants in the debate know what is at stake—as at specialized sessions of the American Philosophical Association—a thought experiment may be voiced whose significance everyone in the room grasps, without its place in the debate needing to be spelt out in letter and verse. Indeed, informed listeners might find such an exercise pedantic. Moreover, in certain artistic milieus, especially in terms of various avant-garde movements, there may be overarching, animating questions—like what is art? or what is cinema?—of which virtually all informed spectators are aware and which, for that reason, do not require overt enunciation for uptake by prepared audiences of the relevance of the pertinent artistic thought experiments.

On the other hand, even if we accept the skeptic's contention that the dialectical context of any thought experiment that advances a philosophical thesis must be made explicit in order to count as *doing philosophy,* this challenge can be easily met with respect to *Sunset Boulevard,* while simultaneously avoiding the skeptic's dilemma. Even the most determined skeptic, Bruce Russell, allows that films can provide evidence for an informed audience to arrive at a philosophical conclusion (2009). He demands, however, that the fictional narrative at issue *also* specify the relevant dialectical context, which he appears to presume can only be done by itemizing its argumentative premises.

But this, maybe needless to say, he assumes, will mobilize the second wing of the skeptic's dilemma: it will necessitate outlining the premises of the argument by nonnarrative means (Russell 2009), thereby defeating the notion that fictional narratives as such (and notably movies) can provide philosophical insight. Yet this is logically fallacious. The possibility that the skeptic has overlooked is that the narrative may specify its dialectical context by merely stating its *conclusion* (rather than enumerating its premises) and then simply provide the audience with a compelling, emblematic example to support an inference that comports with their experience of the world and that matches the aforesaid conclusion.

And that is precisely what *Sunset Boulevard* does: as already mentioned, with respect to Norma Desmond, Joe Gillis explicitly states the pertinent thesis: "You're a woman of fifty. There's nothing tragic about being fifty—not unless you try to be twenty-five" (or, like Norma aspiring to play Salomé, a fourteen-year-old). The saga of *Sunset Boulevard* is then the thought experiment which inspires the audience to come to the conclusion on its own about the veracity of this philosophical thesis on the basis of their own experience of life outside the movies, and their own cogitations. The audience works out the relevant argument, in other words, without the reasoning being hammered home, step by step, on the soundtrack, either in the mouths of the characters or through voice-over narration.

The Banality Argument The skeptic may grant, in response to the preceding section, that the reasoning, such as it is, necessary to substantiate the alleged philosophical insight in *Sunset Boulevard* is available through the ratiocination the film is most likely to engender in the prepared and alert viewer. However, the caveat here—"such as it is"—is key, just because the skeptic doubts that there is much reasoning at all involved in confirming the conclusion that I've attributed to the philosophizing in the film. Everyone grows old, and *everyone* knows this(!), the skeptic will bark. This isn't philosophy, the skeptic continues, it's common knowledge. This conclusion, if it can really be dignified by being labeled *a conclusion,* is too trivial to be glorified as an *insight,* philosophical or otherwise. It is, not to put too fine a point on it, banal.

Furthermore, in a caustic mood, our skeptic might add that all of the so-called knowledge purportedly retailed by our beloved fictional narratives is exactly of the same sort. Don't make snap judgments, recommends *Pride and Prejudice.* Well, yes. Yet that "discovery" is hardly on a par with Kant's Copernican Revolution. That which is applauded as Austen's philosophical acumen is, frankly, obvious. It's banal, whereas philosophical insight, properly so-called, is never banal. It is, perforce, original, defamiliarizing, unexpected, and/or unconventional.

Yet, once again, the problem here is that the skeptic presupposes too narrow a conception of philosophy. Philosophy may often be involved in the postulation of heretofore unimagined possibilities—monads, the phenomenal/noumenal distinction, and so on. That is certainly one office of philosophy. But, equally, another task of philosophy is to recall to mind features of human experience that, if known once, have been forgotten or are only dimly grasped or are ignored, neglected, and/or even repressed.

For example, central to the not unrelated philosophies of Kierkegaard and Heidegger is the observation that death is an inescapable fact of the human condition *and* that humans typically deny that death is a fact of life (of *Dasein,* as Heidegger would have it). "Terror, perdition, annihilation dwell next door to every man," Kierkegaard points out in *The Concept of Dread* (1957, 140); but most of us live in, as he says, "half-obscurity" about our existential plight (1954, 181; see also Becker 1973, esp. chap. 5). For Kierkegaard, this is our human birthright; as God casts Adam and Eve from the garden, He tells them, "Thou shalt surely die." And yet this is perhaps the hardest thing for us to get our minds around, as we immerse ourselves in our daily pursuits, no matter how insignificant.[16] Enmeshed in our daily affairs—that appointment for cleaning our teeth with the dentist, for example—we never allow to intrude on our behavior the thought of how unimportant this is given the absolute certainty of our ultimate demise. But how could we exist otherwise?

Heidegger is even more emphatic about our mortal tendency to deny mortality. He points out that "one *knows* about the certainty of death, and yet 'is' not authentically certain of one's own"; because "death is deferred to 'sometime later', and this is done by invoking the 'so-called' general opinion'. . . . Thus the 'they' covers up what is peculiar in death's certainty—*that it is possible at any moment*" (1962, 302). Kierkegaard and

Heidegger are seminal philosophers precisely because they remind us of facts of the human condition which, although admittedly known, are readily forgotten. You might dismiss this as "prophetic philosophy," but it has been one of the tasks of philosophy since the get-go. Ancient philosophy was primarily concerned with how to live (and die) (Hadot 2000, 2009), and in this matter ancient philosophy is closer to what I am calling popular philosophy, the philosophy that primarily engages the layperson (as opposed to the academic).

Obviously, dwelling upon death could stultify action.[17] Why do anything if, in the larger scheme of things, dust is your final reward? So that thought needs be repressed. An important charge of philosophy is to compel us to remember that which we naturally suppress. This is connected to philosophy as a mode of living—which, in turn, is patently relevant to the mission of *popular* philosophy, as it was to ancient philosophy. Popular philosophy is not mainly for the graduate seminar room, where possible worlds await conquest. Popular philosophy is for places like the novel and the movie theater, wherein reminders of mortality have a definite rhetorical bite.

Narrative fiction is ideally suited to engage the populace in popular philosophizing. The insights about the denial of death found in Kierkegaard and Heidegger, for example, are energetically recalled to mind in *Exit the King* by Eugène Ionesco. In that play, the king, Berenger the First, is over four hundred years old. He is about to die. At one point it is predicted that he only has one hour, twenty-four minutes, and fifty seconds to live (putatively the remaining running time of the play). The "Exit" in the title, of course, refers to his death. Throughout the play, Berenger attempts to resist his destiny with various forms of specious reasoning, including the assertion that "kings ought to be immortal" (Ionesco 1967, 36). As he tries to talk his way out of dying, the audience recognizes in him their own—and, for that matter, everyone else's—constant refusal to confront their inexorable fate, including the possibility that we may no longer be here in one hour, twenty-four minutes, and fifty seconds. Wrapped up in our quotidian affairs, few prepare for the inevitable, but, as Berenger has done for over four hundred years, we thrust it out of mind.

That Berenger is so old, of course, emphasizes the tenacity of his denial. Moreover, his denial of his mortality is not unlike Norma Desmond's denial of her advancing age. Interestingly, Berenger's statement that "kings ought to be immortal" curiously echoes Norma's question "Stars are ageless, aren't they?" Both the play and the film not only call upon us to remember the unavoidable facts of our mortality, but also dispose us to recognize and acknowledge our indefatigable propensity to disavow the only guaranteed experiences to which flesh is heir. Indeed, death is even more inevitable than taxes. Furthermore, as argued earlier, we confirm these hypotheses on the basis of our own experience of ourselves and others by calling upon our familiarity with the world outside of fiction.

With respect to *Sunset Boulevard*, the skeptic is apt to charge that everyone knows that aging is inevitable and even that most are cognizant of our tendency to deny this by means of varying degrees of self-deception. Thus, since this is common knowledge, it is too banal to count as philosophy. Indeed, since this is so widely understood, saying that a narrative fiction like *Sunset Boulevard* enables us to "discover" it is ludicrous. There is no insight where the phenomena are in clear sight. And yet, however much we are inclined to agree that everyone knows the human realities that *Sunset Boulevard* dramatizes, we must also acknowledge that we conveniently forget them most of the time. The so-called facts of the matter are not truly in "clear sight." The skeptic is correct; *Sunset Boulevard* does not lead us to discover that which Norma has denied; but it does prompt us to *rediscover* what we already know, and one of the functions of philosophy, since its origins, has been to remind us of deep truths that we have repressed.

Furthermore, because these kinds of truths are so easily forgotten, it is the recurring task of philosophy to invent new devices and stratagems for recalling our attention to them. These include novel thought experiments of all sorts, including popular narrative fictions.

Reminding audiences of truths of the human condition we are disposed to suppress, albeit at our own peril, has been a function of the most significant narrative fiction since the beginning. *Oedipus Rex* concludes by advising, "Call no man happy until he is dead." In this, Sophocles is reminding audiences of one of the deepest insights of Greek philosophy, namely, that bad things can happen to good people. We have a tendency to become so involved in the details and projects of our lives that we forget how vulnerable we are to misfortune. We ignore the facts that disaster can befall us at any moment and that we won't know whether we have lived a happy life until once in the grave, we are out of harm's way. The role of tragedy is to remind us of truths that we tend to repress. It makes philosophy— particularly philosophy as it is related to the task of living—available to the populace. *Sunset Boulevard* stands in that tradition, recalling for us facts of life that, however mundane, are most frequently neglected, generally to our own peril.

The Excessive Elaboration Argument   As we have seen, *Sunset Boulevard* is a very complex artistic object, as is the case with many other supposedly philosophical narrative fictions. In fact, they are far more complicated than would appear to be necessary for the purpose of advancing the philosophical themes that they are alleged to communicate. Compared to the thought experiments one typically finds in standard philosophical discourse, these so-called thought experiments are very extravagant. This suggests that it is not the primary purpose of these narrative fictions—if it is their purpose at all—to present philosophy, popular or otherwise. With respect to *Sunset Boulevard,* the skeptic submits that it was designed to entertain, not to instruct. It is only the superego of people like me that motivates us to attempt to locate its value in terms of philosophical didacticism. Perhaps we feel the need to justify those hours at the movies when we should have been doing our homework.

Undoubtedly, the first thing to note in response to this argument is that it would not be a problem for the view (that narrative fictions can do philosophy in the manner indicated above) if this was not the only or even the primary purpose of the relevant fictions. Most fictions have multiple aims. That a narrative fiction may have more than one purpose is compatible with the assertion that philosophizing is one of them. Furthermore, it is not evident that entertainment and philosophical instruction must always be construed as opposites. Philosophical instruction can be entertaining by engaging the mind. Even thought experiments in professional philosophy journals often make a play for amusement.

But a deeper response to the excessive-elaboration objection rejects the charge that the kinds of narrative fictions that *Sunset Boulevard* represents are more complex than they need to be. Given the philosophical service that such a narrative is meant to perform, *Sunset Boulevard* has just the kind of structures required to discharge its function.

What is the function of *Sunset Boulevard?* Well, *one* function, *ex hypothesi,* is to impress spectators deeply with its insight into our tendency to deny our mortal finitude, particularly with respect to the passage of time. In order to drive that insight home forcefully, *Sunset Boulevard,* like most narrative fictions of the pertinent variety, recruits our emotions.[18] The supposedly overelaborate structures that the skeptic maintains serve no philosophical function are precisely what are called for in order to enlist the spectator's emotions in the process of—let us call it—their philosophical education.

For example, earlier we stressed the subtle infusion of horror imagery throughout *Sunset Boulevard*. This, however, is not mere ornamentation for the sake of ornamentation. Its purpose is to direct our emotional appraisal of what Norma Desmond is doing. The recoil of horror that Norma Desmond elicits focuses our attention upon what is "against nature" in her behavior and marks it as monstrous. Because the emotions are essentially evaluative, we do not merely pick up an interesting anthropological fact about human nature from *Sunset Boulevard*, but instead one that is saturated with value. The aversion we feel for Norma not only shapes our assessment of her while viewing the film, but by being so emotionally arresting embeds the philosophical lesson to be garnered from *Sunset Boulevard* more deeply in spectators than would any prosaic statement of its theme.

Popular philosophy aspires to educe philosophical insight from broad audiences. In this endeavor, the emotions are a natural ally inasmuch as they serve not only to guide cognition and appraisal, but also to make a deep impression. Thus, much of the complexity of narrative fictions like *Sunset Boulevard*—which skeptics dismiss as irrelevant to their putative philosophical mission—functions to induce the kind of emotional engagement from audiences that facilitates achieving philosophical understanding and making it one's own.

One aspect of this is the development of rather detailed narratives, which emphasize the particularity of the events and persons recounted. This is important since our minds, including our emotions, have been adaptively calibrated by evolution as mechanisms responsive to our immediate and concrete surroundings. That is why popular philosophy relies so heavily upon very individualized stories. Likewise, fictional narratives like *Sunset Boulevard* cast characters and events in ways designed to trigger preordained emotional responses, like the revulsion we feel toward Norma Desmond, not simply to entertain us by provoking an affective rush, but in order to lead us to appreciate the significance of the events depicted in the proper evaluative light and to assure that that insight sinks in.

To a large extent, fictional narratives engage audiences emotionally by what I call criterial prefocusing (Carroll 1997). That is, the visceral appraisals that we call emotions track certain features of situations, the supposed perception of which triggers the state in question. For example, fear is the response to the perception of danger. In this regard, perceived danger is a criterion for the state of fear; perceived wrong is a criterion for anger; and so on. Fictioneers exploit the criteria of the emotions they mean to provoke by describing or depicting the events and persons in their stories in terms that saliently stress the pertinent emotional criteria—for instance, the piety of Aeneas is repeatedly underlined in order to secure our admiration for him. In this way, the fictioneer, so to speak, has predigested the story for us. He has prefocused our attention so that, in the largest number of cases, audiences shift into the intended emotional state smoothly and reliably.

A great many of the complex structures found in countless narrative fictions, especially popular ones, involve the emotional address of the story. This is true not only of popular fictions in general but also of those that promote philosophical insight. As we have already seen, the use of the emotion of horror—as criterially prefocused in a number of ways, including Swanson's performance—is central to *Sunset Boulevard*. It not only shapes our aversive response to what Norma Desmond is attempting to do but does so in a manner that is deeply memorable, indeed indelible. It helps us see her error in a way we are unlikely to forget. Thus, that which the skeptic is tempted to regard as structures so elaborate that they call into question whether *Sunset Boulevard* is really doing philosophy turn out to be just the kinds of designs that can foster popular philosophy.

Summary

In recent years, there has been a mounting interest in the relation between narrative fictions, especially popular narrative fictions such as movies, and philosophy. Some philosophers have maintained that such narratives can contribute to philosophical insight, while others have rejected this hypothesis. In this essay, I have identified one narrative, *Sunset Boulevard,* which I believe has a fair claim to the mantle of philosophy, albeit popular philosophy. I have identified its major philosophical theme as an exploration of the denial of mortal aging and the existential costs that entails, as exemplified in the story of Norma Desmond. I have also examined three arguments that skeptics might level against my claims on behalf of *Sunset Boulevard.* These include what I have called the no-argument argument, the banality argument, and the excessive-elaboration argument. The no-argument argument fails because it ignores the audience's share in producing the philosophical insight available through *Sunset Boulevard.* The banality argument falters because it overlooks philosophy's role as a discloser of hidden truths, known but repressed. And lastly, the excessive-elaboration argument stumbles because it underestimates the role of emotional engagement in the dissemination of popular philosophy, perhaps due to drawing too sharp a distinction between cognitive content and emotional content, an error to which we academic philosophers are frequently prone.

NOTES

I would like to thank Joan Acocella, Robert Cornfield, Aaron Smuts, Leland Monk, C. Allen Speight, and the audiences of the Film Program of the Graduate Center of the City University of New York and the Institute for Philosophy and Religion for their comments on this piece. They, of course, are not responsible for its errors; I am.

1. In this essay, I am concentrating on the possibility of popular fictions doing popular philosophy—philosophy for the masses. In other essays, I have defended the broader claims that fictions can convey knowledge and that artworks, including literary and audiovisual ones, can engender fairly sophisticated theoretical and/or philosophical knowledge. See Carroll (2006, 173–85; 2009; 2010a; 2010b). It is not that I have abandoned these broader claims but rather that I want in this essay to examine more closely the relationship of popular narratives to popular philosophy.

2. It also won Academy Awards for art direction and musical score.

3. When Gillis refers to himself as a "ghostwriter," the phrase takes on a second meaning; a verbal reference to ghosts also pops up when Gillis speaks of the "ghost of a tennis court."

4. Maybe one measure of the power of this image is that nearly fifty-nine years after the release of the film, it can serve as the source of an allusion in the installation piece *The Collectors* by Elmgreen and Dragset at the 2009 Venice Biennale.

5. Indeed, the fish-eye view of Gillis's body suggests visually that he may be something's next meal.

6. Indeed, Swanson referred to herself as a "sacred monster" in her memoirs. See Swanson (1980, 444–45).

7. The theme of Norma as vampire is developed at length in Lucy Fisher's excellent article "*Sunset Boulevard:* Fading Stars" (Fisher 1988). I have benefited from the many insights in Dr. Fisher's essay. The idea is also broached by Haskell (1974, 246).

8. Where emptiness is an index of Norma's being alone, abandoned by her audience.

9. Here I want to emphasize that *Sunset Boulevard* is an example of *substantive* popular philosophy—which is my way of saying that it philosophizes about life, in contrast to many contemporary popular movies, which, if they aspire to philosophy or theory at all, are more often advancing general insight into the workings of motion pictures. For instance, Jim Jarmusch's *Limits of Control* explores the genre of the spy thriller, barring its devices, by suppressing crucial information in a way that enables the viewer to discover many of its recurring strategies, whereas in *Inglourious Basterds* Quentin Tarantino uses hyperbole and (inglorious?) exaggeration to limn the conventions of the war movie and the western (in fact, Tarantino's movie is the bastard child of these two genres). In this respect, both of these films are descendants of Jean-Luc Godard's *Made in U.S.A.*, which employs these strategies and more to expose the rhetoric of Hollywood filmmaking. We can assume that his title refers to *movies made in the U.S.A.*

10. Indeed, the original scene in the movie, later dropped, involved Gillis talking to other corpses in the LA morgue. See Sikov (1999, 293, 301).

11. Bazin (2005, 60). It might be interesting to speculate that it is perhaps due to this "embalming effect" that Norma has been deluded into believing that, as she says, stars are ageless, since she appears ageless in the silent films of herself that she watches over and over again.

12. Although Swanson was only fifty at the time the film was made, her acting—including the stiffness that makes her seem like a living corpse—makes her seem much older. And, in any event, in the 1950s American audiences would have been even more likely to be conditioned to regard a relation like Norma's and Gillis's as disgusting.

13. Wittgenstein (1958, 42e); Cavell (2005, 190). The notion that narrative may recover knowledge is also developed by Gibson (2007, esp. chap. 3).

14. Indeed, stars, by Norma's definition, turn out to be unnatural, inhuman, and monstrous just because they are ageless, like vampires.

15. There should be no question about whether stories—including thought experiments couched as stories—can lead audiences to conclusions abductively. Think of Aesopian fables and then recall that not all of Aesop's fables came with the morals tacked onto them.

16. Indeed, it has been suggested that the brain has subconscious subroutines designed precisely to inhibit thoughts of our own mortality. For how effective could we be if, like some character from a Woody Allen film, we were constantly stricken by thoughts of our own mortality? See Carey (2009, D1).

17. As Aaron Smuts reminded me, Gilgamesh, in the epic that bears his name, undergoes an utter mental collapse when he realizes that he will die. Myths, like philosophy, remind us of verities we might prefer to forget.

18. Perhaps at this point some philosophers, in the tradition of Plato, will argue that by enlisting our emotions, *Sunset Boulevard* shows itself to be clearly not of the party of philosophy. For philosophy has no truck with the emotions. However, I think this is false. For instance, the emotions come into play when we consult our intuitions when confronting various thought experiments and counterexamples in moral and political philosophy, since those intuitions are rooted in our sentiments with respect to fairness, justice, obligation, and so forth. Ethics is not the only area of philosophy where emotions have a legitimate role, but inasmuch as there is this one arena—indeed, an arena often germane to popular philosophy—we need not yield to the skeptic's claim that emotion has no place in philosophy.

REFERENCES

Bazin, André. 2005. "Cinematic Realism." In *The Philosophy of Film,* edited by Thomas Wartenberg and Angela Curran. Oxford: Wiley-Blackwell.

Becker, Ernest. 1973. *The Denial of Death.* New York: Free Press.

Brackett, Charles, Billy Wilder, and D. M. Marshman. 1999. *Sunset Boulevard.* Berkeley and Los Angeles: University of California Press.

Carey, Benedict. 2009. "Why the Imp in Your Brain Gets Out." Science Times, *New York Times,* July 7, D1.

Carroll, Noël. 1997. "Art, Narrative, and Emotion." In *Emotion and the Arts,* edited by Mette Hjort and Sue Laver, 190–211. Oxford: Oxford University Press.

———. 2006. "Philosophizing Through the Moving Image: The Case of *Serene Velocity.*" *Journal of Aesthetics and Art Criticism* 64 (1): 173–85.

———. 2009. "*Memento* and the Phenomenology of Comprehending Motion Picture Narratives." In *Memento,* edited by Andrew Kania. London: Routledge.

———. 2010a. "Literary Realism, Recognition, and the Communication of Knowledge." In *Art in Three Dimensions.* Oxford: Oxford University Press.

———. 2010b. "The Wheel of Virtue." In *Art in Three Dimensions.* Oxford: Oxford University Press.

Cavell, Stanley (in conversation with Andrew Klevan). 2005. "What Becomes of Thinking on Film?" In *Film as Philosophy: Essays on Cinema After Wittgenstein and Cavell,* edited by Rupert Read and Jerry Goodenough, 167–209. London: Palgrave-Macmillan.

Fisher, Lucy. 1988. "Sunset Boulevard: Fading Stars." In *Women and Film,* edited by. Janet Todd, 97–113. New York: Holmes and Meier.

Gibson, John. 2007. *Fiction and the Weave of Life.* Oxford: Oxford University Press.

Hadot, Pierre. 2000. *What Is Ancient Philosophy?* Cambridge, Mass.: Harvard University Press.

———. 2009. *The Present Alone Is Our Happiness.* Stanford: Stanford University Press.

Haskell, Molly. 1974. *From Reverence to Rape: The Treatment of Women in the Movies.* Baltimore: Penguin Books.

Heidegger, Martin. 1962. *Being and Time.* Translated by John Macquarrie and Edward Robinson. New York: Harper and Row.

Ionesco, Eugène. 1967. *Exit the King.* In *Exit the King, The Killer, and Macbett: Three Plays by Eugène Ionesco,* translated by Charles Marowitz and Donald Watson. New York: Grove Press.

Kierkegaard, Søren. 1954. *The Sickness unto Death,* Translated by Walter Lowrie. Garden City, N.Y.: Anchor Editions.

———. 1957. *The Concept of Dread.* Translated by Walter Lowrie. Princeton: Princeton University Press.

Kivy, Peter. 1997. "The Laboratory of Fictional Truth." In *Philosophies of Art: An Essay in Differences,* 121–39. Cambridge: Cambridge University Press.

Russell, Bruce. 2009. The Limits of Film Again. Author Meets Critics Session, American Society for Aesthetics, Annual Meeting of the Pacific Division, Asilomar, California, April 15–17.

Sikov, Ed. 1999. *On Sunset Boulevard: The Life and Times of Billy Wilder.* New York: Hyperion.

Staggs, Sam. 2000. *Close-up on Sunset Boulevard: Billy Wilder, Nora Desmond, and the Dark Hollywood Dream.* New York: St. Martin's Press.

Swanson, Gloria. 1980. *Swanson on Swanson.* New York: Random House.

Wittgenstein, Ludwig. 1958. *Philosophical Investigations I.* Translated by Elizabeth Anscombe. London: Basil Blackwell.

Thick Narratives

John Gibson

That literary content is often a kind of ethical content seems in one sense obvious. After all, if literary works concern themselves with the stuff of human experience, they can as much ignore the ethical as they can the psychological, familial, social, or political dimensions of life. On one sense of "ethical," the ethical just *is* the particular relationship that obtains between these and similar aspects of life in a given community: it is what constitutes its "ethical life," as certain philosophical traditions have it. If this is so, then the very act of offering a representation of cultural activity or a vision of life—in literature or elsewhere—is nearly always stamped with a kind of ethical significance.

The problem the philosopher of art faces is not whether ethical concerns are *ever* relevant to the evaluation and appreciation of literary works. Contrary to a certain rumor, few philosophers have ever denied this.[1] The problem, rather, is to account for the ethical dimension of literature in such a way that we can accommodate certain curious features of literary experience. Chief among these features is the plain fact that there are many successful literary works—works we value *as literature*—that seem vicious if judged from a purely moral point of view. One should think here not only of the often cited examples, such as expressions of anti-Semitism and fascist sympathy in the work of high modernists like T. S. Eliot, Ezra Pound, and Wyndham Lewis (the last of whom wrote the lovingly entitled *Hitler*[2]). If one were to mine the great works of the Western canon from antiquity to the present, the list of works in which one finds content that is from the moral point of view odious or at least highly suspicious—works that seem to endorse or aestheticize forms of sexism, racism, violence, intolerance, classism, and all other manner of moral nastiness—would likely be considerably longer than the list of those we would take to be on the side of the angels. Observations such as these have led many philosophers to embrace a version of *immoralism,* a position that has been given a wide range of senses, all of which share the belief that, all things being equal, literary works can survive their moral flaws. Indeed, they often thrive precisely on account of them.

What I want to show here is how to reconcile the plausible insight of the immoralist with the lingering sense that literary content may at a deeper level still be shot through with ethical significance. It is possible, and in fact happens quite frequently, that literary works that "fail" in the respect immoralists deem relevant can still be engaged in important ethical labor, and so the sorts of concern that guide immoralism (and its competitor positions[3]) are not always decisive in determining the ethical character of a literary work. The immoralist is impressed by the fact that literary works can get away with saying Yea where morality says Boo.[4] I do not think that the immoralist is wrong to find significant this freedom that literature enjoys from the burden of speaking always on the side of morality. But I do think that the nature of literature's relation to morality is much more complicated than this. This is because there are, or so I shall argue, two potential centers of moral gravity in the literary work of art, and the contemporary debate surrounding immoralism—and the ethical value of art more generally—has largely concerned itself with only one of them. My goal here is to expose and argue for the significance of the other.

The contemporary debate tends to conceive of literature's ethically relevant activity as having an essentially *evaluative* character, consisting at root in the ways in which a work manifests attitudes of approbation and censure in respect to the social practices it explores and casts in shades of good and evil the forms of behavior it represents.[5] Literary works can clearly go about this well or badly, from the moral point of view, and hence it is natural to look here when trying to identify exactly how literature opens itself up to moral assessment. A more technical way of putting what this amounts to is to say that the contemporary debate treats the ethically relevant features of, say, a novel as in an important respect analogous to moral *judgments,* with the immoralist's insight being that novels can apply moral concepts—

"judgment" taken broadly, as the considered application of a kind of concept to some state of affairs—in ways that are unwarranted, false, or simply bizarre.[6] This is in essence the immoralist's entire point: an artistically successful novel can often get away with casting a murderer as *heroic,* a misogynist as *enlightened,* a pedophile as *amusing,* whereas by the lights of our best moral theories and soundest moral intuitions *contemptible, ignorant, repulsive* (or whatever) ought to apply to these representations.

I think that all of this is reasonable, and it has at any rate been thoroughly and competently studied by others.[7] But the alternative picture I will develop will part with it in a fundamental way. This picture locates an ethical dimension of literature that does not at all consist in the ways in which literature gives expression to moral judgments, manifests virtuous or vicious attitudes, or anything of the sort. Rather, this dimension concerns a specific sort of *meaning* literary works can bestow upon the events they relate, a kind of *narrative sense* that, I hope to show, reveals how literature may bear a significant kind of ethical value even when it goes rogue in exactly the respect the immoralist brings to our attention.

Self-Narratives

The area of contemporary philosophy in which narrative theory has been most exciting is arguably not the philosophy of literature but the philosophy of the self. It has been a particularly fruitful area of research because the narrative turn in the philosophy of the self has shown us how to ask the traditional questions of the field without being led into the thick of metaphysics. When a contemporary philosopher asks what a self is, she often has in mind a kind of narrative achievement rather than a kind of entity; and when she wonders how this self might persist over time, she often asks this as a question about the extension of a kind of story and not about the perdurance of a peculiar kind of substance. It goes without saying that there is much controversy concerning just what a narrative self might be, and I won't be taking much of a stance on it here. But I do want to bring to light a few respects in which narrative approaches to selfhood open up ways of understanding what literary narratives can accomplish ethically.

Before beginning, I need to introduce a basic distinction in narrative theory, the distinction between a story and a narrative.[8] The distinction is not altogether natural in English, where the two terms are more or less interchangeable (hence some scholars prefer to use *fabula* and *sjužet* or to use expressions that combine the two ideas, for example "storytelling"). But the point, if not the terminology, is clear enough. A story is what a narrative relates. It is the material out of which a narrative is woven, the constellation of events a narrative shapes in the act of recounting them. The distinction is similar to that of *content* and *mode of presentation,* though the concept of narrative is richer and has a more focused extension than that of mode of presentation. By making this distinction, we open up the possibility of seeing how a story is *transformed* by the narrative that recounts it, not in the sense that it becomes a different story, but in the sense that in the act of narration a story becomes freighted with patterns of meaning and significance (emotional, for example) that are not properties of the mere story itself.[9] In this respect, there can be different narratives of the same story, though not quite different stories of the same narrative.[10] This idea of the "transposability" of a story is familiar enough as the practice of retelling traditional tales. Think of the genre of the *chanson de geste,* the various versions of Socrates' trial, or the many incarnations of *Romeo and Juliet*— set either in Verona or New York—with Shakespeare's own version a retelling of a prior Italian tale.

It should be noted that in practice stories usually cannot be neatly distinguished from the narratives that relate them. For one thing, stories are usually *created* by the very narratives that recount them and never go on to achieve existence independent of those narratives. This is the case of most works of fiction that are not retellings of older tales. For another, the presence of a story almost always indicates the presence of narrative agency. The events we treat as constituting a story are selected from endless other candidate events, and this act of selection would seem to be an act of *narrative* selection, a kind of executive decision as to which events will find a home in the story one wishes to relate. For example, you likely will not include in the "story of your life" the event of being served a salad the last time you ate at your parents'; but you probably will include that it was at this meal that your parents told you that you were adopted. This decision will be a narrative one, a decision concerning the events you deem essential (or irrelevant) to the story you must tell if you are to succeed in conveying a sense of who you are. For these reasons, it would be a mistake to think that stories always predate their narratives or are logically separable from them. Since the ideas are so intertwined, the distinction should be heard as one of convenience and not of kind.

With this in mind, I want to bring to view a precise kind of sense narratives can convey, extracting my point from a few rather simple reflections on the role narrative can play in helping us form a particular kind of self-concept.[11] I will do so with the aid of an example, one that is plausible in fiction if not in fact. Imagine an amnesiac. He has, of course, no memory, and with the loss of his memory he has also lost his sense of self, that is, he has lost his understanding of the kind of person he is. Now imagine that he is given a certain drug, one that *almost* works. His memories come flooding back, but not his sense of self. The memories are scattered and disjointed, like a box of photographs emptied onto the floor. The obvious question is, what does the amnesiac have to do to forge a sense of self out of this mess of memory?

I would think that the first thing we should say is that it would not take very long for a rudimentary sense of self to appear. If memories are essentially experiential and perspectival,[12] the person who has them cannot help but see the memories as *his*. It is, as it were, written into our memories that they are ours, expressive of our experiences and perspectives as subjects— otherwise they'd hardly be intelligible as memories. This reflexive identification with the content of his memories would help the amnesiac to begin to reconstruct a story of his life.[13] Importantly, he would have access to basic causal-psychological information concerning his role as an agent in the events he now recalls. His memories would include first-personal information about how he felt during certain experiences and the desires and intentions that underwrote many of his recollected actions. It would be difficult for him to remember an especially destructive relationship without also remembering the love that gave him the desire to continue in it despite everything; and recalling those endless hours of running in a crowd would likely also be to recall his passion for marathons.[14] In this respect, the recovering amnesiac will soon have not just a basic *chronicle* of his life, an ordering of many of its key events. He will also be able to detect in his life something that resembles a *plot*,[15] a sense of the standing goals and pursuits that explain why he acted as he did; and this, in turn, will endow his chronology with an air of purposive movement. The understanding he will acquire about his past will surely not be as detailed as it was before his accident. And the amnesiac's labor, one would think, will involve as much reconstruction as it will retrieval of his past, and there is clearly room for error here. But it will suffice to give him a serviceable *story* of his life, the odd lacuna and misremembering notwithstanding.

But if this is all that our amnesiac has, he will have a very thin sense of self. He can identify himself as an agent in the events he now recalls, but he does not yet have a conception of why he was the *kind* of person to have acted as he did. Without this, his sense of self is preposterously episodic, limited to knowing no more about himself than that he did this on that occasion.[16] That is, his self-concept will be no broader than his awareness of the desires and impressions that happened to have passed through him during those moments he now recalls. As such, it hardly resembles the form of articulated self-awareness we imply we have when we say, to ourselves or to others, *this is who I am*. When our amnesiac looks at the story of his life he now possesses and then asks, "But who am I?" we understand perfectly well what he is after. He wishes to be able to see something *general* about himself reflected in the various events that constitute his story, an image of the *kind* of person he is. In trying to recover his sense of self, he is struggling to see his story as expressive of what he is made of, in the sense we intend when doing moral psychology. So the question becomes, what does the amnesiac have to do with his story to arrive at this richer sense of self?

This is where narrative comes in. The crucial thing when one has a story is to determine *how to tell it*. When we tell our stories, we do not just list off their key events: we inevitably *interpret* them. This is not interpretation of an especially technical sort, unless we are in for a bit of professional help. In its most basic form it is interpretation as, following David Velleman, *construal*. For example, say our amnesiac comes to find that the story of his life includes a great number of run-ins with the law, so many in fact that he cannot help but take them as defining who he is (see Velleman 2003). This is important, but note how little this gives him by way of a self-conception: "lawbreaker" or some similarly vague self-description might follow from it, but not much else. It is in the narrative he weaves that this is made into a story of a specific kind of self, and there is much room for maneuver here. He might feel constrained to tell it as the tale of misguided, petty criminal: of a life wasted. Or with some charity he might find that it is best cast as the heroic story of a romantic rebel. Or perhaps he will blame his criminality on his parents, his genes, or "society" and offer up the image of a life ruined by regular visits from Bad Luck. One could go on imagining possible narrative construals of his story, all more or less within the realm of rational possibility for a history such as his. What is important for our purposes is to note how different the story becomes upon each telling, and that each of these differences in construal marks an important difference in self-conception, in the amnesiac's sense of who he basically *is*.

It is through this narrative act that the recovering amnesiac fashions an image of himself that looks like what he is after when he asks, "Who am

I?" What the amnesiac is in effect doing here is making the story *his* story. In deciding how his story is to be narrated, the story becomes *about* the sort of person he takes himself to be. The self-concept he acquires through this narrative act accomplishes at least two things. First, it represents the *moral* to be drawn from the story of his life: if the moral we derive from artworks is a kind of meaning, the moral we derive from our life stories is a kind of self-conception. And secondly, this self-concept in turn offers an orientation towards the events of the story themselves, a way of understanding their significance and import. The self-concept in effect represents what the story is *about*. In this respect, the kind of sense these self-narratives communicate has little to do with the *connection* (causal, emotional, or otherwise) between the events of a story, contrary to a common view of what narratives concern themselves with. These narratives have as their goal the attribution of sense *to the story itself*. They essentially concern the whole and not the links between the various parts.

I do not wish to claim that all narratives have this as their goal; surely many do not. But this discussion of selfhood does bring to view a very interesting narrative power, and this is its value. We might call the kind of narratives I am discussing here *thick narratives*. Gilbert Ryle introduced the distinction between thick and thin descriptions, and, following him, the sort of narrative I am exploring here is "thick" by virtue of possessing an especially rich kind of descriptive content (see Ryle 2009). To use an example in the style of Ryle himself, consider the evolving thickness of the following descriptions of f: (i) a flutter of an eyelid, (ii) a conspicuous wink, and (iii) an incorrigible flirt who is again making inappropriate eyes at you. Likewise, when the amnesiac turns his story of a generic "lawbreaker" into the tale of a fiercely individualistic enemy of authority, he has offered up a thick narrative. In thinking this of himself, he may, depending on the facts of his life, reveal that he is delusional. But it will be a decidedly thick delusion, and it will be that by virtue of the thickness of the narrative he has woven.

It was Bernard Williams who made fashionable philosophical talk of the thick and thin, in his case in respect to kinds of concept (see Williams 1985). For Williams, thick concepts are ethical concepts like *courageous, cruel, generous,* and *compassionate,* and one can easily imagine extending the list to include aesthetic and emotional concepts like *rude, inelegant, graceful, joyous,* and *melancholic*—here in the realm of value the distinction between the emotional, aesthetic, and moral blurs very quickly.[17] The first thing to note about thick concepts so conceived is that they pick out the kind of qualities we attribute to ourselves and to others when weaving these narratives of selfhood I am exploring here. Unlike thin concepts, which merely evaluate an object (he is a *good* father, that painting is *ugly,* and so forth), thick concepts, because of their descriptive richness, can cast their objects as having highly defined sorts of *character:* hence it is often said that they represent a fusing of fact and value, of description and evaluation. It is for this reason that thick concepts offer a more internal perspective on the self to which they are applied, giving a sense of how the individual hangs together as a person, such as when we call someone—and mean what we say to pick out something basic about the person—cowardly, spiritual, or poetic. This is one of the reasons these concepts, and by extension the narratives that make use of them, are *thick:* they convey information about the object under scrutiny that is sufficient to situate it at a precise point in the space of value.

I will work out the ethical significance of thick narratives in my discussion of literature, which I turn to next. But one thing is worth mentioning briefly before concluding this discussion of selves. These thick narratives have as their goal the articulation of a kind of content that is clearly ethical but that has very little to do with the specification of duties, obligations, or methods for determining the moral worth of possible courses of action. In fact, it has very little to do with ethics conceived as a matter of making moral *judgments,* of offering verdicts concerning the rightness or wrongness of actions and intentions (or representations of them, such as we find in art). It is a conception of the ethical in the ancient and expansive sense of the term. When we weave these thick narratives, we are not attempting to offer an insight into the realm of oughts but to cast into relief the specific arrangement of desires, passions, hopes, beliefs, and values that define us. The self-image we offer up in these narratives is our attempt to reveal the ways in which we embody these and similar features of moral character, that is, of the ethical structure of a person. An insight into this is an insight into something not of theoretical but earthly ethical significance: a sense of what we amount to as agents, as people.

Literary Narratives

I can now return to literature, and my discussion will shift focus from narratives that try to make sense of one's self to narratives that try to make sense of one's culture. The leap from the personal to the social here is unsurprising, at least if we recall that the term from which the English word "ethics" ultimately derives is *êthos*, which for a speaker of Attic Greek could be used without much change of meaning to refer to the moral character of a self or a society. The analogy I shall argue for is the following: just as thick narratives allow us to express how we are (or take ourselves to be) constituted as selves, literary works often employ thick narratives to convey a sense of how a culture is constituted ethically. This is a mouthful, so let me explain, beginning again with the importance of stories.

Until modernism stepped on the scene, it would have seemed quite natural to claim that to be a literary work is, among other things, to have a story to tell. And while we should be skeptical of easy identifications of literature with narrative—it is common to speak of nonnarrative poetry, for example[18]—in a comfortable majority of cases literary works tell a story, however unorthodox or avant-garde their telling may be. And one option writers frequently take up is that of telling the tale of some aspect of common experience: those stories of loss, love, exploitation, alienation, hard-won happiness, and so on that define us. One way of putting this is to say that writers often assume the guise of a documentarian. They try to "bear witness" through their stories, and, to this extent, one of the *narrative goals* of many literary works is to explore the practices, institutions, and forms of interaction that shape our world and structure our experiences and relationships.

The pursuit of this narrative goal requires a number of things of a literary work. The actions and experiences at the core of the story must be such that they can represent or otherwise stand for *general* kinds of actions and experience: those that typify the region of culture a writer wishes to explore. A writer in pursuit of this narrative goal will commonly try to throw light on the norms, attitudes, habits, and values that sustain the practice she is attempting to document. And in getting us to see something general in the events of the story, a writer will also have to decide on how to tell the story itself. As we saw above, this is a crucial step, since it is through narration that a story becomes interpreted and hence that a distinct conception of the meaning, of the *point*, of a story is forged. Like a person in search of a self-concept, a writer in pursuit of this narrative goal will struggle to find a way of recounting the events of her story so that a specific purchase on them can be communicated, a purchase that is usually as much emotional and aesthetic as it is cognitive.

Think, for example, of the presentation of Southern culture in William Faulkner's 1948 *Intruder in the Dust*. The structure of this story of racial injustice is hardly original: a black man is wrongly accused of murdering a white man, and a lawyer who reluctantly comes to believe in his innocence fights against a community set on lynching him. We've heard this story (or at least seen the movie) before, in one form or another. Faulkner's accomplishment was not to construct a terribly original story but to tell a story in a particular way, a way that rendered intelligible how certain features of Southern culture give rise to these familiar, intractable problems of race. Faulkner was a writer of fiction and not a sociologist, so his work consisted not in statistical surveys but in telling a story that reflects in a general way how Southern culture hangs together: that reflects its *character,* at least once upon a time and from one vantage point. Faulkner situates the events of his story in a certain atmosphere of feeling, as all literary narratives do. He presents the reader not only with a sense of characteristic actions, thoughts, and forms of interaction but also with a feel for the fabric of the culture, the primitive allure of its clannish values, the suffocating yet protective weight of its traditions, and the hesitant, measured exchanges across racial lines. The formal features of Faulkner's narrative technique (stream-of-consciousness prose, and modernist in that uniquely Southern way) contribute much to this, creating as they do an unsettling sense of both transparency and remoteness: of bearing witness to events that despite being brought into plain view remain fundamentally ambiguous and inscrutable, as certain features of postwar Southern culture surely were.

Now, all of this is admittedly unremarkable literary criticism. But it does give a sense of what it means for a writer to take up this narrative goal, and what will lead a writer to weave a thick narrative. Faulkner's tale is descriptively rich in much the same respect in which thick narratives of the self are. It offers up an image of something general about the culture it explores, fashioned out of the highly original way in which Faulkner narrates his rather common story. Faulkner's achievement was to elicit from this tale a very precise conception of the cultural space in which stories of this sort play out, stories that belong as much to the real world as they do to the fictional world of Faulkner's novel.[19] It tries to give us a sense, in short, of how the culture it explores is constituted, at least in respect to the questions Faulkner asks of it.

It is worth acknowledging that there are many literary works with no interest in weaving thick narratives of this sort. But it is also worth noting that the point of many literary works is virtually unintelligible apart from a conception of this narrative goal. Novels, plays, and poems as varied as *Paradise Lost,* "Howl," *Hard Times, The Man Without Qualities, Uncle*

Vanya, and *Waiting for Godot* (the last of these just in a particularly symbolic manner) are in their own ways all in pursuit of this goal. Needless to say, this narrative goal exists alongside the various aesthetic, dramatic, and imaginative goals that are also at play in the literary work of art. Literary works that document but do little else tend to be quite bad literary works, forgetting as they do that readers generally prefer their course of insight to be served with lots of art. And it is also worth pointing out that while writers often exploit the conventions of literary realism to accomplish this goal, it is not necessary they do so. In *The Lonely Girl* Edna O'Brien explored gender roles by trying to show men and women as they are, at least in a certain neck of the woods; in *Cock & Bull* Will Self found that having women grow penises and men vaginas (behind the knee, no less) can be an effective way of exploring more or less the same thing. It is a testament to the power of the literary imagination that writers have devised endlessly inventive ways of constructing a representation of the human situation, and realism is only one of many devices writers employ when going about this.

Morality and Ethics, Briefly

It is in respect to this narrative goal that literary works have an obvious claim to ethical significance. But explaining how they bear this value requires saying something brief about what the term "ethical" means here. It is true that in contemporary English, and indeed in much contemporary philosophy, the term "ethics" is conterminous with the term "morality," but there is a tradition in modern philosophy that distinguishes the two in a way that is especially helpful for the point I am pursuing about literature. The source of the particular way of thinking about the difference between ethics and morality that I have in mind is Hegel's distinction between *Sittlichkeit* and *Moralität*[20]—in effect between "ethical life" and morality— and Bernard Williams's critique of the "modern morality system" in favor of a return to "thicker" and less intellectualist conceptions of ethics is the most obvious twentieth-century contribution to this tradition (see Williams 1985), though one can see something of it in the thought of philosophers such as Charles Taylor, Axel Honneth, and Alasdair MacIntyre, among others.

The particular way this tradition frames this distinction usually makes things rather worse for morality,[21] and every way of putting it that I am aware of requires making both "morality" and "ethics" mean something they do not mean for many philosophers who make a living using these terms. For these reasons, the distinction will inevitably strike nonbelievers as contentious, even invidious, at least until one provides much more argument in support of it than I can offer here. Since I wish to make use of this distinction but avoid the controversy, what I shall do is use it to build a Wittgensteinian ladder, borrowing it just long enough to make my point and then returning "moral" and "ethical" back to common usage. At any rate, what I describe here should not be read as an outline of a position one would be advised to take in moral philosophy but as groundwork for an account of two basic ways in which literary works open themselves up to ethical assessment.

The outlook that this tradition associates with modern moral thought (modern because it really begins with Kant and is typified by his project) is the attempt to specify, in the words of Samuel Scheffler, a "normative intellectual structure" by virtue of which the common questions of morality can be answered. It is concerned especially with understanding how we can determine what we *ought* to do, and what it means for this "ought" to be a genuinely moral one. This naturally leads to questions concerning what makes our actions morally *good,* our responses morally *right,* as opposed to, say, "good" or "right" from the perspective of pure self-interest or an arbitrary social code (Scheffler 1987, 412). Moral philosophy, on this picture, is the branch of philosophy that searches for a source from which spring answers to these questions; and it conceives of this source in highly cognitive terms, for example as a very precise employment of reasoning or a principle accessible only through philosophical reflection. The categorical imperative is a good example of this, as is the principle of utility. This view of morality tends to treat moral thought as most naturally and perfectly expressed in moral *judgments:*[22] in those activities of thought that underwrite, or should underwrite, our application of moral concepts. For this reason moral philosophy, again so conceived, labors to identify the sorts of consideration ("can I will the maxim of my action to be universal law?" "would acting thus promote more pleasure or pain?" etc.) that give moral judgments a claim to moral *truth:* to getting the demands of morality *right.*

The outlook that has its roots in certain strands of ethical thought in classical Greek and German philosophy—Aristotle and Hegel, in effect—takes as its starting point not the search for an abstract source of our obligations but the structure of actual *ethical life.* That is, it treats as the stuff of ethical insight the complex tissue of norms, customs, and interests that gives our cultural practices their point. What I above described as the "cultural space" in which our various stories play out is, on this view, fundamentally an *ethical* space. Contrary to the quite formal approach of morality, ethics so conceived has as its target the cultural grounds of human action and experience, and it explores the "living" arrangement of values operative in a community. On this view the ethical is what we uncover when we begin to query the purpose of our practices: the forms of life they make possible, the kinds of experience they structure, and the sorts of value of which they are expressive. As Simon Blackburn puts it, the ethical is in effect a kind of "climate" or "environment" in which our social practices and personal pursuits are carried out (2001, 1–2). This view treats the ethical as distributed more or less holistically throughout a culture: it is the structure of guiding values, desires, and habits that hold us together as societies or, for that matter, as selves. This is, one will have noticed, in effect the view of the ethical I have been working with in my discussion of thick narrative.[23]

I would think that the smart money is on seeing these two views not as competing but as complementary, and one would expect a serious moral philosopher to have much to say about the ways in which they interlock. At any rate, ethics without a dash of what this tradition calls morality runs the risk of being reactionary, unable to critique effectively many existing practices because it can produce no standards of moral evaluation external to those practices.[24] As Bertrand Russell once said of Hegel's ethics, it gives us the "freedom to obey the police" (as quoted in Pippin 2004, 1). And moral thought untethered to the concerns of actual ethical life can run the risk of being too formal, too abstract (and so perhaps empty), and of issuing demands that cannot be squared with human nature or that are destructive of the very practices—friendship, for example—that give our lives meaning. Happily, these and similar issues are for moral philosophy (or is it ethics?) and not the philosophy of literature. For my argument to go forward, all one need concede is that an insight into ethical life is of obvious value, and that the sort of thick narratives literary works can weave appear intuitively well suited for offering this form of insight. But before one can grant me this, I need to spell out just what all this amounts to as a claim about literature, and this is what I shall clarify next.

Let me quickly introduce two terms of art before moving on, each corresponding to the two different forms of emphasis that this discussion of morality and ethics brings to view. I will use the term "moralism" to refer to a critical stance that evaluates literary works in line with the concerns of morality, as described above; and I will use the term "ethicism" to refer to a critical stance that evaluates literary work in line with the above vision of ethics as primarily concerned with the fabric of actual ethical life.[25] A distinction of this sort is essential to literary aesthetics, as I hope the following will make clear.

Being Right and Being Understood

Consider the following example. In a letter of 1940 George Orwell expressed intense, though not uncritical, admiration of Henry Miller's *Tropic of Cancer*,[26] and he contrasted it with a work that is in one respect kindred to Miller's and in another poles apart from it: Louis-Ferdinand Céline's *Journey to the End of the Night*. Though more fascinated (and perplexed) by Miller's novel, Orwell was interested in how each of these writers responded to the same basic problem. The problem, in a word, is the problem of modernity: the perceived collapse of value, meaning, and moral order that occurred, depending on who you talk to, either with onset of the industrial revolution or when people stopped going to church. Here is how Orwell put it:

> *Voyage au Bout de la Nuit* is a book-with-a-purpose, and its purpose is to protest against the horror and meaninglessness of modern life—actually, indeed, of *life*. It is a cry of unbearable disgust, a voice from the cesspool. *Tropic of Cancer* is almost exactly the opposite. The thing has become so unusual as to seem almost anomalous, but it is the book of a man who is happy. . . . With years of lumpenproletarian life behind him, hunger, vagabondage, dirt, failure, nights in the open, battles with immigration officers, endless struggles for a bit of cash, Miller finds that he is enjoying himself. Exactly the aspects of life that fill Céline with horror are the ones that appeal to him. So far from protesting, he is *accepting*. (Orwell 1968, 498)

As a staid British socialist, Orwell likely found the histrionic excess of each of these writers amusing, as characteristically French or American as they were. Céline's response was to shout obscenities at the space where Value, Decency, or whatever once resided. Miller's response, however, was what every college-age American knows as spring break fever. If Céline's response is like that of an atheist who is furious at God for not existing, Miller's is the response of a child who has just figured out that no one is watching. For Miller the collapse of moral order is a good thing. He can treat people instrumentally, either for sex or for money, move to Paris and drink all day, and, most importantly, he can produce art that celebrates a life lived like this (censorship notwithstanding). For Céline, it is people like Miller who make modern life unbearable.

If we think of sameness of story, if just for a moment, in terms of sameness of narrative goals and not sameness of content, then Céline and Miller tell the very same story—*The Collapse of Civilization* might be the title— and what so interested Orwell was how different their tellings of this story are: in one case the story is told as a tragedy, in the other it is told as a story of liberation. Both authors elicit powerful images of the ethical constitution of the world they took themselves to live in. In Céline's case it is a world that is fundamentally evil, dehumanizing, and ugly. In Miller's it is free, honest (since aware that nothing is to be taken seriously), and beautiful, even, or precisely, when at its dirtiest and meanest. In each case these images are wrought by bringing to view the practices and forms of experience that these writers take to be characteristic of the modern world: Céline largely explores the economic and social; Miller, the sexual, artistic, and, for lack of a better term, Bacchic. These are excellent examples of thick literary narratives, and surely one of the things Orwell was responding to was the clarity and power of these writers' visions, different though they were, of the character of late modern culture.[27]

We are now in a position to see something interesting. Consider how different our assessment of a literary work looks when we plug in the evaluative perspectives offered by moralism and ethicism. From the moral point of view Céline is not beyond reproach (his ranting betrayed a conservatism that in real life took the form of supporting the Vichy government and writing the occasional anti-Semitic pamphlet), but Miller's is clearly the more morally unnerving of the two novels. *Tropic of Cancer* is often criticized for its sexism, but Orwell points out that there is much more to worry about: "To say 'I accept' in an age like ours is to say that you accept concentration camps, rubber truncheons, Hitler, Stalin, bombs, aeroplanes, tinned food, machine-guns, putsches, purges, slogans, Bedaux belts, gas-masks, submarines, spies, *provocateurs,* press censorship, secret prisons, aspirins, Hollywood films and political murders" (1968, 500). Though one might wish to rescue aspirins from this laundry list of evil, the sentiment is sound. Miller's is an acceptance of what we should reject, or at least thumb our noses at, should we wish to do the *right* thing. In this respect, the moral vision of the book is clearly *false,* since it gets the demands of morality wrong, confounding at quite basic levels what we *ought* to do: what we owe one another, and what our duties and obligations amount to. But it is important to note what "false" means here. It means something like "false by the lights of the best moral theory or soundest moral intuitions." This is the domain of "moralism," as defined above, and so to say that it is false here is to say it only in a normative sense. This says very little about whether it is false to life.

From another perspective, that of ethicism, it seems altogether wrong-headed to call it false. Indeed, if Orwell is right about the value of Miller's novel (and assume he is, for the sake of argument), Miller's vision of modern life is *true,* at least in respect to a certain slice of it. The very moral madness of Miller's novel is, for Orwell, symptomatic of the late modern world, *a feature of it,* and Miller is of significance precisely because his novel bears such perfect witness to it. Orwell's praise of the novel is incomprehensible apart from a conception of Miller's documentary success. If it weren't revelatory of something general about our culture, it would just be a well-written statement of one pervert's fun, and this sort of thing never appealed to Orwell. The form of life Miller documents may be "wrong" by the lights of moralism, but then much of what we humans do will be. We do not live in a world of just saints and angels, and so if we are to have a record of our way in the world, a novel like Miller's that reveals to us unsettling features of our ethical climate offers an important insight. It is an *impoverished* ethical climate—surely that was Orwell's point, though not Miller's—but this too is a kind of ethical insight, since this too tells us something about the ethical constitution of our culture.

Literary moralism and ethicism offer these very different evaluative frameworks because they are, strictly speaking, logically independent of one another. And they are independent of one another because they have distinct criteria of success. The criterion of success for moralism is in effect *rightness,* and the criterion of success for ethicism is at root *intelligibility.* I do not mean anything especially technical by these terms. Moralism, as a normative enterprise, assesses the merit, legitimacy, appropriateness—*rightness*—of the morally relevant attitudes, ideas, and beliefs manifested in a work. Miller, one would think, fails wildly by this criterion of success. Ethicism, on the other hand, casts literature's ethically relevant activity as residing in its ability to bring to light the structure of our cultural practices and the values, beliefs, and norms that sustain them. It assesses literature's ability to offer a purchase on kinds of human experience by bringing to clarity the cultural space in which they take place and against the backdrop of which they make sense. Neither Céline's ranting nor Miller's gallivanting is intelligible for what it is without a grasp of the features of culture that prompted it. It is this attempt to fill out our sense of the ethical character of a culture—to render it intelligible—that literary ethicism, as I have defined it here, evaluates. And this shows, I think, that there is no tension in saying that a literary work might be morally insolvent but ethically rich, as long as we understand that we are speaking about two evaluatively distinct phenomena. Assuming Orwell is right, Miller's *Tropic of Cancer* is an excellent example of this.

If we are uncomfortable saying of a work like Miller's that it bears ethical value, it is likely the moralist in us who is making us feel this way. A good way to assuage the moralist is to remind him that standards other than his own guide ethical evaluation of the sort I arguing for. What would be naïve, I think, is to suppose that literary works of the best sort must always be those that are successes from the standpoints of both moralism and ethicism. This would be to think, for example, that Miller would have produced a better work had his novel expressed the right moral attitudes toward the content of the story, condemning instead of reveling in the events it recounts. It is naïve because the pursuit of one kind of value often requires the abandonment of the other, and so in some cases it would be impossible to line them both up on the side of the good. Orwell's point is that Miller's work is so clarifying because it reveals the allure of the kind of life Miller documents and the sense of freedom it offers those who embrace it. This is why it has a claim to rendering intelligible something important about the ethical climate of modern life. Had Miller busied himself with condemning this climate, his work would not have been able to accomplish this so effectively or so vividly. It is perhaps the case that in many, though certainly not all, of the great works of the modern literary canon, the moral and ethical dimensions are in harmony, expressing just the right combination of approbation and admonishment in respect to the features of ethical life they explore (think of almost anything by Dickens, Dostoevsky, or Austen, or novels like Ralph Ellison's *Invisible Man* or George Orwell's own *Burmese Days*). But it would be a step too far to think that a general rule can be made to the effect that harmonizing the moral and ethical pursuits of a novel always make for a better novel, or that novels that fail (or refuse) to achieve this harmony are always to that extent worse off as works of art.

I can now make good on a claim made at the beginning of this essay. I said that I was impressed by immoralism but wished to show that the issues it addresses are much more complex than immoralists tend to acknowledge. What I meant by that should now be clear. To speak of a work as a moral failure, in the sense immoralists tend to favor, is to speak of it as a failure by the standards of moralism, as I have defined it here. It is to say that a work manifests or is otherwise expressive of the wrong kinds of moral attitude in respect to its content. I think that the immoralist is right that moral failures of this sort do not always imply aesthetic (or artistic) failures, and I think that Orwell's reflections on Miller and Céline are a compelling example of this.[28] What is philosophically unfortunate is that *this* is thought to exhaust the range of possible ethical value a work might bear, as if to say that when a great work fails morally, then it can only be lots and lots of "art" that we are appreciating in it. Whether or not this is the case will depend on the literary work in question. But the account of thick narratives I have given here shows that it is possible for a literary work to fail morally yet still offer readers a very significant kind of ethical insight. This will only sound surprising or inconsistent if one thinks that there is really only one kind of basic moral or ethical value art may bear, and that there is not is part of what I have tried to demonstrate here.

Conclusion

My argument made, it would be wise to liberate "ethics" and "morality" from the restricted sense in which I have been using them and return them to common usage (whatever that might be for philosophically charged terms like these). And one inevitably feels a pang of embarrassment for putting an "ism" at the end of such common English words, as I have done here. But these terms, or any we might choose in their place, are not really of much importance here. It is the idea they gesture towards that counts. And the idea I have explored in this essay is that literature's ethical core—and here I use "ethical" in the sense in which one could just as well use "moral"—is complex, composed, in effect, of two distinct phenomena: one normative and the other narratological. It is the ethical significance of the latter that has not received nearly enough philosophical attention.[29] And while much more still needs to be said about it, I hope that the account of thick narratives I have developed shows that it is worth saying, and that the general story we tell of literature's engagement with value will be richer for it.

NOTES

I would like to thank Carola Barbero, Robert Chodat, Espen Hammer, Bernard Harrison, and Luca Pocci for very helpful comments on earlier drafts of this essay.

1. See Guyer (2008) for an excellent discussion that shows that even historical figures often cited as progenitors of the idea of the "autonomy" of art (Kant, for example) would have found it bizarre to deny the relevance of ethical concerns to the criticism of art.

2. In fairness to Lewis, he later came to see his folly and in 1939 published *The Hitler Cult,* in which he disavowed much of what he said in 1931 when he published *Hitler.*

3. Daniel Jacobson puts the difference between immoralism and its chief competitor positions—autonomism and moralism—in the following way: immoralism "holds that although the moral qualities of art are sometimes aesthetically relevant (contra autonomism), its morally dubious features can be among its aesthetic merits and its morally salutary features among its aesthetic flaws (contra moralism)" (Jacobson 2008). On this sense of immoralism, many versions of so-called moderate moralism and moderate autonomism count as versions of immoralism, since they deny precisely what the immoralist denies: that there is a categorical or, in Jacobson's terms, "invariant positive" link between the moral success (or failure) of an artwork and its aesthetic success (or failure). I will follow Jacobson's use of "immoralism" here, though I will reserve the term "moralism" to mark a slightly different concept.

4. None of this should be taken to imply that novels (or readers) treat these morally suspicious "yeas" as asserted of reality, as though being an immoralist about literature makes one an immoralist about life.

5. Recently many philosophers have argued for response-dependent accounts of art's relation to morality, according to which the objects of moral evaluations are the responses an artwork calls on a reader to have towards its content so that it can work its intended magic. I take response-dependent theories not to be an alternative to, but a more sophisticated version of, what I say above in my characterization of the contemporary debate. To give a sense of why I think this, a novel, for example, must at some level express a pro (or con) attitude towards, say, a sexist character if it is to call on us to respond to him with admiration (or disgust); otherwise it is utterly unclear how the novel could be said to be trying to extract an admiring (or disgusted) response from the reader. So the attitudes a novel expresses in respect to its content and those it tries to call forth from a reader usually turn out to be the same. For a compelling recent treatment of response-dependent moralism, see Hazlett (2009).

6. I am indebted to Crary (2007) for her discussion of this, as well as to her arguments against conceiving narrowly of moral thought as concerned primarily with the making of moral judgments.

7. For work more or less in this vein to which I am sympathetic, see Carroll (1996), Eaton (2001), Gaut (2007), Harold (2008), Kieran (2003), and Schellekens (2007).

8. The distinction is often cast as tripartite, between story, narrative, and narrative discourse. Since I will make no use of the notion of narrative discourse in what follows, I shall ignore it here. Some useful discussions of this distinction can be found in Genette (1980), Prince (1987), and Abbott (2002). Though it was published too late for me to be able to use it here, see Currie (2010) for an excellent treatment of contemporary issues in the philosophy of narrative.

9. Many would argue that any minimally organized linking of events counts as a narrative. As Lamarque puts it, "All that narratives have in common are minimal formal conditions about the ordering of events in a story" (2004, 19). The tradition I am appealing to is only willing to call this a "story," though the issue here seems purely semantic. One can, if one wishes, think of what I am calling a "story" as just the most basic expression of narrative.

10. Though it is easy to imagine skepticism in respect to the idea that different narratives can literally share the "same" story. See Smuts (2009) for an interesting discussion of this.

11. Velleman (2006) distinguishes three guises of the self: self-image, autonomous agency, and self-sameness over time. I am considering only the first here.

12. At least memories of the sort relevant here, variously called "recollective," "episodic," or "personal" memories. If so-called semantic memory ("I remember that $4 + 4 = 8$") is memory of impersonal fact, personal memory is a record of lived experience ("I remember being afraid of algebra as a student").

13. I say "a" rather than "the" story of his life because memory is clearly fallible, and denial and repression can rear their heads here.

14. If this causal-psychological information would not be recalled directly, then a simple act of induction would make it available to him.

15. This isn't to say that his *life*, or any other life for that matter, has this plot-like structure in the same way in which a literary work has the structure of plot, which is surely too strong. See Williams (2009) and Peter Goldie's contribution to this volume for a critique of this view.

16. I ignore here Strawson's (2007) arguments to the effect that episodic selfhood is not a bad thing. On Strawson's account selfhood turns out to be a much thinner notion than it is for just about all those who would take issue with his claim, and so his provocations turn out to be much less radical than they first seem. For Strawson, as for Dan Zahavi, the notion of a self is much more basic than the notion of a person (see Strawson 2009 and Zahavi 2008): it picks out the locus, in effect, of subjective or first-personal awareness, and the term "person" is reserved for more articulated forms of (culturally mediated) identity. If one is sympathetic to this idea—in other contexts I am—then one can just as well read "person" wherever I write "self": my general point will remain intact.

17. I borrow some of these thick aesthetic terms from Lamarque (2008, chap. 7) and Bonzon (2009), and some of the thick emotional ones from Goldie (2008).

18. For example, the sort of lyric poetry typified by John Ashbery and much of the New York School. Whether poetry of this sort turns out to be nonnarrative will naturally ride on what one thinks a narrative is, and I am skeptical that the forms of subjective experience this kind of poetry often explores do not make for the stuff of a narrative: they strike me as narratives of the self, however fragmented and decentered these selves, and so their stories, are shown to be. See Koethe (2000) for an excellent discussion of Ashbery and the philosophical significance of his poetry, a discussion that touches on many of these issues.

19. I leave aside here the question of truth, of how we can *know* whether writers get these cultural practices right. I deal with these and similar questions in Gibson (2007).

20. For a treatment of Hegel's ethics that informs much of what I say here about ethics and morality, see Wood (1990, 1993).

21. This is because the distinction is usually employed in the service of building a skeptical case against (modern notions of) morality.

22. Here I am again indebted to Crary (2007).

23. There is much more to this view of ethics than this, of course: in addition to culture, one will have to say something about virtue, at least if one is to remain true to its Greek origins. But it is the idea the ethical structure of culture—of those aspects of the Greek view that inform the Hegelian conception of *Sittlichkeit*—that I shall take from this and apply to literature, and so I will permit myself to stop the story here.

24. This is not to deny the possibility of "internal" critique on such a model of ethical life. I thank Bernard Harrison for pointing out that an earlier version of this essay suggested this.

25. These labels are not entirely fair to the use of "moralism" and "ethicism" favored by some aestheticians (no label will be entirely at home here, and at any rate there isn't uniformity of use among aestheticians). In recent debates "moralism" and "ethicism" are often used interchangeably to refer to positions that endorse what James Harold felicitously calls a "valence constraint," according to which, "if a moral flaw of a work affects that work's aesthetic value, it reduces that value; if a moral virtue of a work affects that work's aesthetic value, it increases that" (2008, 46–47). While I am not here interested in discussing the valence constrain (apart

from expressing a degree of admiration for the immoralist, who denies it), either moralism or ethicism, as I use them here, could be expressed in terms of a valence constraint, with each marking a distinct conception of the kind of moral/ethical success (or failure) that can affect the aesthetic success (or failure) of a literary work.

26. An example of Orwell's characteristically intense yet tempered praise is "Here in my opinion is the only imaginative prose-writer of the slightest value who has appeared among the English-speaking races for some years past. Even if that is objected to as an overstatement, it will probably be admitted that Miller is a writer out of the ordinary, worth more than a single glance; and after all, he is a completely negative, unconstructive, amoral writer, a mere Jonah, a passive acceptor of evil, a sort of Whitman among the corpses" (1968, 527).

27. It is true that Miller and Céline offer radically different takes on ethical life in late modernity, but this is an example of difference without conflict, and it would be silly to think that logic dictates that at best only one of their views can be *correct* or *true*. Again, the goal of the sort of thick literary narratives I am examining here is to document some general aspect of our way in the world, and there is more than one way in which people generally find themselves in the world.

28. I have obviously assumed rather than argued for immoralism in this essay. But in assuming it, I make clear that I am aware (and accept that) the immoralist can rehearse his arguments in respect to the notion of ethical value I have developed here.

29. Literary theorists and critics have on occasion taken an interest in exploring the prospects of a specifically narrative-based account of literature's ethical significance. See, for example, Newton (1995) and many of the essays collected in Davis and Womack (2001).

REFERENCES

Abbott, H. Porter. 2002. *The Cambridge Introduction to Narrative*. Cambridge: Cambridge University Press.

Blackburn, Simon. 2001. *Being Good: A Short Introduction to Ethics*. Oxford: Oxford University Press.

Bonzon, Roman. 2009. "Thick Aesthetic Concepts." *Journal of Aesthetics and Art Criticism* 67 (2): 191–99.

Carroll, Noël. 1996. "Moderate Moralism." *British Journal of Aesthetics* 36 (3): 223–37.

Crary, Alice. 2007. *Beyond Moral Judgment*. Cambridge, Mass.: Harvard University Press.

Currie, Gregory. 2010. *Narratives and Narrators: A Philosophy of Stories*. Oxford: Oxford University Press.

Davis, Todd F., and Kenneth Womack, eds. 2001. *Mapping the Ethical Turn: A Reader in Ethics, Culture, and Literary Theory*. Charlottesville: University Press of Virginia.

Eaton, Marcia Muelder. 2001. *Merit, Aesthetic and Ethical*. Oxford: Oxford University Press.

Gaut, Berys. 2007. *Art, Emotion and Ethics*. Oxford: Oxford University Press.

Genette, Gérard. 1980. *Narrative Discourse: An Essay in Method*. Ithaca: Cornell University Press.

Gibson, John. 2007. *Fiction and the Weave of Life*. Oxford: Oxford University Press.

Goldie, Peter. 2008. "Thick Concepts and Emotion." In *Reading Bernard Williams,* edited by Daniel Callcut, 94–109. London: Routledge.

Guyer, Paul. 2008. "Is Ethical Criticism a Problem? A Historical Perspective." In *Art and Ethical Criticism,* edited by Garry Hagberg, 3–32. Oxford: Basil Blackwell.

Harold, James. 2008. "Immoralism and the Valence Constraint." *British Journal of Aesthetics* 48 (1): 45–64.

Hazlett, Allan. 2009. "How to Defend Response Moralism." *British Journal of Aesthetics* 49 (3): 241–55.

Jacobson, Daniel. 2008. Review of Berys Gaut, *Art, Emotion and Ethics. Notre Dame Philosophical Review,* http://ndpr.nd.edu/review.cfm?id = 12584.

Kieran, Matthew. 2003. "Forbidden Knowledge: The Challenge of Immoralism." In *Art and Morality,* edited by José Luis Bermúdez, and Sebastian Gardner, 56–73. London: Routledge.

Koethe, John. 2000. *Poetry at One Remove.* Ann Arbor: University of Michigan Press.

Lamarque, Peter. 2004. "On Not Expecting Too Much from Narrative." *Mind and Language* 19 (4): 393–408.

———. 2008. *The Philosophy of Literature.* Oxford: Blackwell.

Newton, Adam. 1995. *Narrative Ethics.* Cambridge, Mass: Harvard University Press.

Orwell, George. 1968. "Inside the Whale." In *An Age Like This, 1920–1940.* Vol. 1 of *The Collected Essays, Journalism, and Letters of George Orwell,* edited by Sonia Orwell and Ian Angus, 493–502.

Pippin, Robert. 2004. Introduction to *Hegel on Ethics and Politics,* edited by Robert Pippin and Otfried Höffe, 1–20. Cambridge: Cambridge University Press.

Prince, Gerald. 1987. *A Dictionary of Narratology.* Lincoln: University of Nebraska Press.

Ryle, Gilbert. 2009. "The Thinking of Thoughts: What Is 'Le Penseur' Doing?" In *Collected Essays, 1929–1968,* 494–510. Collected Papers 2. London: Routledge.

Scheffler, Samuel. 1987. "Morality Through Thick and Thin: A Critical Notice of *Ethics and the Limits of Philosophy.*" *Philosophical Review* 96 (3): 411–34.

Schellekens, Elisabeth. 2007. *Aesthetics and Morality.* London: Continuum.

Smuts, Aaron. 2009. "Story Identity and Story Type." *Journal of Aesthetics and Art Criticism* 67 (1): 5–14.

Strawson, Galen. 2007. "Episodic Ethics." In *Narrative and Understanding Persons,* edited by Daniel Hutto, 85–116. Royal Institute of Philosophy Supplement 60. Cambridge: Cambridge University Press.

———. 2009. *Selves: An Essay in Revisionary Metaphysics.* Oxford: Oxford University Press.

Velleman, J. David. 2003. "Narrative Explanation." *Philosophical Review* 112 (1): 1–25.

———. 2006. *Self to Self: Selected Essays.* Cambridge: Cambridge University Press.

Williams, Bernard. 1985. *Ethics and the Limits of Philosophy.* Cambridge, Mass.: Harvard University Press.

———. 2009. "Life as Narrative." *European Journal of Philosophy* 17 (2): 305–14.

Wood, Allen. 1990. *Hegel's Ethical Thought*. New York: Cambridge University Press.

———. 1993. "Hegel's Ethics." In *The Cambridge Companion to Hegel,* edited by Frederick Beiser, 211–33. New York: Cambridge University Press.

Zahavi, Dan. 2008. "Is the Self a Social Construct?" *Inquiry* 52 (6): 551–73.

Narrative, Emotions, and Autonomy

Amy Mullin

If we want to understand others, as much or more than seeking to understand what they believe and what they want, we seek to understand what they feel—what they love, hate, and fear, what makes them ashamed, nervous, remorseful, contemptuous, or disgusted, and what makes them feel delighted, comforted, excited, or joyful. Once we know these things about another person, we feel we really know and can trust—or should distrust—him or her, because emotions express what we find significant (Oatley 2007).

If we want to understand ourselves, this kind of emotional understanding is equally important, and not always easily obtained.[1] When we read and respond to some literary narratives—those that focus on characters who act and react, when these narratives also make us care about the characters and situations—this can help to develop our ability to identify and evaluate emotional responses, including our own. Our abilities to recognize and properly identify our own emotions, and to reflect upon or be guided by what our emotional responses reveal about what we find significant, are meta-affective skills. These skills are important sources of personal autonomy, considered as the ability to act and react in ways that are personally meaningful. As I will argue, reading and responding to these types of literary narratives can help to develop and refine our meta-affective skills, and hence these narratives can be a resource that increases personal autonomy—while at the same time posing certain risks to autonomy.

In this essay I sketch an account of personal autonomy and the skills and capacities required for it. My account builds mainly on the work of Paul Benson, Catriona Mackenzie, and Diana Meyers. I will characterize the types of literary narratives that can help us develop and refine some of these skills. I will focus on several literary narratives that fit the bill, and show how reading and responding to them may enhance our autonomy—while also suggesting that there are ways of responding to emotionally engaging narratives that can undermine autonomy.

I will further argue that there is a significant role to be played by discussing our responses to literary narratives in a social context, and that the humble book club can be an important resource for developing our meta-affective skills in a way that enhances, rather than undermines, autonomy. However, particularly when we run the risk of having our emotional responses belittled or devalued, or, on the other hand, privileged over others' responses,[2] it is important to think carefully about with whom we are sharing our emotional responses to literary narratives.

Before I proceed with the main body of my essay, I will briefly be explicit about some claims I am *not* making about the role of narratives in making us the kind of people we are. I do so because of the current debate around the role of narrative (with sometimes a minimalist definition of narrative) in making us either into people, good people, or autonomous people. There have been many papers published on this topic (much of it in response to articles by Galen Strawson, disputing whether narrative is required for any of these purposes), but in this essay I am not joining that debate.[3] I do not believe that we need to have a narrative of our lives as a whole in order to be persons, good persons, or autonomous persons, although I believe that we can be neither maximally autonomous nor meet all of our moral responsibilities if we are not interested in the past—not only our own past but equally the past of other people who are or should be of relevance to our decision making. I agree with John Christman that the abilities that are relevant to personhood and autonomy are abilities to find our decisions and reactions intelligible, that complex narratives are certainly one way of doing so, and that the simplest narratives don't necessarily help (Christman 2004).

Instead of trying to identify what we should take as the most basic properties of all narratives[4] or talking about the extent to which it can be helpful to tell ourselves (accurate and responsible) stories about where we have been and where we might want to be going, I am in interested in ways in which complex literary narratives, with certain features, may affect our autonomy, either positively by increasing our meta-affective and imaginative skills or negatively by encouraging us to imagine only along familiar tracks or by limiting the range of what we think of as appropriate emotional responses to ones that fit dominant and sometimes oppressive cultural paradigms. Given limitations of space, I will focus on their potentially positive impact and limit myself to some remarks about potential dangers.

In order to explain how a certain kind of emotional engagement with literary narratives can enhance our autonomy, I need to explain what I mean by autonomy and what skills and capacities I take as necessary for autonomy. I also need to explain how I understand emotions. First, I am interested in personal autonomy rather than political autonomy. Second, I am not interested in what might be necessary to live an independent life, but am instead interested in what is required in order to live a life that the agent himself or herself finds personally meaningful, and this is a life lived in accordance with what one cares most about.[5] Following Catriona Mackenzie and Diana Meyers, I regard autonomy as something we can possess in degrees, with different degrees in different domains (for instance at work rather than in romantic relationships), and I understand autonomy to reflect the extent to which we have a variety of skills, capacities, and resources (including social rather than simply personal resources).

I take the most basic of these skills, capacities, and resources to include, most importantly, the ability to care stably, albeit flexibly, for some things rather than others. Next, autonomy requires that we be able to identify what we care about, identify opportunities to achieve what we would like to achieve, and know how to carry out plans in order to realize those opportunities or make reasonable efforts toward achieving goals. This requires us to notice what is relevant to our concerns and to have the ability to reason about how to achieve what we aim at, regulate our actions to accord with our concerns rather than being overwhelmed by momentary impulses, imagine alternatives for action, and imagine how we might feel about different scenarios, if achieved. All of these abilities are not merely personal, as we may enlist friends, acquaintances, and professionals to help us reason, to get us to stick to our guns, to imagine alternatives, to let us know information that is relevant to our decisions and responses, and to help us understand ourselves. Finally, in addition to actually possessing these abilities, we need confidence that we have them. This is the important insight of Paul Benson, who recognizes that if we do not have certain basic forms of self-trust and self-confidence, then, even when we do possess abilities necessary for autonomy, we will not trust ourselves to have them, and we will not be autonomous.[6]

What an autonomous agent cares about will not and need not always be transparently available to her in reflection. She remains autonomous, in a particular domain, as long as her activities reflect the reasons she has for action. Since there can be a gap between what we really care about and what we think of ourselves as caring about, and also a gap between the former and what we think we should care about, an autonomous person's activities do not always need to accord with her self-conception or her explicit beliefs about what she considers to be appropriate motives. This means that critical reflection guided by one's self-conception and/or one's beliefs about what are appropriate motives can mislead an agent about what she should do (when those things do not cohere with what she actually cares about). This is why Nomy Arpaly argues that it can sometimes be reasonable to disregard one's all-things-considered judgment about what is best to do—and it is also why our emotions can sometimes be better guides to what we should do, since they can reflect what we really do care about (even if we don't realize it). In order to explain this, I need to say something about how I understand the emotions.

Our emotions are a disparate class. They include occurrent emotions such as particular instances of fear, anger, disgust, joy (which have a distinct phenomenological feel and a particular target), standing emotions such as generalized trust in acquaintances not to be malicious (which have a less distinct target and combine with other standing emotions and therefore are less distinctive in phenomenology), emotional dispositions (a tendency to anger easily), and moods (good or bad, which tend to have as their target most or all of the subject's encounters with the world for a period of time, and which don't tend to be finely nuanced). All emotions are valenced and express our satisfaction or dissatisfaction with a particular context (which may include physical and social features of our situation, and may reflect how we hold the world to be, or have been, or possibly be) (see Currie and Ravenscroft 2002; Oatley 2007). All emotions pick up on only some features of a situation (they are like perceptions in that) and direct our attention to some features of our surroundings while causing us to overlook or discount other features (see De Sousa 1987). For instance, when we fear we attend to what is fearful and to features of the situation that may direct our response (fight or flight); when we trust we may overlook signs that would warrant our suspicion, or discount those indications that are brought to our attention, whereas when we distrust those are precisely the features that would be noticed and attended to.

Emotions differ significantly in their cognitive component. Some more basic emotions, such as fear, can occur before we have consciously noticed anything about a situation, and fear can also occur despite our conscious belief about our safety (as in fear of flying). Other emotions, in order to be distinguished as the particular emotion that they are (resentment, or envy), require us to have made a particular judgment, but not necessarily to be aware that we have done so. Some emotions (such as trust) involve our taking the world to be a certain way,[7] often without making any specific judgment or noticing that we have done so (we may only notice that we trusted, and made ourselves vulnerable when that trust is betrayed). In all of our emotional responses, we are responding not only to our taking (whether consciously or not) the world to be a certain way, but also to the fit, or lack of fit, between how we take the world to be (including what possibilities we think might be realized) and how we want it to be. Emotions involve appraisals of how the world is in relation to what we find to be of significant concern. Emotions therefore reflect what matters to us, what we care about and find significant—even when what we care about or find significant is not something we realize or can admit to ourselves (because it conflicts with our self-conception or what others judge to be worthy, or how we wish we were). However, emotions may reflect what we find to be significant in the moment (such as embarrassment that prevents us from acting on long-term ambitions) or what we still find significant because of habits or emotional inertia (even when we are in a process of changing our goals and priorities) (Mackenzie 2002 valuably makes the latter point). They will also reflect only part of what is relevant in any given situation, as emotions not only make some things salient, but also cause other things to go unnoticed or dismissed.

Therefore, we need good meta-affective skills and need to have experiences that show us something about when our emotions are helpful in disclosing what we should attend to, or what we care about even when we don't realize that we do, and when they aren't, but instead reflect emotional inertia, or a failure to perceive important features of our situation. I claim that reading and responding emotionally to certain kinds of narratives, particularly but not only when we also discuss with others what our emotions revealed or obscured, can be an important resource in developing our meta-affective skills and our experience, and confidence in our experience, in identifying and evaluating our emotional reactions. This is because I agree with Gregory Currie and Jon Jureidini (2004) that when we respond to fictive imaginings, we feel real emotions, even if our emotional reactions don't lead us to take the kinds of actions we might take were we to feel the same emotions in response to what we take as real-life events, which make real-life interventions possible.[8] On this point, I appeal to my readers to reflect upon the extent to which they have noticed themselves or others responding to literary narratives with emotional responses such as relief, anxiety, delight, sadness, anger, and disgust.

In addition, I note that our emotional responses to fictional narratives are entirely consonant with our emotional responses to how we imagine the real world might be, or could become when we feel hope or fear about some possible future, or when we feel embarrassed in realizing that we might have made a significant mistake but didn't—in none of these situations do we need to believe that the possibilities to which we are emotionally responsive are actually occurring, did occur, or will occur. Keith Oatley's work also supplies considerable evidence for the claim that the emotions we feel in response to fiction are similar in both kind and intensity to the emotions people report in diaries of every incident of emotion (1994). He further notes that psychologists who wish to study the impact of particular emotions often use emotionally engaging narratives to provoke the emotion in question (1999).

What are the features shared by the kind of literary narratives in which I am interested? First, they are high in narrativity, in Currie and Jureidini's sense; they have "great specificity of detail, particularly with respect to inter-actions between particular things, and some emphasis on what might have happened as well as on what did happen." Second, they focus on portraying the purposive activity and emotional responses of characters, real or imag-ined. Third, they involve "imaginings that are neatly packaged in ways that recruit affective systems and draw heavily on memory and evaluation" (Currie and Jureidini 2002, 420). It is not enough that they portray the actions, reactions, and feelings of characters in a detailed and complex man-ner, but they must also do so in a way that is emotionally engaging to the reader.[9] Because of this, as the authors note, the imaginings they encourage have the potential to influence action in those who read them. I will have more to say about this later.

In the next section of my essay, I discuss three novels, all of which have the three features mentioned above. These are *Shantaram* by Gregory David Roberts, *The Enchanted April,* by Elizabeth von Armin, and *Exit Lines,* by Joan Barfoot. I will also mention a fourth, *Taft,* by Ann Patchett, when I discuss the power of the imagination to affect our emotions and hence our actions and a fifth, *We Need to Talk About Kevin,* by Lionel Shriver, when

I discuss the impact of sharing our emotional responses to fictional narratives with others.

Shantaram was published in 2003 and is a very lengthy semiautobiographical novel about an escaped Australian convict who spends approximately a decade in India, sometimes living in a slum, sometimes working for the Bombay mafia. *The Enchanted April* was published in 1922 and is a relatively short comic novel about four Englishwomen holidaying for a month at a small castle in Italy. *Exit Lines* was published in 2008 and is about four elderly residents of the Idyll Inn, a private facility for seniors in the United States. *Taft* was published in 1994 and focuses on John Nickel, a bar manager in Memphis, his attempts to reconnect with his son, his interactions with his waitress and her brother, and his detailed imaginings of the last weeks of life of their father, Taft. *We Need to Talk About Kevin* was published in 2003 and concerns a woman's ambivalence about motherhood—far before her oldest child, Kevin, becomes a serial killer.

Shantaram has the three features mentioned above. It is narrated by the central character, Lindsay (Lin) Ford, who arrives in Bombay at the opening, having just escaped from a maximum security prison in Australia, where he was beaten and tortured by other prisoners and by guards. Because of experiences in which his efforts to be kind or good came to naught, Lin is cautious about acting on the basis of compassion. He recalls his experience of taming a mouse in prison, only to have its tameness make it easy prey for a cruel other inmate, and finds this echoed when his gift of a taxi to a man he loves and values results in the man's death in an accident, and when he discovers the medical aid he provided to his fellow slum dwellers used medicine provided by mobsters with the aim of testing its efficacy for their future use. Increasingly he turns to members of the Bombay mafia and accepts becoming their tool, because he is clear about what they aim at and doesn't risk doing inadvertent harm through motives of kindness and compassion.

At the midpoint of the novel, one of Lin's friends, a fellow slum dweller, kills another friend in order to keep him from further exploiting two women the murderer cared about. The murderer goes to the same brutal Bombay prison where Lin had spent several months. Lin is then well resourced and could afford to bribe officials to get his release, or use his media connections to draw sympathy to the prisoner. He tries to do so but is rebuffed by his friend, who is prepared to accept his responsibility and his punishment. Lin responds to this refusal with a mixture of awe and fear. In coming to terms with why he felt the way he did over a considerable period of time, he eventually realizes that his own escape from the Australian prison, many of the decisions he has made since, and his lingering on instances where his good intentions came to naught are all part and parcel of his refusal to accept responsibility for those of his actions that did not have good intentions.

This is only one of the realizations Lin comes to. He also comes to realize that his wallowing in his own misery (when he became addicted, a second time, to heroin) led him to fail to question why his lover, Karla, appeared to him at the behest of his mafia boss, and similarly, that his pride failed to allow him to listen to her appeal that they stay away from Bombay together. He therefore fails to notice the signs she gives him that she has been working for the boss as well. There are many points in the novel when he realizes that strong emotional reactions kept him focused on only certain features of a situation and kept him from noticing or asking about other relevant features. However, his emotional reactions also help him to discover what he really does care about, such as when he realizes he loves other characters, when he is puzzled by his strong emotional reaction to his friend's refusal to escape from prison, and when he reacts similarly strongly to another friend's ongoing faith in his lover (eventually justified), despite significant evidence she betrayed him. These emotional reactions and his responses to them help him to discover why, in the years he has spent as a money launderer and forger, only occasionally interacting with his friends, he has been living in a way alienated from what he really cares about.

The book is highly detailed. Told from the perspective of Lin, it gives lengthy accounts of his agency and failures of agency, of his emotional responses, and of his coming to realize what his emotional responses indicate about him. It is also emotionally engaging (at times verging on melodrama) in its account of emotionally extreme events. Since the novel is told from his perspective, it also leaves the reader to be taken in by (or occasionally discern the gaps that result from) Lin's own, emotionally driven, focus on some aspects of his situation rather than others. As a result, it gives its reader repeated experiences of identifying Lin's emotional responses, and evaluating them, as well as many opportunities for the reader to evaluate his or her own emotional responses to the characters and events in the novel. It therefore offers the reader the opportunity to develop meta-affective skills, and experience in having one emotional reaction exposed as limited by a combination of reflection, imaginative experience, and other emotional reactions. Reading and responding to a novel like this can therefore be a resource for personal autonomy, by contributing to an awareness of the ambivalent role of emotion in identifying what we really care about, either preventing us from acting in ways that accord with our concerns or prompting us to do so.

We can also, of course, read the book and enjoy the plot and characters and emotional rollercoaster without thinking too much about what the emotional reactions of either the characters or ourselves reveal (although this would require us to fail to engage with a central theme of the book and would make some of the plot twists appear unmotivated). We might also find some emotionally charged aspects of the novel to be inexplicable or unrealistic, especially if we focus only on some aspects rather than others, as a result of some of our own emotional reactions being stronger than others. Discussing the novel with others we trust can be helpful in getting us to reflect about aspects of our own reactions that might have kept our attention focused only on certain parts of the story.

The Enchanted April opens with each of its main characters emotionally damaged. They are four relative strangers: Lottie, who no one finds worthy of attention, not even herself; Rose, who believes that she can only find meaning in service to others; Lady Caroline, who has become bitter and selfish in response to being desired by others only for her beauty; and Mrs. Fisher, an older widow, who finds nothing as worthwhile in the present as her memories of peripheral connections to literary luminaries in the past. From a variety of motives, including their longing for beauty, simple pleasure, and escape from the people in their lives, the women respond to an advertisement about the possibility of renting a small Italian castle.

For Lottie, this first step of taking her desires seriously enough to defy expectations, and the beauty she finds in Italy, open her up to the possibility of loving others, rather than waiting, as she describes it, for proof that they love her first. She then serves as a catalyst for change in the other three women. Rose overcomes her religiously based opposition to her husband's successful novels about the mistresses of dead kings, Mrs. Fisher learns to respond to living people rather than focusing only on the merits of the dead, and Lady Caroline attends to other people's desires rather than only her own.

Much of the novel is comic (when Lottie and Rose arrive at their destination, late and unable to speak Italian, they aren't sure if they are being escorted to the villa or being kidnapped and robbed, and aren't sure whether to tip, because they fear being made ridiculous by attempting to tip potential robbers). The characters are broadly drawn. This aspect of the novel can mislead its readers to expect that emotional engagement with it will be slight. But though we don't get the finely grained account of individual emotional responses we found in *Shantaram*, we do get a very clear account of what makes it possible for the characters to change, and of the role their emotional responses play in this change. We see how Lottie's generosity and self-confidence bring about a change in her rather officious husband (whom she invites to join her), both in her ability to see more than his faults and in his responsiveness to affection (as well as the opportunity for career advancement represented by Lady Caroline and Mrs. Fisher, who are wealthy). The novel leads its readers at first to despise Lottie's husband, Mr. Wilkins, who insists upon being called Mellersh-Wilkins because he finds it more distinguished, and who praises thrift except when it affects his meals. However, as the novel progresses both Lottie and the reader see him as being more than one-dimensional and having some merits (the ability to express affection, and a genuine desire to be of service to his clients). Each of the four central characters is transformed by love—in some instances romantic love, in other cases ties of family or friendship.

Rose in particular changes her self-conception—whereas previously she had thought she found meaning and happiness in devotion to God, the poor, and duty, she recognizes first that she is deeply unhappy, and second that love for a particular person, rather than devotion to a cause, is the only way she will find happiness and meaning. Her willingness to attend to her own emotions (mainly because she is repeatedly challenged to do so by Lottie) reveals her unhappiness and the extent to which her self-conception has missed out on what really has significance for her. As with *Shantaram*, we are able to see first how emotions can narrow our focus (for instance both that of Lottie in regard to her husband and that of the reader who identifies with her) and how they can help show us when our self-conceptions and goals are disconnected from what we really find significant. Yet the narrator's seeming endorsement of Lottie's conclusion that people can only find happiness in pairs, and the account of Rose's inability to see the poor as real people whom she might learn from as well as minister to, leaves the reader feeling that the novel dismisses the possibility of finding meaning in connection to something larger than one other person. This aspect of the novel, and some unease the reader may feel with it, can valuably be discussed with others.

Exit Lines opens with three elderly characters attempting to fulfill the wishes of a fourth, Ruth, who wants her friends to help her die, and it alternates between the events of that evening and the next morning, when Ruth survives, and the events that led up to Greta, George, and Sylvia's decisions to help Ruth put an end to a life she describes as empty of longing. The novel is told in the third person, but the narrator has intimate access to the thoughts and feelings of each of the four central characters (particularly important since George, after several strokes, finds it difficult to communicate). It gives voice to the complex and conflicting thoughts and feelings of disparate people whose voices are rarely represented with any complexity in fiction, people coping, near the end of life, with a variety of impairments and dependencies.

The novel demonstrates that its characters are often emotionally savvy; Ruth, for instance, carefully selects newspaper stories in order to convince her friends of the reasonableness of her view that there is nothing much she can hope for, and Sylvia, in the hours before Ruth is to die, shares her own careful selection with her friends. Both are well aware of the connection between emotional response and selective attention. Ruth also recognizes that a variety of emotional responses (empathy for her view of her situation, guilt about times when they have not risen to the occasion to meet others' demands, admiration for Ruth's determination, resentment at the extent to which family members and staff at the Idyll Inn underestimate their capacities) play a role in her friends' decision to attempt to support her plan. There are aspects of their emotional lives that are initially obscure to the characters—Sylvia only comes to realize the extent of her love for her daughter when that daughter becomes quite ill. Other aspects remain obscure—Ruth realizes that she has mixed feelings about her mercy killing of her husband, but can't admit to herself that her regret and worry play a role in her desire to die in the same way that she killed him; Greta never realizes that her shame about her bodily desires plays a role in her decision to overcome her reluctance to participate in Ruth's death. The novel therefore offers many opportunities to identify various emotions in the characters and in oneself as reader, and to evaluate the extent to which emotions motivate, reveal significance, or aid in self-deception.

I now turn to some recent evidence that supports my contention that engaging with certain types of literary narratives (those that, as discussed above, give a detailed and emotionally and imaginatively engaging account of the doings and reactions of intentional agents) can help us develop meta-affective skills and confidence and hence may serve as a resource for personal autonomy. Two recent experiments by Djikic et al. (2009a, 2009b) suggest that when readers respond to a literary narrative high in narrativity (Chekhov's story *The Lady with the Toy Dog*), as opposed to a less emotionally and imaginatively engaging narrative on the same topic, of the same length and at the same reading level, they evidence greater emotional change in response to the literary narrative (interestingly, emotional change in an idiosyncratic direction, along various dimensions that differ for different readers). Those readers who score high on a scale designed to measure discomfort with experiencing negative emotions are likely to demonstrate the most significant emotional change, suggesting, as the authors conclude, that such readers may find literature a safe place to experience such emotions. This suggests, as Mar and Oatley argue, that fiction "allows us to experiment in a controlled and safe manner with intentions, emotions, and emotion-evoking situations that would be impossible and often highly undesirable in the real world," and hence engaging with fiction (at least those fictions that probe difficult circumstances) "provides us with an opportunity to grow emotionally" (2008, 183).

Mar and Oatley go on to cite further psychological studies that show that readers engage emotionally with literary narratives of the type discussed above via processes that combine triggering of autobiographical memory, sympathy, and identification.[10] They do not stress the importance of developing meta-affective skills, as I do, in part because their focus is on the extent to which fiction allows us insight into others and into the dynamics of social interactions, but their work does provide evidence that our responses to literary narratives give us practice feeling and identifying various emotions, and that they also tend to elicit (at least fairly short-term) idiosyncratic emotional change.

Although Mar and Oatley concentrate mainly on the benefit of our engagement with literary narratives, and assume that most such narratives will be at least psychologically realistic and hence provide insight into the workings of the human mind, they note that not all stories are useful social guides, and that "just as we are careful in choosing the friends who surround us, so should we be careful in choosing the books with which we spend our time" (185). Beyond noting that books can influence us or give us false information, they don't have much to say about the potential negative effects of engaging with literary narratives. To make the source of the danger clearer, I would like to say something about the impact of engaging in certain types of emotionally involving imaginings. I will start with a brief account of the role played by a character's vivid imaginings in the next novel I will discuss, Ann Patchett's *Taft.*

John Nickel is the main character of *Taft,* and the novel alternates between his first person account of his own experiences and a third person account of the last few weeks in the life of Taft, the dead father of two of the other characters. The latter is entirely the product of Nickel's imagination, focusing on Taft's thoughts and feelings about his children, Fay and Carl. Part of Nickel's fascination with Taft has to do with his strong ambivalent feelings for Fay (just on the cusp of becoming an adult, she is infatuated with Nickel), and part of it has to do with his own struggle to continue to be an engaged father to his young son (the mother has moved away with the boy, but might possibly come back). Nickel's detailed imaginings of Taft help him to keep from becoming romantically involved with Fay (as his identification with Taft keeps him focused on her need for a father and her youth and vulnerability) but also deepen his involvement with Carl, a troubled and drug-addicted young man. Because Nickel worries about Carl as Taft did, and sees the best in him, he misses several clues that Carl is more seriously troubled than Nickel acknowledges, and in particular that Carl has begun dealing drugs in the bar Nickel manages. When the clientele of the bar changes, Nickel interprets this as the tourist season come early; as Carl spends more and more time in the bar and with other customers, Nickel sees this as Carl's attempt to bond with him and his becoming more emotionally engaged with others. Finally, Nickel is forced by another employee to recognize what is happening, but he still does not take the measures he should, and ends up being shot by Carl. Once again his identification with his imaginary reconstruction of Taft causes him to pity Carl and worry for his future, and so he risks his life by refusing to have his wound properly treated.

Taft demonstrates the power of emotionally involved imaginings to motivate action, in part by generating selective focus, in part by shaping attachments to people and even to particular interpretations of events. I have argued elsewhere that imagining situations, particularly morally laden situations, from a particular perspective has a power to shape what we notice and what we do (see Mullin 2002 and especially 2004). Currie and Jureidini argue that we should not think of believing and imagining as entirely different sorts of mental operations, such that what we merely imagine will not impact what we do. Reading a scary story may make us worry more about sounds we hear late in the house at night, or about the safety of our children, by making scenarios we know to be only possible more emotionally salient. Reading about a romantic relationship that ends badly, or about lovers who treat each other cruelly, may make us more likely to be suspicious of romantic partners, particularly if we have other reasons to have suspicions, and hence the feelings bring to mind memories which are then made more vivid.

Imaginings are particularly likely to have powerful effects upon our reactions and our plans when we engage in repeated imaginings of a particular sort. These effects may be positive (Mar and Oatley note that merely reading about characters of another race, sympathetically portrayed, can diminish racism), but they can also be negative.

Thinking about the way our imaginings impact our actions and reactions can be another reason to turn to a social group in order to discuss our emotional and imaginative reactions to literary narratives. However, just as our own emotional and imaginative abilities can be ambivalent resources for enhancing our autonomy, so too can social groups be ambivalent resources. For example, if we read novels that challenge practices that are typically accepted, it could be important to share one's reactions to the novels with a group containing members who are alert to the existence of unacknowledged forms of oppression and whose emotional reactions demonstrate that awareness. On the other hand, it could be damaging to share one's emotional reactions to the narrative, especially if those reactions are dismissed or belittled, with people who do not share one's sense of what is oppressive or wrong. I do not say that one should share one's emotional reactions only with people who agree with one about which political practices are right and which are wrong. However, when not only is there disagreement, but those who disagree are aligned with more powerful forces in society and use that power to dismiss one's emotional responses, that could easily undermine one's confidence in one's abilities, and hence one's autonomy. By contrast, if one's own emotional responses are privileged, that could be damaging to one's discussants' autonomy. For example, Lionel Shriver's 2003 novel *We Need to Talk About Kevin* discusses maternal ambivalence and the burdens placed on women by expectations that mothers will find joy in self-sacrifice. For someone just starting to contest those norms and feeling emotions other than those expected of mothers, it could be damaging to share feelings about the novel with others who strongly endorse the norms and are horrified at deviation from them.

In conclusion, our emotions are a potential resource for autonomy, by revealing what we care about even when our concerns are in tension with our self-conception and social mores. However, they are far from a generally reliable resource, and it is important to develop the meta-affective skills (and relationships with others) that help us to identify our emotions and learn when they reveal what we find important and when they obscure it. Reading literary narratives of the type I have discussed can help us develop these meta-affective skills. Discussing our responses to these narratives in a supportive community of people with different perspectives but a commitment to respectful sharing—in which one may challenge, but not belittle, one another's responses—can make it more likely that we will learn when we should trust what our emotions are telling us.

NOTES

1. Oatley and Duncan (1992) present evidence that when people report emotional incidents in a diary, at least 6 percent of the time they acknowledge they do not understand why they feel the particular emotions they do, and that other studies show that people find some aspect of their emotional responses mysterious between 5 and 25% of the time. Self-reports may underestimate our misunderstanding of our emotions.

2. See Burrow (2005) and Meyers (1997) on connections between emotional perception and political location.

3. See, for instance, Christman (2004), Lamarque (2004), and Strawson (2004, 2005) on the one side and Dennett (1988), MacIntyre (1985, 1997), Rudd (2007), and Schechtman (2007) on the other.

4. See Carroll (2001) for one interesting attempt.

5. See Mullin (2007) for an extended account of my views about the nature of personal autonomy.

6. See Benson (2005). However, I think we do not need to be as self-consciously aware that we trust ourselves as he suggests. I think we do not need to have conscious beliefs that we are competent, so long as we take ourselves to have the kinds of competences I sketched above. We might not be willing to articulate our self-confidence in response to others' challenges, either, but this will not undermine confidence so long as we do not crumble in the face of challenges.

7. See Carroll (1997) for his account of the thought content of an emotion. This is similar to what I mean by taking the world to be a certain way (rather than necessarily believing it to be).

8. See Levinson (1997) for an account of what he terms the "paradox of fiction," which is that we seem to feel real emotions in response to what we acknowledge not to be real events. I think the emotions are real, and that our emotional responses to fiction are by no means the only time we respond to imaginings with real emotions.

9. This account of what it is for a work to be high in narrativity has remarkable affinities with that of Mar and Oatley (2008). They argue that what interests readers in literary narratives is the narratives' focus on "autonomous intentional agents and their interaction," in a way that engages us emotionally and imaginatively in the interactions between agents and their goals (174). I think we are interested in intentional agents both when they are autonomous and when they are less so. I agree with the authors that the characters' social interactions are important, but I take the characters' other goals to be as potentially engaging as the social interactions the authors emphasize in this article.

10. Here it is important, as noted above, that Mar and Oatley's account of the important features of literary narratives echoes the one I use.

REFERENCES

Arpaly, Nomy. 2000. "On Acting Rationally Against One's Best Judgment." *Ethics* 110 (3): 488–513.

Benson, Paul. 2005. "Taking Ownership: Authority and Voice in Autonomous Agency." In *Autonomy and the Challenges to Liberalism: New Essays,* edited by John Christman and Joel Anderson, 101–26. New York: Cambridge University Press.

Burrow, Sylvia. 2005. "The Political Structure of Emotion: From Dismissal to Dialogue." *Hypatia* 20 (4): 27–43.

Carroll, Noël. 1997. "The Rationality of Emotional Responses to Art." In *Emotion and the Arts,* edited by Sue Laver and Mette Hjort, 190–211. Oxford: Oxford University Press.

———. 2001a. *Beyond Aesthetics: Philosophical Essays.* Cambridge: Cambridge University Press.

———. 2001b. "On the Narrative Connection." In *Beyond Aesthetics: Philosophical Essays,* 118–32. Cambridge: Cambridge University Press.

Christman, John. 2004. "Narrative Unity as a Condition of Personhood." *Metaphilosophy* 35 (5): 695–713.

Currie, Gregory. 2006. "Narrative Representation of Causes." *Journal of Aesthetics and Art Criticism* 64 (3): 309–16.

Currie, Gregory, and Jon Jureidin. 2004. "Narrative and Coherence." *Mind and Language* 19 (4): 409–427.

Currie, Gregory, and Ian Ravenscroft. 2002. *Recreative Minds: Imagination in Philosophy and Psychology.* Oxford: Oxford University Press.

De Sousa, Ronald. 1987. *The Rationality of Emotion.* Cambridge, Mass.: MIT Press.

Dennett, Daniel. 1988. "Why Everyone Is a Novelist." *Times Literary Supplement,* Sept. 16–22, 1016–22.

Djikic, Maya, Keith Oatley, Sara Zoeterman, and Jordan B. Peterson. 2009a. "Defenseless Against Art? Impact of Reading Fiction on Emotion in Avoidantly Attached Individuals." *Journal of Research in Personality* 43:14–17.

———. 2009b. "On Being Moved by Art: How Reading Fiction Transforms the Self." *Creativity Research Journal* 21 (1): 24–29.

Lamarque, Peter. 2004. "On Not Expecting Too Much from Narrative." *Mind and Language* 19 (4): 393–408.

Levinson, Jerrold. 1997. "Emotion in Response to Art: A Survey of the Terrain." In *Emotion and the Arts,* edited by Sue Laver and Mette Hjort, 20–35. Oxford: Oxford University Press.

MacIntyre, Alasdair. 1985. *After Virtue: A Study in Moral Theory.* London: Duckworth.

———. 1997. "The Virtues, the Unity of Human Life, and the Concept of a Tradition." In *Memory, Identity, Community: The Idea of Narrative in the Human Sciences,* edited by Lewis P. Hinchman and Sandra K. Hinchman, 241–63. Albany: SUNY Press.

Mackenzie, Catriona. 2000. "Imagining Oneself Otherwise." In *Relational Autonomy: Feminist Perspectives on Autonomy, Agency, and the Social Self,* edited by Catriona Mackenzie and Natalie Stoljar, 124–50. New York: Oxford University Press.

———. 2002. "Critical Reflection, Self-Knowledge, and the Emotions." *Philosophical Explorations* 5 (3): 186–206.

———. 2008. "Imagination, Identity, and Self-Transformation." In *Practical Identity and Narrative Agency,* edited by Catriona Mackenzie and Kim Atkins, 121–45. New York: Routledge.

Mar, Raymond, Maja Djikic, and Keith Oatley. 2008. "Effects of Reading on Knowledge, Social Ability, and Selfhood: Theory and Empirical Studies." In *Directions in Empirical Literary Studies,* edited by Sonia Zyngier, Marisa Bortolussi, Anna Chesnokova, and Jan Auracher, 127–39. Philadelphia: John Benjamins.

Mar, Raymond, and Keith Oatley. 2008. "The Function of Fiction Is the Abstraction and Simulation of Social Experience." *Perspectives on Psychological Science* 3:173–92.

Meyers, Diana. 1989. *Self, Society, and Personal Choice.* New York: Columbia University Press.

———. 1997. "Emotion and Heterodox Moral Perception: An Essay in Moral Social Psychology." In *Feminists Rethink the Self,* 197–218. Boulder: Westview Press.

———. 2005. "Decentralizing Autonomy: Five Faces of Selfhood." In *Autonomy and the Challenges to Liberalism: New Essays,* edited by John Christman and Joel Anderson, 27–55. New York: Cambridge.

Mullin, Amy. 2002. "Evaluating Art: Morally Significant Imagining Versus Moral Soundness." *Journal of Aesthetics and Art Criticism* 60 (2): 137–49.

———. 2004. "Moral Defects, Aesthetic Defects, and the Imagination." *Journal of Aesthetics and Art Criticism* 62 (3): 249–61.

———. 2007. "Children, Autonomy, and Care." *Journal of Social Philosophy* 38 (4): 536–53.

Oatley, Keith. 1994. "A Taxonomy of the Emotions of Literary Response and a Theory of Identification in Fictional Narrative." *Poetics* 23:53–74.

———. 1999. "Why Fiction May Be Twice as True as Fact: Fiction as Cognitive and Emotional Simulation." *Review of General Pyschology* 3 (2): 101–17.

———. 2007. "On the Definition and Function of Emotions." *Social Science Information* 46 (3): 415–19.

Oatley, Keith, and Elaine Duncan. 1992. "Incidents of Emotion in Daily Life." In *International Review of Studies on Emotion,* vol. 2, edited by K. T. Strongman, 250–93. Chichester: John Wiley.

Rudd, Anthony. 2007. "In Defence of Narrative." *European Journal of Philosophy* 17 (1): 60–75.

Schechtman, Marya. 2007. "Stories, Lives, and Basic Survival: A Refinement and Defense of the Narrative View." *Royal Institute of Philosophy Supplements* 82: 155–78.

Strawson, Galen. 2004. "Against Narrativity." *Ratio* 17:428–52.

———. 2005. "Episodic Ethics." In *Narrative and Understanding Persons,* edited by Daniel Hutto, 85–115. Royal Institute of Philosophy Supplement 60. Cambridge: Cambridge University Press.

Narrative Rehearsal, Expression, and Goethe's "Wandrers Nachtlied II"

Richard Eldridge

It is by now all but a commonplace that modern human subjects face increased difficulties in finding and sustaining meaningful orientation and routes of significant interest in life in comparison with their forebears in less technologically advanced circumstances. To be sure, modernity brings significant advantages with it. Not only are there the benefits of modern technologies of food production, medicine, transportation, and so on in easing the material conditions of life, there are also the charms of being able to an increased extent to choose for oneself what sort of social identity to develop from among a wider array of possibilities. Constraints of income, circumstance, available options, and opportunities and expectations set by others still no doubt exist, but there are also both new possibilities and increased degrees of geographic and social mobility. No one in 1200 C.E. could move from Kansas or Kuala Lumpur or Kinshasa to Manhattan or Mumbai or Moscow in order to get an education and become a polymer chemist, plumber, police officer, professional tennis player, or performance artist.

With these increased possibilities of social identity, however, there often also come increased uncertainties and anxieties. Human beings at any level of culture are always and everywhere capable of reflection and are hence the kinds of beings who are capable of calling their own being into question.

This fact is rooted in the emergence in us of specifically discursive consciousness as opposed to mere sensory intake. Unlike other animals, we classify things under concepts, sometimes the very same physical object under different concepts, depending on our contexts of use and engagement with it. Or—depending on your views about animals and concepts—we do so at least with enormously greater plasticity and flexibility of attention than do other animals. Hence we can ask, is this (stick) a weapon, a piece of firewood, a building material, or a drawing implement? Given our plasticities of engagement and attention, questions of correctness arise for us in a way in which they do not arise for other animals, and these questions of correctness have to do also with what is wanted of us in a given context and with how others are engaging with an object of attention.

Cultures existing at subsistence level have to get things right—is that a tiger?—but they are not so much occupied with reflection on plasticities of attention, engagement, and practice. Strongly tribal or traditional cultures may slot their members into courses of action with few alternatives and without much occasion for reflection. In modernity, however, things are different. With the growth of scientific and technological knowledge, increasing urbanization, and expanding market economies, diversity within cultures becomes the norm. Individuals begin to have to make a way of life, more and more by skill and will and less and less by necessity and tradition. The question of how it is best or most fruitful or right to live becomes pressing. This question arose in some form in urban centers in the ancient world—for example, in Athens in the fifth and fourth centuries B.C.E. But even there this question arises in part as a function of urbanization and the increase in possibilities of subjective particularity that it brings with it. These possibilities of subjective particularity then explode with increasing force at least from the early seventeenth century onwards (with complicated, interesting roots and antecedents).

Once reflection on attention and on engagements with the world has begun, it is both urgent and all but impossible to rein it in. It is urgent in that, without reflection of the right kind, subjective particularity is in danger of running riot and culminating in all kinds of unchastened competitive individualism, factionalism, and violence, particularly as religion declines in cultural authority with the rise of science. It is all but impossible to rein it in, in that no absolute ontological ground is available to discursive consciousness, from which it emerges and knowledge of which might guide its course. Think of Hölderlin's "Sein und Urteil" fragment or of Wordsworth's sense of his fall out of naturalness and into discursivity.

In the absence, then, of available fundamentalisms, one possible way of arriving reflectively at modes of attention and engagement in which one can believe, or in which one can believe more fully, is through narrative rehearsal. One may be unable to know by theorizing, or have at hand no ready way to know, what human life as such is *for*. But one might hope to come to a better, clearer sense of what one's particular life might best or better look like, and this sense might manifest itself in feeling that one has thought through certain possible larger shapes of life, for oneself and possibly for some like-minded and like-situated others. That is, one might tell a story to oneself and others about how one might move in time from A to B to W, hoping that certain imagined itineraries will emerge in feeling as better supporting conviction in their ability to sustain a sense of lived meaningfulness than do some others. This strategy—imaginative, narrative rehearsal of possibilities, thence tested in feeling for whether or how well they support a sense of lived meaningfulness—at any rate was prominently taken up and developed in Germany in the decades immediately following 1781, as German thinkers and writers struggled both with how to receive Kant's critical philosophy, given its dismissal of the possibility of ultimate metaphysical knowledge, and with larger problems of secularization and social pluralization. Just what, it was wondered, are we to do with ourselves, and how are we to support a lived answer to this question, if both the will of God in any detail is unavailable to us and we cannot know theoretically what we are and are made for?

To the extent, then, that we continue to live within a modern cultural dispensation, with senses of social possibility, of the unavailability of ultimate metaphysical knowledge, and of a consequent need for meaningful orientation in life, which senses resemble the sense of the human subject that was prominent in post-Kantian Germany, it may be of some help to consider exactly how Kant and some of his successors turned to narrative in the service of emotional clarification about possibilities of meaningful life.

One place in which it is especially clear that Kant is caught up in an agon of reflection on fit or fruitful modes of life, aiming at but failing to achieve full assurance in cultural practice, is his 1786 essay "What Is Orientation in Thinking?" In this essay Kant argues, along Cartesian lines, that "it is possible to remain secure against all error if one does not venture to pass judgment in cases where one's knowledge is insufficient for the judgment in question" (1991, 240). This is often a valuable policy in the exact sciences.

There are, however, also cases in which there is a need to pass judgment despite the insufficiency of knowledge, notably cases involving judgments of rightness in action. In these cases we may, Kant argues, first, establish that a concept is free from contradiction, and, second, use only pure concepts of the understanding, free from all sensible content, in formulating judgments. In this way, we may in particular come to a purely rational belief (that does not, however, amount to knowledge) in the existence of a God without any sensible characteristics and who provides no reliable evidence of his presence in history. The belief in such a God is, Kant argues, practically necessary in that we need, in order to achieve orientation in both theory and practice, to assume that there is purposiveness in nature and that God exists as its only possible ground, even if he neither displays himself within this purposiveness nor makes its direction evident. This purely rational belief is then "the signpost or compass . . . [such that] the man of ordinary (but healthy) reason can use it to plan his course, for both theoretical and practical purposes, in complete conformity with the whole end of his destiny" (245).

It is, as Kant's successors found, possible—indeed, unavoidable—to find this recommendation both intriguing and relatively empty. We are barred from substantial knowledge of God's providence and from substantial knowledge of our destiny. As Kant remarks in his 1784 "Universal History" essay, nature "reveals something, but very little" of a path toward a kingdom of ends (1963, 22). How, then, is orientation "in complete conformity with the whole of [one's] destiny" possible? The categorical imperative sets certain fixed prohibitions and certain abstract ideals, but it is far from delineating this path. At the very least, substantial imaginative casuistry coupled with historical and cultural understanding will be needed.

How, then, within present cultural practice might a sense of orientation be effectively achieved and sustained? A number of possibilities were suggested and canvassed in immediate reaction to Kant. I will sketch six, with breathtaking speed. The latter five in particular involve a turn toward the use of narrative and some narrowing of a difference between philosophy as a discipline (at least when ethical questions about cultivation are in view) and certain forms of literary practice.

(1) One might undertake to provide a better grounding for a philosophical system that describes both the emergence of discursive consciousness and its path toward a destiny of achieved freedom. This representationalist-descriptivest-theoretical stance is, crudely oversimplifying, the stance of

Reinhold and Fichte. Paul Franks (2005) has described very well the imperative toward system that dominates their thinking: all or nothing. One must understand everything—the discursive mind, its place in nature, its destiny, and the path toward it—or one will have understood nothing, or nothing really important. This alternative all-or-nothing maps, I suggest, onto the alternative: life as a fully achieved human subject or death in reactivity and ungrounded conventionality. A difficulty of this stance, as Fichte already comes to see in his political turn, is that the emphasis on correct theoretical representation of our condition reinforces the turn toward reflection about representation that itself distances one from meaningful engagements in culture and practice. Its wages—however much the Fichtean Absolute is not an individual subject—are isolation and detachment, as well as desperate repeated attempts to ground the system convincingly.[1] And this suggests that the antithesis—either fully achieved, absolutely valuable and exemplary human life, or death in life—is itself too sharply drawn. Surely there must be a middle way? But how is it to be found, once the sense of the possibility of death in present conventional social life has arisen, so that something new needs to be done?[2]

(2) Hegel, too, pursues the imperative toward system, but in contrast with Reinhold and with much of Fichte, he sees the description of our stances as possessors of discursive consciousness as always bound up with practical attitudes in culture that are held by both the describer and the object of description. *Teilnahme,* participation, absorbs and informs any purely representational stance. Stability comes only at the end of history, when theoretical description and practical stance within culture have settled into mutual transparency, as a result of the long march of trial-and-error, of the labor of the negative. Here, to put it mildly, one may wonder whether any such settling really has or is taking place. Perhaps in certain ways, in certain regions of North Atlantic culture, say, *en mesure.* But the relations between such settlings as exist and persisting instabilities surely still remain to be worked out.

(3) One might, against the imperative toward system, emphasize the spontaneity of the human subject that is bound up with the ability to reflect and to think things otherwise. This is, of course, the way of Schlegel and *Witz,* more recently urged on us as well by Blanchot and by Lacoue-Labarthe and Nancy (see Lacoue-Labarthe and Nancy 1988). The power of spontaneity—the power to think and act otherwise, with improvisatory aptness—in the face of what is done is not to be scanted. Exercise of this power is bound up with feeling oneself to be a subject at all, and that feeling

deserves some nurturance. As Blanchot puts it, "to speak poetically is to make possible a non-transitive speech whose task is not to say things (not to disappear into what it signifies) but to say (itself) in letting itself say, yet without taking itself as the new object of this language without object" (1993, 357). One may, however, nonetheless wonder, even after all contextualist constraints have been specified, whether enough stability in life is afforded by the cultivation of irony and agility. What J. M. Bernstein calls "theoretical exorbitance" (2006, 157) attaches to philosophizing always on the run, so that a certain nomadism results. Beginning, always and always over again, "Jena Romanticism," in Bernstein's words, "cancels any synthesis, harmonization, riveting together of materiality and the social sign" (158). It is no accident that the Jena Romantics produced no great literary works. Without at least some stable enough harmonization of materiality and the social sign, a collapse into succumbing to the evanescent blandishments of consumerism is possible. I might, that is to say, wittily and ironically "buy" this or that—my style of dress, my friends, my books, my religion, my household furnishings, or my spouse—and so be pulled apart, never really recognizing myself as a subject over time.

(4) Underlying spontaneity, *Witz,* and agility, one might appeal to the affordances of what Benjamin called unseen affinities or Adorno, following Benjamin, called fugitive experiences. The dominant economy and its culture may be commodified. But there remain pockets of resistance—the oddly difficult work of art that cannot readily be replicated in a fungible commodity or the traces of childhood where there is a sense of thickness of experience, as in Benjamin's *Berliner Kindheit*—that might be allowed to resurface with complex disturbatory and partially recuperative effects. Trauma and loss might be worked through, and some lines of self-continuity might be achieved, despite trauma and loss. Energies might be heightened. One might also think here of spots of time in Wordsworth or of certain moments in Proust. Both literary practice and philosophical criticism might undertake the work of discerning and reanimating the fugitive intimations of something beyond commodity life that may be found in both art and life. This, too, is not a suggestion to be scanted. But one might again wonder here just how much stability is enabled, and just what criteria there might be for evaluating and integrating the affordances of various fugitive intimations. One could further wonder what the costs of yoking disturbance even in part to self-recovery and self-stability might be. Such a yoking may somewhat underrate the artistry of the work and the disruptive powers of art.

(5) Instead of system, spontaneity, or the recovery of the fugitive, one might invest one's energies in the work of forming an artistic presentation or *Darstellung,* hoping to direct and stabilize these energies within the activity of artistic construction itself. This idea runs throughout defenses of the autonomy of art from any instrumental purposes, and it is usefully developed in David Wellbery's recent critical writing on Goethe and Eichendorff. Wellbery terms this strategy of artistic construction the pursuit of the simulacrum. "The presentation, which in mimesis possesses a transparency that is oriented toward an ideal realm of depth, attains in the simulacrum its own proper thickness" (2006, 147; my translation). The result of this pursuit of a proper thickness is, in Eichendorff's "Wünschelrute" and "Der Abend" and in Goethe's "Der Fischer," "a romantic lyric that is separate from all enthusiasm for nature and closeness to the folksong, and that is instead to be understood as an investigation of the intrinsic possibilities of a medium" (151). (Wellbery concedes that the performative aspect of mimesis—the text's transmission of a message about something—is also important. Here he is principally correcting an overemphasis on message as against the powers of the work itself to engage and absorb us.) The strategy of constructing absorbing works has the advantage of engaging the subject and its powers in actual courses of constructive artistic labor and of promoting identification with the artistic subject capable of such construction. It brings into view the possibility of some stability for the subject in attachment to the continuing labor of artistic making. If, however, all claims to represent something beyond the medium are suspended, then there is at least something of a danger of a flight from life into formalism and aestheticism.

(6) Finally, there is Hölderlin. What is most distinctive about Hölderlin's approach to the problem of orientation is his development of the doctrine and poetic practice of *Wechsel* or modulation. In Hölderlin's hands, *Wechsel* comes to mean appropriately modulated alternation among various poetic moods: heroic, naïve, ideal, and so on. More abstractly, Hölderlin's practice of *Wechsel* embodies the thought that "a conflict is necessary between [1] the most original postulate of the spirit which aims at [the] communality and unified simultaneity of all parts, and [2] the other postulate which commands the spirit to move beyond itself and reproduce itself" (Hölderlin 1988, 62). The subject alternates, that is to say, between moments of receptivity and absorption, on the one hand, and moments of striving, form-making, and self-assertion, on the other. (Dieter Henrich sums this up as the persistence of the conflict between love and selfhood within Hölderlin's writing [1997, 127–28].) Narration of the alternation of

such moods displaces theoretical grasp of something "over against" the subject as a means of finding and sustaining valuable orientation in life. The hope of Hölderlin's poetic practice is that the alternations that mark his writing will be not brute, but modulated. They will embody a working through and bringing into relative (but not perfect) balance of the conflicting tendencies toward love-absorption-stability and selfhood-independence-departure that mark modern human life. This practice involves a certain foregrounding of an elegiac, lyric voice that is aware of its own alternations, and it involves also a certain commitment to endlessness of conflict and of the poetic registering of conflict, against the claims of theory. The wager is that the registering of conflict as modulation will enable enough recognition and stability on the part of the subject to go on, that it will yield just enough orientation, claiming neither too much nor too little. Commitment to reflection and to the work of writing is balanced against receptivity to and involvement in nature and others.

To recapitulate, the possibilities that are in view for thinking about how to achieve continuing, self-determining orientation for human subjects in post-Kantian modernity are:

1. Reinhold-Fichte: epistemological theory
2. Hegel: historical-descriptive social theory
3. Schlegel-Blanchot: spontaneity, agility, and wit
4. Wordsworth-Proust-Benjamin: recovery of fugitive experiences
5. Wellbery (following Eichendorff, Goethe): constructing thick artistic presentations
6. Hölderlin: the lyric that embodies modulation

Among these six possibilities, I find Hölderlin's suggestion to be most capacious in incorporating elements of each of 3, 4, and 5. But what remains to be seen is exactly *how* in at least some exemplary cases 3, 4, 5, and 6 might fruitfully be combined. What, that is, might a successful, self-determining, orientation-intimating modulation of mood, constructed by spontaneity, taking up the recovery of the fugitive, and achieving thick artistic presentation look like? And how might such an orientation-intimating modulation help subjects in modernity to find some sort of assurance about value in life?

Though it does not have quite the directness in treating the powers and interest of literary language of either theories that tend toward formalism or theories such as Hölderlin's that emphasize the agon of the reflecting subject, Goethe's own poetic theory also embodies an effort to bring together spontaneity, receptivity, thickness of form, and modulation.[3] Goethe's poetology is, however, not as well known as it might be, largely because it is most fully developed in connection with his metaphysics of nature, as he attempts to work out a comprehensive theory of human being in relation to a natural world that itself bears meanings. As Walter Benjamin insightfully remarked, "the place occupied in Goethe's writings by his scientific studies is the one which in lesser artists is commonly reserved for aesthetics" (1999, 172). More specifically, Goethe's morphology embodies the fundamental thought that everything that is is both interpretable and expressive in relation to human subjects. "Morphology rests on the conviction that everything that is must also show itself and be adumbrated. We take this fundamental principle to be valid for everything from the first physical and chemical elements up to the spiritual expressions of mankind" (Goethe 2003, 45; my translation). This may have little plausibility in the face of our experience of, say, iron ore or salt, or more broadly, of our materialist conception of the world. Our interactions with iron ore and salt have more to do with measurement, theorizing, and use than they do with interpretation or with deciphering meanings, in any ready senses of these terms. To this extent, we are, as modern subjects especially and as makers of meanings, cast into culture and outside the self-enclosedness of a physical nature that is externally available for use and as an object of theorizing. Goethe's theory of nature seems too much to look backwards toward older, discredited religio-mythological views.

This impression can be somewhat softened, however, when we note how Goethe specifically develops his theory of form in relation to objects that *are* interpreted, objects such as works of art and human actions of various kinds. Here Goethe observes that "form is a moving something, a becoming, a passing away. The theory of form is the theory of transformation" (45). This claim emphasizes the constructive activity of the interpreting subject who is positing forms as much as simply finding them immanent in things, and it emphasizes also that the construction of form is both bound up in time and answerable to changeable interests on the part of the interpreting subject. Form is both "the brought forth and the becoming of what is brought forth" (48). When it comes to poetic texts, this claim enables us to see the form of the poem itself—its way of holding together its beginning, middle, and end in an overall plot—as all at once materially embodied, emergent both for the author in the course of writing and for the reader in

the course of reading, shaped by interest and need, and temporally developing. As in Hölderlin's theory of modulation, the struggle to make meaning
via modulation that lets something happen, that lets form emerge, and that
is answerable to the needs of a temporally and spatially situated subject is
more important than the statement of any ready doctrine or *Lehre*. Or, as
Goethe himself puts it, "Because very few of our experiences allow themselves to be wholly articulated and directly communicated, I have for a long
time chosen the means of a repeated reflection, so that I could through
opposed and at the same time reciprocally reflecting images reveal to those
who could notice the secret sense of things" (letter to Carl Jakob Ludwig
Iken, September 27, 1827, cited in Witte and Otto 1996, 20; my translation). The task of poetry is then to allow our experience to express itself
roundly and to be communicated, and this task is carried out through juxta-
posing images that let sense and form emerge for those who pay attention
in the right way.

We can, I think, make further sense of these poetological claims—both the
Hölderlinian strategy of *Wechsel* and the Goethean strategy of juxtaposition
for the sake of the emergence of sense—by turning to theories of what
makes artistic expression distinctively different from other forms of mean-
ing-making that are either more prosaic or more nakedly revelatory of self,
without craft and control.

   Art in general involves, I have argued (following many others), the
attempt to achieve the expression of emotion and attitude—a way of seeking satisfaction of a desire that one's ways of responding to and feeling
about perplexing initiators be endorsable. Am I right to feel perplexity, sadness, I don't know what, in relation to an initiating scene or incident? This
is the question that is all but explicitly on the minds of many imaginative
literary writers as they work. To get some feel for how this is so, we might
think, for example, of Shakespeare in writing *Hamlet* as undertaking to
figure what to think and feel about the competing claims of honor-tradition-
clan vs. individuality and about the proper roles of conscience, proof, eros,
deference, family piety, and so on in sorting out these competing claims.

   Making a poem, play, or other work of literary art can, then, be a way
of exploring and resolving emotions, thoughts, and attitudes that arise in
relation to perplexing scenes and incidents of life. Exactly how might artistic
writing manage to do this? Considering well-known theories of emotion
and expression in art can help us to address this question. These theories
fall into three main groups.

(A) There are, first of all, *psychodynamic* theories of artistic expression. Such a theory is often ascribed to both Benedetto Croce and R. G. Collingwood, especially if one focuses only on part I of *The Principles of Art,* ignoring Collingwood's subsequent general elaboration of a theory of human subject development and discursive consciousness and their relations to language and culture. Collingwood does hold that artistic expression is distinguished from ordinary planned making (*techne*) by the fact that the distinctions between planning and execution, means and end, raw materials and finished product, and form and matter have no place in it (1938, 20–25). This makes it seem as though artistic expression is nothing but a spontaneous welling up of emotion somehow—without thought or planning—manifesting itself in materials (words or stone or paint or bodily motions) that are being rhapsodically manipulated. Collingwood explicitly denies this implication, in distinguishing between the expression of emotion, which necessarily involves some control over the process, and the betrayal of emotion, which does not (121–24). He does not, however, at least in part I, give a very good account of the sort of intelligent control (that is not *techne*) that is exercised in artistic expression in contrast with betrayal. The advantage of a psychodynamic account, however, is that it emphasizes that burdens of feeling, attitude, emotion, and response are felt by human subjects and that these burdens can be discharged or lightened through expressive activity. Something in us, that is to say, is getting out of us via artistic expression, in such a way that actually occurring burdens and perplexities of feeling and stance are lightened and calmed.

(B) There are, second, *structural-linguistic* theories of artistic expression, of the kind developed by Nelson Goodman and Alan Tormey (see Goodman 1996; Tormey 1987, 421–37). Goodman, in particular, defines expression as a species of signification that arises out of the conscious, skilled manipulation of a language or code with distinct structural features, syntactic and semantic. More specifically, expression is *metaphorical exemplification,* where *exemplification,* first of all, is possession of a quality (falling under a general term) plus reference back to the quality possessed (or the general term that is applicable). For example, a tailor's swatch possesses the color, weight, pattern, and weave of the larger bolt of cloth that it also refers back to; or a paint chip both possesses and refers back to the color of the paint that appears on it. Such swatches and chips are used as representative samples of general features that are also found elsewhere: the sample and what it refers back to share, as it were, an overall physiognomy. Metaphorical exemplification or artistic expression is then exemplification (possession plus reference back) in an unusual, unexpected way. For example, Beethoven's *Pathétique* Sonata both possesses (the characteristic contour and rhythm of) sadness and refers back to sadness (Goodman 1996, 85–95).

The advantage of this account is that it highlights the craft or skill of putting significative exemplification into a work. Artists need not be, and typically are not, caught up in a rush of feeling in the moment in which they are doing their work. Instead they are paying careful attention to how in a medium to exemplify emotions in an unusual way: Rembrandt exemplifying in paint his love for Hendrikje Stoeffels by making the painted canvas possess and show it; Liszt exemplifying his melancholy yet serene religiosity in his late *Transcendental Etudes* by making them possess and show it, and so on.

This disadvantage of this account, however, is that it underrates the importance of feeling-with on the part of the audience. Successful expression becomes, apparently, colder than in psychodynamic theories, a matter of embedding properties in a work so as to convey a message rather than issuing to an audience invitations to participate in feeling and its clarification. Hence it both misses the importance of having emotions to having a point of view as a subject in general and, more specifically, misses the passions and urgencies that drive both artistic making and response to art. And it misses, further, the singularity of successful artistic expression, where we want, often, to dwell in or with the work—to experience just its way of rendering thought and emotion in its materials—rather than decoding it to find some more general message about kinds of emotions.

(C) Third, there are *intransitive* theories that focus on distinctive success in the formal arrangement of materials; *expressive* is treated as a near-synonym for *successful*. Garry Hagberg (1995, 103–9) and Roger Scruton (2004, 1–9) have developed theories of this kind. Such theories often take as their point of departure Wittgenstein's remark in *The Brown Book* that there is an "intransitive . . . usage" of the word "particular" to convey "an emphasis" (1958, 158). Similarly, we can use the word "expressive" as a commendatory adjective, as in "her playing was expressive," without filling in that it is expressive *of* anything. The advantage of this view is that it highlights both the importance of care in producing the work and the singularity of success: one work may be successfully expressive in this way, while even a closely similar work is not: in certain simple sonatas, a single note or two here or there may make all the difference between Mozart and Czerny. The disadvantage of this view, however, is that it does not show how satisfaction in doing the work of formal arrangement is driven by and bound up with matters of feeling. Hence this view at least drifts toward a more decorativist formalism.

It seems reasonable to conclude that there are some insights and some blind spots in each of these three views. We should try to integrate the insights of each of them while avoiding their missteps. In the Preface to *Lyrical Ballads,* Wordsworth begins usefully to develop just such a synthetic view. In poetry, he argues, the aim is not the straightforward communication only of information about an object, but rather the presentation and clarification of feeling in relation to it. "The feeling therein developed gives importance to the action and situation, and not the action and situation to the feeling" ("Preface to the Second Edition of *Lyrical Ballads* (1800)," in Wordsworth 1965, 448). When the work of poetry goes well, then the poet will "describe objects, and utter sentiments, of such a nature, *and in such connection with each other,* that the understanding of the Reader must necessarily be in some degree enlightened, and his *affections strengthened and purified* (448, emphasis added). The idea, then, is that the successful poetic work presents both a subject matter and a course of thoughts and feelings about the subject matter, with the aim of working through the thoughts and feelings, via the formal arrangement of words that present subject matter, thoughts, and feelings, until the thoughts and feelings become evidently more apt in relation to the subject matter. Our affections—how we are invested emotionally in things, positively or negatively—become strengthened and purified, in being purged of anything accidental and inappropriate to their objects.

This Wordsworthian stance is a primary source (along with materials on clarification from Aristotle, Spinoza, and Collingwood[4]) for an elucidatory definition of art that I have proposed and defended. (This definition is elucidatory in that it seeks not taxonomic exactness or the transformation of difficult or borderline cases of whether something is a work of art into easy ones, but rather an illuminating explanation of the functions in human life of the practices of art, as achieved in a wide range of exemplary cases.) That definition is that a work of art is a presentation of "a subject matter as a focus for thought and emotional attitude, distinctively fused to the imaginative exploration of material" (Eldridge 2003, 259 and below) for the sake of *working through* one's emotions in relation to a community of some extent that shares with the artist both a world and emotions in relation to it.[5]

The production of a work of art, and especially of a work of poetry, begins, then, with an initial disturbance or puzzlement or perplexity occasioned by an object, person, scene, or incident. One feels, somehow, something, but exactly what one feels, why one feels it, and whether one's feeling is apt to its initiator are all less than clear. The response to this perplexity that literary art achieves is then to find the narratively apt cause of a now more specifically articulated and acknowledged feeling that is now more evidently appropriate in relation to an overall situation. That is to say, one tells a story; one rehearses what is or may be going on in the course of having a feeling. This involves asking, what in the initiator is perplexing, and why? How and why, for example, am I perplexed, troubled, or transported in this specific way by this initiator? And it involves narrating the course of development of feeling itself as the story of its occasioning is generated, so that the feeling itself becomes caught up in reflection and so further specified and articulated, as one is guided in narrating by an effort to find the exact word, image, and cadence in sound that will yield clarity. Or, to revert to Wordsworth, descriptions and sentiments are presented in connection with each other in such a way that our affections are strengthened and purified. The fact that the situating of thoughts and feelings within an overall course of development (guided by the search for apt comparisons and for cadential resolution) *clarifies* them helps to make sense of what Aristotle means in saying both that plot is "the origin and as it were the soul" (1987, 9) of tragic drama and that a successful narrative plot presents "things that are possible in accordance with probability or necessity" (12). The soul of lyric in particular is specifically the narratively structured working through and articulation of emotion in relation to an initiator, so as to achieve greater stability, calm, formal success, and satisfaction in it (however ecstatic, horrific, beatific, disruptive, etc. the initial response may itself both be and remain). A narrative arc from disturbance to calm informs the process of working through, where working through is central to poetic process.

Remarks at this level of generality are all too likely to carry neither conviction nor intelligibility in the absence of detailed attention to a concrete example of the work of successfully expressive poetic art. It is impossible for any single work to illuminate clearly the powers and interest of all poetry, let alone of literature in general. But it remains possible to read a single poem closely, in the hope that an account of its powers and interest may at least serve as a model for how to begin to approach other cases.

J. W. Goethe's "Wandrers Nachtlied II / Wayfarer's Night Song II" is the single most well-known short lyric poem in all German literature. It remains to this day the poem that German schoolchildren are given to memorize at the age of twelve or thirteen, so that it stands, for many, as the means of their first serious reflective encounter with serious adult literature. It was, famously, carved by Goethe into the wall of a traveler's hut on the top of the Gickelhahn, a small mountain overlooking the Thüringer Wald, outside Ilmenau, at about 8 p.m. on September 6, 1780.[6] One can still climb the Gickelhahn today to see a reconstruction of the hut, just below the peak, with the carving reproduced. The poem has been set to music by at least forty-five composers, including Kempff, Liszt, Mendelssohn-Hensel, Reger, Schubert, and Schumann, as well as Ralph Shapey and Charles Ives. Just what did Goethe do in this short lyric poem, and why has it figured, and why does it continue to figure, so prominently in the German, and not only German, sense of the expressive powers of imaginative literature?

Über allen Gipfeln
Ist Ruh,
In allen Wipfeln
Spürest du
Kaum einen Hauch;
Die Vögelein schweigen im Walde.
Warte nur, balde
Ruhest du auch.

[Over all the hilltops
is calm.
In all the treetops
you feel
hardly a breath.
The little birds fall silent in the woods.
Just wait . . . soon
you too will be at rest.][7]

In order to enter into the work of this poem, it is useful to begin by asking two fundamental questions: (1) Who is the *du*-addressee? and (2) What does *ruhen* mean?

(1) A number of possibilities for the *du*-addressee immediately suggest themselves. It may be the faithful little dog who has accompanied Goethe

up the mountain and who is now not quite yet settled to rest. No doubt this possibility is somewhat fanciful, but consider the last lines of "Gute Nacht!" the last poem in Goethe's *West-östlicher Divan:* "Ja, das Hündlein gar, das treue / Darf die Herren hinbegleiten" [Yes, the little dog even, the loyal one, / May accompany the masters] (in Goethe 2006, 118; my translation). Being accompanied by a loyal dog is a kind of metaphor or metonymy (perhaps both) for the achievement of trust, loyalty, and exemplary mastery in relation to an audience. "Gute Nacht!" is a poem about a hope for success as a human subject in writing. It begins "Nun, so legt euch, liebe Lieder, / An den Busen meinem Volke!" [Now, lay you, dear songs / In the bosom of my people] (117; my translation), and it concludes this expression of hope for reception with an image of a dog, freely devoting itself out of loyalty to accompanying its master.

Less fancifully, Goethe's eminent biographer Nicholas Boyle argues that the addressee is entirely general. Specifically, "The 'you' is not—not specifically or by allusion—the woman [Charlotte von Stein] to whom Goethe was writing only minutes before, and after, he composed the poem" (1991, 266). This claim is part of Boyle's overall argument that Goethe's early poetry is "the poetry of desire" (the subtitle of volume 1, which goes up to 1790), more specifically of desire unstilled, but expressed. "The sources of his poetry ran deeper, and purer, than 'the sweet conversation of my inmost heart' that was his mental discourse with Charlotte von Stein" (266). Goethe practiced "an art not of possession but of desire, of a sensuous presence always suffused with recollection, reflection, or anticipation: that unfulfilled desire for the always absent object was the origin of his personal, as of his literary magnetism" (429). That is, Goethe's poetry is the deep poetry of a discursive, commitment-and project-having consciousness that is cut off from perfect wholeness, thus given over to wandering and suffused with a standing desire for presentness. This all seems quite right. But it is also the case that a specific address to an absent lover might itself be an expression of this standing desire, be the claim to or hope for intimacy in wandering with another who singularly, but absently, is a synecdoche for the possibility of redemptive intimacy. The desire persists, because she is absent, but an intimacy is sought in relation to her in this moment of address.

More importantly, however, Boyle's emphasis on the generality of the addressee points toward the addressee as either oneself (the poet himself) or anyone (or both). The thought is, "I have been in motion, first in climbing up here, and second in being busy in professional and social life (the life of the Weimar court) about the affairs of the world, and calm for me has not been possible." And this thought about activity failing to yield calm, that is, about lack of full assurance in and identification with busy activity, is a thought that might come to anyone. In fact, the most natural reading of *du* in line 4 is "anyone," that is, anyone who might happen to be here in this spot at this moment; and anyone who, further, feeling this stillness might be prompted to share a sense of exteriority to the calm of bare nature, because caught up in busy activity, hence an intimate second subject or *du*. We will come in a moment to consider what thought and possibilities of feeling and consolation are then offered to such a *du*-anyone and how they might be achieved.

(2) What does *ruhen* mean? Surely, as with the English "rest," it means both *sleep* and *death*. As with the birds falling silent, sleep will come, and so, too, will death. T. W. Adorno made much of this connection in his commentary on the poem. "In the line, 'Warte nur, balde' the whole of life, with an enigmatic smile of sorrow, turns into the brief moment before one falls asleep. . . . In the face of nature at rest, a nature from which all traces of anything resembling the human have been eradicated, the subject becomes aware of its own insignificance. Imperceptibly, silently, irony tinges the poem's consolation: the seconds before the bliss of sleep are the same seconds that separate our brief life from death" (Adorno 1991, 41–42).

Much of this is right: *ruhen* does indicate both sleep and death. All traces of the human have been eradicated from nature. This is registered formally in the repeated U sounds and soft F's, as though nature were speaking a semiotic mother tongue that precedes ego formation and will outlast ego identity. (Against this musicality, *Hauch* and *Auch* then come as interruptive, then conclusive, moments of the enactment of identity. I will come back to this.) The poet is thinking about that fact—about a nature that will survive his eradication; that is, he is thinking about his own death and about the meaning, if any, of the life that will have preceded it. (Compare the opening of Wordsworth's "Tintern Abbey": "Five years have passed . . . The day is come when I again *repose* / Here, under this dark sycamore" [in Wordsworth 1965, 108; emphasis added].) Adorno's phrase "becomes aware of its own insignificance" implies that the restless, anxious striving to master the terms of significance has been first voiced and then, somehow, calmed. A movement from disturbed restlessness to acceptance has somehow taken place.

Adorno then argues further that the restlessness of the subject or the sense of being caught up in busyness arises from the experience being caught up in modern commodity society. Goethe's lyric expresses a protest against that social world. "In its protest the poem expresses the dream of a world in which things would be different. The lyric spirit's idiosyncratic opposition to the superior power of material things is a form of reaction to the reification of the world, to the domination of human beings by commodities that has developed since the beginning of the modern era, since the industrial revolution became the dominant force in life" (Adorno 1991, 40). Here the thought that this particular lyric expresses at least in part a reaction to its particular social world is at least plausible, though I am somewhat inclined to say that it expresses a sense of undirected restlessness in the face of the stillness and self-continuity of nature, which sense of undirected restlessness might come to anyone in any culture, though it is perhaps more typical in modern commodity society. But it is surely right that the poem "expresses the dream of a world in which things would be different," a world in which the stresses of ego-formation and the bearing of ego-identity would be moderated or redeemed.

Just how does it do this? According to Adorno, the work resists commodity society and resists more generally a world in which undirected busyness predominates "by refusing to submit to anything heteronomous and constituting itself in accordance with its own laws" (40). That is, it achieves through aptness of reflection and formal artistry a coincidence of formal and thematic closure, and it achieves a kind of fullness of both attention to life and expression of that attention.

Adorno goes on to say that the speaking I in this poem "has lost [nature] as it were, and attempts to restore it through animation, through immersion in the 'I' itself" (41). (György Lukács makes a similar point about lyric in general in remarking that "at the lyrical moment the purest interiority of the soul, set apart from duration without choice, lifted above the obscurely-determined multiplicity of things, solidifies into substance; whilst alien, unknowable nature is driven from within, to agglomerate into a symbol that is illuminated throughout" [1971, 63].) To say that the "I" has lost nature is to say first that in possessing discursive subjectivity and reflectiveness, a human subject is not a being in and through whom everything simply happens, the way it happens in and through a leaf that changes color at a certain time of year. Rather, a human subject can reflect on and question its existence and so is not, or is no longer, immersed in mere naturalness. This not or no longer being immersed is experienced as a loss, an experience of loss that is perhaps exacerbated by the undirected busyness of modern commodity society. What is my choosing to be about this or that for? What, if anything, doth it avail? What does my life mean? These are the questions that are on the speaker's mind—the thoughts that are disturbing him—within his experience of the stillness of nature.

The solution is then to achieve animation, immersion in the I itself. I take this to mean fullness of attention in expressing this experience; the achievement of wholeheartedness or fullness of cathexis in and to the activity of giving apt voice to what one's situation and experience are. We might further note that the formal craft of the poem, specifically its pattern of repetitions, functions to lend a stillness to nature. The repeated *Über-Ruh-du*—suggesting a musicality and the repetitive babblings of the prediscursive—of the first four lines is interrupted by the harder *Kaum-Hauch,* then restored by the *Ruhest-du* of the last line, with the rhyming *auch* lending formal closure. The "I" has then emerged from a prediscursive position, found this situation troubling, spoken with formal unity, clarity, and medial thickness, and so come to terms with its situation. Spatially, the movement toward calm and the acceptance of (disturbing) thought and feeling is indicated in the movement of the poet's gaze and attention downward, from the mountaintops to the treetops to the birds in the trees to, by implication, the ground (*ruhen*).[8] Hence it can utter the *auch* that repeats the interruptive, percussive *Hauch,* and in echoing it achieves dramatic closure. That is, the speaking voice, having worked this material thematically and formally, can take responsibility for and find itself to be at one with this work. The father tongue, one might say, takes up, responds to, and closes the prior speech of the mother tongue, and so achieves its own proper fullness.[9] Nature will continue beyond the life of the individual discursive subject, who will not know all. But life can be accepted and lived anyway. Having fitly exercised one's powers is worth something, is perhaps even a form of temporary satisfaction that is beyond normal, somewhat happenstantial work and love. In this way, love for life as a discursive, human subject is achieved or reachieved, despite the senses of loss and of immersion in undirected busyness. One has, at least, reflected, felt, thought, and written fully, anyway. "Es war *doch* so schön."[10] Or as Adorno puts it, "[The] pure subjectivity [of lyric poems], the aspect of them that appears seamless and harmonious, bears witness to its opposite, to suffering in an existence alien to the subject and to love for it as well—indeed their harmoniousness is actually nothing but the mutual accord of this suffering and this love" (1991, 41).

To bear witness to suffering in an alien existence, but to love that existence anyway (insofar as fullness of expression is possible within and in relation to that existence; fullness of the achievement of what discursivity and reflectiveness and language discover themselves to be for), and to bear witness to that love as well—to do all this is to return to a sense of a harmoniousness of subjectivity with a nature and world that remain discordant from it, to move from disturbance to the thought and feeling that the world is good enough for us to live in it, at least to this extent: it has permitted this fullness of exercise of human powers of attention and expression. This strikes me as a centrally exemplary achievement—all at once formal, thematic, and emotional—of lyric and of art in general. I have no doubt that we need a more impersonal, constructivist politics of institutions, where compromises in social life will be necessary. I have no doubt that abstract, philosophical accounts of the nature of cognitive achievements in science and mathematics can be illuminating. Political philosophy and epistemology have their roles in life. But so, too, I think, does the aesthetic thinking—the thinking of the human subject in modernity in thick material forms—that this poem embodies.

NOTES

I am grateful to Joan Vandegrift, as well as to discussion with audiences at the Greater Philadelphia Philosophy Consortium session on Emotion, at the University of Chicago Workshop on Forms of Lyric (especially Hannah Eldridge, Michael Payne, and David Wellbery), at the University of Warwick Conference on Poetry and Philosophy (especially Jorie Graham and Stephen Houlgate), at the University of East Anglia, and at the University of Freiburg, Freiburg Research Institute for Advance Studies (especially Werner Frick), for helpful comments on earlier versions of this essay.

1. On Fichte's repeated attempts to refound his system as a cycle of procession and epistrophe, see Eldridge (1997, 62–71).

2. On imaginative rehearsal as a response to a felt sense of possibilities of death-in-life, see Eldridge (2008, 69–85).

3. I am grateful to Hannah Eldridge for calling my attention to Goethe's poetology in his scientific writings.

4. Collingwood's full theory of artistic expression, arrived at only in part III, after he has developed his accounts of the development of the discursive subject and of the indispensable importance of the media of art and of the audience to successful artmaking, is much closer to the required integrative view of expression than it is often taken to be.

5. See Eldridge (2008, especially chaps. 1, 4) for a fuller account of the process of working through as it is carried out in and through poetic composition.

6. The circumstances of the composition of Goethe's two "Wandrers Nachtlied" poems are recounted in Boyle (1991, 266).

7. In Goethe (2005, 34); translation modified from that by Hyde Flippo, which is archived at http://german.about.com/library/blwander.htm.

8. I owe this point to Jorie Graham in discussion at the University of Warwick.

9. I take the terms "father tongue" and "mother tongue" and the account of the relation between them from Stanley Cavell's adaptation/adoption of Thoreau's use of "father tongue" in Cavell (1972, 15–16).

10. Herbert Marcuse takes this line, which appears both in the "Türmerlied" ("Song of the Tower Warden") in Goethe's *Faust* and as the last words in Wedekind's *Pandora's Box,* as expressing a fundamental attitude of art toward life. There is a "reconciliation which . . . catharsis offers [that] also preserves the irreconcilable" (Marcuse 1978, 59).

REFERENCES

Adorno, Theodor W. 1991. "On Lyric Poetry and Society." In *Notes to Literature,* vol. 1, edited by Rolf Tiedemann, translated by Shierry Weber Nicholsen, 37–54. New York: Columbia University Press.
Aristotle. 1987. *Poetics.* Edited and translated by Richard Janko. Indianapolis: Hackett.
Benjamin, Walter. 1999. "Goethe." In *Walter Benjamin: Selected Writings,* vol. 2, *1927–1934,* edited by Marcus Paul Bullock, Michael William Jennings, Howard Eiland, and Gary Smith, 161–93. Cambridge, Mass.: Harvard University Press.
Bernstein, J. M. 2006. "Poesy and the Arbitrariness of the Sign: Notes for a Critique of Jena Romanticism." In *Philosophical Romanticism,* edited by Nikolas Kompridis, 173–95. London: Routledge.
Blanchot, Maurice. 1993. "The Athenaeum." In *The Infinite Conversation,* translated by Susan Hanson, 351–59. Minneapolis: University of Minnesota Press.
Boyle, Nicholas. 1991. *Goethe: The Poet and the Age.* Vol. 1, *The Poetry of Desire.* Oxford: Oxford University Press.
Cavell, Stanley. 1972. *The Senses of Walden.* New York: Viking Press.
Collingwood, R. G. 1938. *The Principles of Art.* Oxford: Clarendon Press.
Eldridge, Richard. 1997. *Leading a Human Life: Wittgenstein, Intentionality, and Romanticism.* Chicago: University of Chicago Press.
———. 2001. *The Persistence of Romanticism: Essays in Philosophy and Literature.* Cambridge: Cambridge University Press.
———. 2003. *An Introduction to the Philosophy of Art.* Cambridge: Cambridge University Press.
———. 2008. *Literature, Life, and Modernity.* New York: Columbia University Press.
Franks, Paul W. 2005. *All or Nothing: Systematicity, Transcendental Arguments, and Skepticism in German Idealism.* Cambridge, Mass.: Harvard University Press.
Goethe, Johann Wolfgang von. 2003. "Zur Morphologie." In *Schriften zur Naturwissenschaft,* edited by Michael Böhler. Stuttgart: Reclam.
———. 2005. *Selected Poetry of Johann Wolfgang von Goethe.* Edited and translated by David Luke. London: Penguin Books.
———. 2006. *West-östlicher Divan.* Boston: Adamant Media.
Goodman, Nelson. 1996. *Languages of Art: An Approach to a Theory of Symbols.* Indianapolis: Bobbs-Merrill.
Hagberg, Garry. 1995. *Art as Language: Wittgenstein, Meaning, and Aesthetic Theory.* Ithaca: Cornell University Press.

Henrich, Dieter. 1997. "Hegel and Hölderlin." Trans. Taylor Carman. In *The Course of Remembrance and Other Essays on Hölderlin,* edited by Eckart För-ster, 119–40. Stanford: Stanford University Press.

Hölderlin, Friedrich. 1988. "On the Operations of the Poetic Spirit." In *Essays and Letters on Theory,* edited and translated by Thomas Pfau, 62–82. Albany: SUNY Press.

Kant, Immanuel. 1963. "Idea for a Universal History from a Cosmopolitan Point of View." In *On History,* edited by Lewis White Beck. Indianapolis: Bobbs-Merrill.

———. 1991. "What Is Orientation in Thinking?" In *Kant: Political Writings,* edited by Hans Siegbert Reiss, 237–49. New York: Cambridge University Press.

Lacoue-Labarthe, Philippe, and Jean-Luc Nancy. 1988. *The Literary Absolute: The Theory of Literature in German Romanticism.* Translated by Philip Bernard and Cheryl Lester. Albany: State University of New York Press.

Lukács, György. 1971. *The Theory of the Novel: A Historico-Philosophical Essay on the Forms of Great Epic Literature.* Translated by Anna Bostock. London: Merlin Press.

Marcuse, Herbert. 1978. *The Aesthetic Dimension: Toward a Critique of Marxist Aesthetics.* Translated by Herbert Marcuse and Erica Sherover. Boston: Beacon Press.

Scruton, Roger. 2004. "Wittgenstein and the Understanding of Music." *British Journal of Aesthetics* 44 (1): 1–9.

Tormey, Alan. 1987. "Art and Expression: A Critique." In *Philosophy Looks at the Arts: Contemporary Readings in Aesthetics,* 3rd ed., edited by Joseph Margolis, 421–37. Philadelphia: Temple University Press.

Wellbery, David E. 2006. "Verzauberung: Das Simulakrum in der romantischen Lyrik." In *Seiltänzer des Paradoxalen: Aufsätze zur ästhetischen Wissenschaft.* Munich: Hanser.

Witte, Bernd, and Regine Otto, eds. 1996. *Goethe Handbuch.* Vol. 1. Stuttgart: Metzler.

Wittgenstein, Ludwig. 1958. *Preliminary Studies for the "Philosophical Investigations," Generally Known as the Blue and Brown Books.* Oxford: Basil Blackwell.

Wordsworth, William. 1965. *Selected Poems and Prefaces.* Edited by Jack Stillinger. Boston: Houghton Mifflin.

Rubber Ring
Why Do We Listen to Sad Songs?

Aaron Smuts

But don't forget the songs
That made you cry
And the songs that saved your life.
Yes, you're older now
And you're a clever swine
But they were the only ones who ever stood by you.
                    —*The Smiths, "Rubber Ring"*

Introduction

My topic is song, or, more precisely, songs. Although my interests are philosophical, my goal is not to provide a conceptual analysis of song, or to take
a stand on whether songs are a hybrid art form merging poetry and music.[1]
Rather, I want to look at a few ways in which songs are used, ways in
which people engage with and find meaning in songs.[2] In particular, I am
concerned with sad songs—those that are about lost love, separation,
missed opportunity, heartache, hardship, and all manner of sad subject.
Such songs are not merely expressive of sorrow; they are typically about its
varied causes, upon which we are invited to dwell. Many of us are drawn
to such songs in moments of emotional distress caused by situations similar
to those portrayed in the lyrics. This is curious. It is curious because sad
songs do not always make us feel better; no, they often make us feel worse.

So, we must ask, why do we listen to sad songs? This is the question that I will attempt to answer.

The underlying problem that I am concerned with is the *paradox of tragedy,* or better put, the *paradox of painful art* (Smuts 2007b). It boils down to a simple question: why do we seek out artworks that we know will likely arouse painful feelings? Our engagement with sad songs poses, perhaps, the purest example of the problem of painful art. It is undeniable that some songs just hurt.[3] Therefore, it is something of a mystery why we listen to them. In order to see the full force of the puzzle, it is necessary to first say something about the nature of songs and some of the ways in which people customarily listen to this form of music. It will be most instructive to do this by drawing a contrast to pure (or absolute) music—music unaccompanied by words, or what Peter Kivy calls "music alone."[4] This essay is about a small fraction of music accompanied by words. For the most part, I will discuss sad rock songs.[5]

My principal claim is that sad songs not only frequently make audiences feel worse, but that we are perfectly aware of this fact, and, more importantly, we desire them precisely because they heighten our suffering. Normally, by listening to sad songs we do not purge our sorrow; we enhance it. Sad songs are often anticathartic. I argue that sad songs, particularly those with suggestive narrative structures, aid in reflective processes of tremendous import. We seek them out to intensify negative emotions partly as a means of focusing our reflection on situations of great importance. Backed by mood-inducing instrumentation and vocalization, the narrative and imagistic content of sad songs seeds reflection on personal events.

I am not solely concerned with the paradox of painful art in regard to song. I also intend to defend the appropriateness of a mode of musical engagement that is radically at odds with that of music alone. The prescribed mode of listening to sad songs is not one of predominantly formal appreciation of musical structures, but one of personal, imaginative engagement with the narrative content. In this way, we might say that sad songs are not only typically accompanied by instrumental music; sad songs are accompanied by us.

Some Problems with Absolute Music

Philosophical reflection on absolute music has given rise to a few intriguing puzzles. Absolute music, music unaccompanied by texts or other linguistic content, is nearly pure sonic structure. To engage with pure music is to be attentive to the complexities, patterns, and progressions of sounds. We listen for the development of a variation throughout a work, and delight in the brilliance of the composition. Absolute music may be profoundly moving. Indeed, it may afford aesthetic experiences of nearly unmatched intensity, but it cannot be profound. To be profound, a work must be about something of great importance. The work must have some conceptual content. At minimum, it must provide novel insights about the world. Absolute music does not, or at least it is not obvious how it could, provide such insights. How could mere sound—nonlinguistic, nonrepresentational sonic structures—be about anything at all, much less matters of great importance? Works of absolute music may exemplify various states, such as the lumbering state of depression, much as does the visage of a hound dog.[6] But this minimal level of aboutness does not allow absolute music to say much about anything. Hence, it seems that pure music cannot be profound, despite our prereflective intuitions to the contrary. This is known as the problem of musical profundity (see Kivy 1991, chap. 10; Kivy 2003).

Similar considerations give rise to a related problem, a problem concerning the possibility of emotional response to absolute music: can absolute music elicit genuine emotional reactions? According to one theory of the emotions, the *cognitive theory,* emotions have intentionality: they are about things. We do not just feel undifferentiated fear directed at nothing in particular; we fear particular dangerous things, such as a menacing dog's sharp teeth. We do not have objectless hope; we hope that we will win the lottery. This feature of emotions helps differentiate them from other species of affect, such as moods. We can be in a good or bad mood for no particular reason at all. Something good might have happened that led to our good mood, it might have a discernible cause, but the mood is not about anything.

If something along the lines of the cognitive theory of the emotions is correct, and if absolute music lacks content, it is hard to see how audiences could respond with genuine emotions to pure sonic structures.[7] What is there for our emotions to be about? We might be startled by the clash of symbols, or excited by a sudden shift in tempo, but there is nothing to fear, to hope for, or to feel sorrow about, except perhaps the beauty of the music itself (Kivy 2005). The problem with such a conclusion is that people often describe their musical experiences as rich emotional episodes. One might say that they felt a full emotional arc in response to a symphonic work: hope, worry, anger, followed by feelings of elevation. One might even call a work such as Bartok's *String Quartet No. 4* nerve-wracking or disturbing.

Many think that "Taps" is heart-wrenching. This is puzzling. What is there to be sad about in a sonic structure that is not about anything? Prima facie, such a response is nearly as absurd as fearing marshmallows.[8]

One explanation for why audiences readily report experiencing strong emotions in response to music might be that they are responding to something different, something other than the music alone. A musical work might lead us to reflect on some episode of our lives, or to imagine narrative episodes that the sounds might exemplify. That is, we sometimes let our minds wander as our imaginations are sparked by the music. Much like Disney cartoons set to classical masterpieces, our imaginations provide the content for the genuine emotions that we experience during the performance. But, the objection charges, this is not listening *to the music*. One is merely using the music as a proto–mood organ, a spur to daydreaming. While off on our imaginative excursions we are no longer engaged with the music, at least not in the right way. An attentive listener will indulge in no such flights of fancy. Sure, we may be prone to respond in such a manner, but this does not show that our emotions are about the music. No, they are about some music-inspired figments of our imagination. Hence, absolute music may indirectly cause audiences to feel genuine emotions, but it is not the content of the emotions. Further, when we approach the music in the proper manner, when we pay attention to it, no such emotional reactions can occur.

Due to the lack of content, absolute music cannot be about much of anything. Hence it cannot be profound. Nor, it seems, can it elicit genuine emotional reactions in listeners who are engaging with the music in the right way. These claims are controversial, but what is clear is that absolutely none of this is true when it comes to most, or at least much, of the world's music. Much of the music produced in the course of human history contains semantic content. It is no mystery where the content comes from. It is right there in the songs. The content comes from the words.[9]

Philosophers focus on absolute music partly because it gives rise to these kinds of tricky puzzles,[10] but also because of an assumption that absolute music represents one of the highest artistic achievements in human history. It is important to note that I am not here to dispute this claim. Rather, I would like to take a look at one variant of music with words: songs. More specifically, I want to focus on sad songs. The question at issue is not whether we can feel genuine emotions in response to songs, but why we would listen to them if they do indeed make us sad.

Before I develop my answer, it will help to say a bit more about the nature of songs and how we listen to them.

What Is a Song?

When we think of song, we typically think of lyrical music sung with instrumental accompaniment. Levinson describes the paradigm as follows: "It is a melodically and rhythmically distinctive arch of full-fledged tones of definitive pitch, produced in the form of vocables coalescing into words and sentences, and typically with support, primarily harmonic, from some cohort of instruments" (1996b, 44). The most widely discussed species of song discussed in the philosophy of music is that of opera (see, e.g., Kivy 1999). For instance, in his entry on music in *The Oxford Handbook of Aesthetics,* Stephen Davies confines his discussion of music and words to opera (2003). It is fair to say that opera has taken center stage in the literature on song. Although much of what I have to say will likely apply to opera and other forms of song, I want to discuss song*s*, not song.

Here I will adopt a distinction that John Fisher makes between song and songs (n.d.). The label "song" applies to any "music with" sung words, but the notion of *a* song is more specific. We talk about particular songs. We might ask, How many songs were on that CD? Or, Have you heard this song? "Song" functions more like a mass term. It describes a type of music and not a unit of work. In contrast, by *a* song we have in mind a work of music that, in turn, might be part of a larger work, such as an album. Songs typically have names and can usually be clearly differentiated from other songs. I have ten thousand distinct songs on my iPod. Many of us know the words to dozens of songs by heart. Further, there is good reason to think that much of the world's musical tradition has been in the form of songs. Many songs have clear authors; others are simply in the wind. Either way, we recognize them as individual works with many subtle variations.

Although we clearly know many songs, it is difficult to say just what makes a song a song. A bit of reflection reveals that the most plausible candidates for necessary conditions are in fact unnecessary. For instance, songs need not contain any instrumentation. Yes, songs are often accompanied by instrumentation, but many are simply sung. A song can simply be sung words with no instrumentation. This raises a worry that the border between spoken poetry and song is unclear. In an effort to distinguish between spoken poetry and song, Levinson argues that there are two important differences: "in song there is a *sustaining* of tones, with some degree of resonance and vibrato, and a *connecting* of sustained tones into a more or less continuous vocal line."[11] But this will not do the trick. Perhaps these features are necessary, but they are not sufficient for singing. Much spoken poetry contains just these two features. And not just poetry—you can find both features in speeches. For instance, Martin Luther King Jr.'s "I Have a Dream" speech contains several passages of sustained tone with resonance and vibrato. You can hear sustain on nearly every word in his early sentences. The next word starts on the sustain of the previous, creating a sustained tone with resonance and vibrato. He connects phrases and sentences together in continuous vocal lines that are punctuated by well-placed pauses. It is a striking presentation, and it satisfies Levinson's two features, but King does not sing the speech. It is not a song.

Regardless of what precisely distinguishes singing from reading poetry or other forms of speech, it is clear that a mere reading of the lyrics of a song, as one might read a poem, does not constitute a performance. For a performance to be a performance of a song, not only do the vocals need to be sung, they most likely have to be sung the right way. It is a plausible condition that any genuine performance must effectively express the intended emotion though vocalization.[12] This raises a host of further complexities that we must ignore. Regardless of the expressive performance constraints, it certainly seems that the lyrics of a song must be sung. That much seems fairly uncontroversial. But this too is wrong. Some hip-hop songs show that to be a song it is not the case that the lyrics must be sung; they can simply be talked out rhythmically.[13] In hip-hop songs there are often no continuous vocal lines of sustained tone. Here the border between spoken poetry and song is very unclear indeed. A further complication is that if we classify rap songs as songs, then not all songs may be a species of song, that is, if song requires anything even resembling singing. If works of rap music are songs, then not all songs feature singing.

Due to limitations of scope, I will have to forgo any further attempt to develop an analysis of a song. Although we do not have a workable analysis, the paradigm of a song is clear. For present purposes, this will have to suffice.

What's a Sad Song?

I am principally concerned with sad songs, not songs in general. But just what makes a song sad is also unclear. It is more complicated than classifying a work of pure music as sad. There are two competing views of what makes a work of absolute music sad. Both views attempt to answer the somewhat unnatural question What makes a work *expressive* of sadness? To put it in O. K. Bouwsma's language, the framing question is whether we think that works are sad because they are sad like an apple is red, or do we think that works are sad because they arouse sad feelings (we need not say emotions) in listeners, as cider does a burp (Bouwsma 1969, 49). The question is whether we first recognize the sadness in the music and thereby feel sad by contagion, if we feel sad at all, or whether some properties of the song cause us to feel a certain way so quickly that we associate it with the music, and, perhaps, project our feelings onto the music.

The principal problem for the first suggestion—the suggestion that we just somehow hear works as expressive of sadness, or that works resemble sadness—is that it seems any putative means of detection require an affective response.[14] We could not hear a song as sad if we did not feel some sadness. It is not that sadness nearly invariably follows detection, but that it is incoherent to think that we could find a sad song sad if we felt nothing at all, just as we could not think that a joke is funny if we did not feel any amusement. It would not make much sense to call a joke funny if it aroused no amusement. The same goes for sad songs. If it does not make us feel sad, it is not a sad song. Kivy disagrees. He notes that we can call all sorts of works sad that do not move us. If we had to be moved to see that a song is sad, this would be impossible. He argues that "there is lots of music that is somber and stately and melancholy that is not good music. And to move me by its somber, stately melancholy, music must be *beautifully* somber and stately and melancholy" (2005, 9).

The principal problem with this objection is that it employs the notion of "being moved," which is vague and primed for equivocation. The claim is not that one must be moved, if that means to have an intense aesthetic experience. No, the claim is that a song cannot be sad if it does not elicit sad feelings in appropriately receptive listeners.[15] We might note that an unsuccessful work tries to be melancholy, tries to be sad, but fails, just as a comedy might try to be funny. If the gags fail, if no one feels amusement, a comedy is not funny. Similarly, if no one feels melancholy in response to a work of music, it is not melancholy. It tries and fails to be melancholy. It might employ the typical devices of sad songs, but if it does not arouse sadness, it is not a sad song. Of course, we might resist a work that we find unduly morose. But we do this by first recognizing where it is trying to take us, by recognizing the affect it is trying to arouse. We harden our hearts against such music, but only after feeling, not merely hearing, its request.

In reply, one might note that we do indeed call all sorts of things sad without feeling any sadness. For instance, weeping willows and hound dogs look sad. But, as Jenefer Robinson notes, if hound dogs made us sad, no one would get one as a pet (2005, 387–88). I agree. But this does not present an objection to my claim that when we call a work of music sad it is only because it makes us sad. Indeed, we might say that the face of a hound dog is sad because its visage resembles that of a depressed person, but this is not the kind of sadness we attribute to music when we call a work sad. Sad songs are not sad as a hound dog is sad; they do not merely appear sad. Rather, they are sad because they make us sad, just as a movie is suspenseful only if it arouses suspense. At least this seems to be the primary sense in which we use "sad" applied to music.

This highlights a significant cause for worry: we might be using the same term, "sad," in different ways.[16] The framing of the debate in terms of expression makes me particularly nervous. The notion of expression is a technical fabrication of the philosophy of art. If it makes any sense to talk of works as expressive of emotion, it is metaphorical at best and lacks secure footing in everyday linguistic practice. Most people, when they talk of music, do not say that songs are expressive of sadness, but simply that songs are sad. And by this, I contend, they typically mean that the song makes them sad. The problem is that the introduction of the technical concept of expression threatens to wreak havoc on our linguistic intuitions. But it is far out of scope to untangle things here.

I do not intend to resolve the debate over the proper account of musical expressivity here. I raise the issue because it is important to note that nothing along the lines of the resemblance theory or the hearability theory can adequately account for what makes a sad song sad. Sad songs also have sad content. They are sad in the way that a story or poem is sad. This is in addition to the way that a work of absolute music might be said to be sad. And it is not plausible to think that novels appear to be sad, or resemble sadness, or could be heard as the expression of sadness. As with novels, there are roughly two ways in which one might try to identify a sad song: by the content or by the feelings that it arouses.

One might say that sad songs are those that are about sad things. Putting aside the problem that "sad" is somewhat vague, the suggestion that we could classify songs based merely on content is problematic. Death is decidedly a sad subject, but one could compose a celebratory song for a New Orleans funeral that would be anything but gloomy. Indeed, it might not be sad at all. Perhaps such a song might really be about the afterlife, which is not a sad topic unless there is reason to think that eternal hellfire awaits the deceased. Nevertheless, the fact that one could compose a song in celebration of death—as that which frees us from the suffering of life—makes it clear that the bare content of a song is not sufficient for classification. Not unless the content also includes the expressed attitude toward the subject.

The problem with this suggestion is that we can only identify the attitude a work takes toward its subject by figuring out what attitude it asks the audience to take. It is hard to see how a work could take an attitude toward a subject that is different from that which the audience should adopt. A work either adopts an attitude or it does not. Of course, there are complex cases, such as those of audience seduction. We find these in more complicated narrative works. A seductive work tries to get us to respond in an inappropriate way, only to reveal our manipulability. Seductive works ultimately take the position that we should, say, feel disgust and not admiration at a wicked character.[17] In addition to seductive works, there are ambiguous works—those that might ask us to respond in different, somewhat conflicting ways. But, regardless of content, we would not call a song "sad" that did not, at least partly, ask us to respond in a sad way. An uplifting song featuring content typical of sad songs is not itself a sad song; it is an uplifting song.

Hence, content alone is not sufficient, even if we include expressed attitudes as part of the content of the work; classification also requires noting the work's take on the content. We determine this by assessing the intended effects of the work. Doing so amounts to developing a nascent interpretation of the song by answering the question, What is the song trying to make us feel? We typically describe sad songs as "depressing," noting the effect they have on listeners. As a character in the movie *Beeswax* (Andrew Bujalski, 2009) says of a song, "This one makes me cry like a baby." That is what makes it a sad song. Perhaps some aspects of a sad song may wear their sadness as an apple wears its redness. I am suspicious of this claim. Regardless, the sadness of the words in a sad song is more like the burp to the cider than the redness to the apple. It does not make much sense to say that the sad content resembles sadness. No, it seems that sad songs are those that make listeners sad.

My contention is that sad songs are those that give rise to feelings that are sad—gloomy, depressing, sorrowful. A combination of intonation, pitch, vocalization, tempo, and content causes receptive listeners to have affective responses that characterize the emotional tone of the song. Lyrics and intonation work together. The pain in Neko Case's voice in the second stanza of "Running out of Fools" amplifies our reaction to the narrative content. We have an immediate visceral reaction to her wail. The affective reaction partly structures our comprehension of the lyrics. We feel her heartache; it does not resemble sadness. We hear her wail as the expression of sadness, but this is not what makes the song sad. If we merely heard the sadness of the singer or thought that the music looked sad, we would be more prone to feel pity than sadness. But we do not feel pity in response to the song, as we do to a sad person. Yes, there are some cases where we might feel pity toward a character in a song, but more often than not, as I will argue in the next section, we feel something closer to self-pity. This gives us additional reason to think that the sadness of a song is more like a sad sentence than a sad face.

For present purposes, we need not develop a more precise notion of sad songs. They are those that typically are about something depressing, such as lost love, missed opportunity, heartache, and separation. In addition, they are prominently intended to arouse sad feelings in listeners. To put it somewhat crudely, a song might be happy and sad. But no unequivocally uplifting song could be classified as sad. And no unequivocally depressing song could be called a happy song.

Before we continue, it is useful to consider an example. Leonard Cohen's "Famous Blue Raincoat" is a well-known sad song. In sound and content it is a paradigm of the genre, ranking in the same league as Jeff Buckley's recording of "Lilac Wine." The song contains an imagistic narrative of infidelity, love, and compassion. The lyrics take the form of a letter to someone who has been out of touch. It begins, "It's four in the morning, the end of December / I'm writing you now just to see if you're better / New York is cold, but I like where I'm living / There's music on Clinton Street all through the evening." In the background, a soft chorus of female voices sings a simple, lulling phrase, or perhaps a mere syllable. The instrumentation is barely noticeable. The lyrics reveal a few details of a story that we struggle to piece together: "I guess that I miss you, I guess I forgive you / I'm glad you stood in my way." Cohen gives us time to learn the import. The song concludes, "Thanks, for the trouble you took from her eyes / I thought it was there for good so I never tried." He sings the song in a laconic, breathy manner, drawing some words out for several beats. His singing is labored; each word sounds difficult for him to vocalize. We learn why as we gradually come to understand the purport, though we may be puzzled by some phrases; what exactly does it mean to "go clear?"

What is clear is that the song can be emotionally devastating, especially if one has ever cared deeply for someone. There is no puzzle of profundity here: "Famous Blue Raincoat" is a profound reflection on the selfishness of romantic love in its demand for exclusivity. Unlike friendship, love cannot be promiscuous.[18] Cohen asks us to see the tragedy: we cannot always be everything that another person needs at all times; nevertheless we cannot share them. Not romantically. Not if we love them.

How to Listen to Sad Songs

In the brief discussion of absolute music above, I noted that the prescribed mode of engagement is one concerned largely with the detection of patterns and variations. If one uses absolute music to drive reflection on the day's events or other matters of import, one is no longer listening to the music. To pay attention to the music is to adopt a largely formal mode of engagement, as if one were taking in a profoundly mood-altering mathematical formula. Since this model of musical engagement is a parody of an extreme, to give it a name, we might call it the priggish listening mode.[19] It finds its jester in the pretentious fool instructed in how to look like one is listening to serious music: he sits down, takes off his glasses and perhaps twirls them by the arm. He cocks his neck slightly, like a dog trying to understand his master, and directs his gaze somewhere off in the distance.

This is, of course, a parody of one extreme theory of the proper mode of engagement with absolute music, but it sets up a clear contrast. The priggish mode of engagement might have its place inside the conservatory. But this is not how one does or should engage with much of the world's music. From dancing to marching to chanting, most music is not listened to while sitting still or twirling one's glasses in reverential attentiveness. Nor should we take a primarily formal appreciative mode. This is especially true of rock and in particular of the kinds of sad songs in which I am most interested.

Sad songs do not ask for a contemplative mode of formal appreciation; they ask for a personally engaged, imaginative experience prompted by the content of the song, guided by musical features such as the pitch, tone, and tempo of the instrumentation and vocalization. Most importantly, many sad songs tell stories upon which we are asked to reflect. The narratives may be elliptical, but they often provide suggestive details that are causally linked.[20]

Consider an extremely simple, but characteristic example—the brief narrative in Damien Jurado's "Letters and Drawings" (from the album

Rehearsals for Departure).[21] The song begins "Goodbye angel / Hands in your pockets / Maybe tomorrow / Maybe you'll come back sometime." The narrative is brief, with minimal detail. A girl leaves: "She boards a Greyhound / With a ticket to Jersey / A gray colored backpack / Full of all her belongings." She promises to write, but, of course, she does not. The singer suffers thinking about her. Many years later he hears that she's married: "She one day calls me / Tells me that she's married / I took it badly." Near the end of the song we learn that the song is a reflection on his sorrow prompted by passing by the spot where he last saw his lover: "Here's where you left me / Only with memories / When we were just sixteen." The story is extremely simple. In fact, it reads like an abstract of any story of lost love. Extracted, it is nothing to celebrate. The narrative itself offers very little to stir the heart. It fails miserably as flash fiction, and would be a terribly ineffective poem. It even makes use of the clichéd conceit of waiting by the phone. On the page, there appears to be very little of value here, but the song, as song, is effective. It simply would not work without the power of music to stir the heart. But it is not the music alone that makes Jurado's song work, it is also the narrative, or to be more precise, the crude nature of the narrative.

Jurado uses the skeleton of a story as an abstract type—the sketch of a situation that many listeners might have lived through, not putting someone on a bus, but of saying good-bye. The song does not ask us to reflect on the details of its story; like most songs, it is short and does not give many details.[22] Instead, the song asks us to think about a similar moment of separation in our own lives. The choice of content would not make much sense otherwise. Why present a kernel of a story if you do not intend for it to be fleshed out by the audience?

Many sad songs contain similar skeletal narratives that allow listeners to heap on their personal reflections. We might say that we personalize sad songs—we customize them through imaginative supplementation for our specific purposes. Not only do we personalize them, we develop personal relationships with songs. As Mark W. Booth (1981) notes, one often feels as if songs have a personal message, a message just for me. But our relationships with songs are often fragile. Morrissey is correct to note in "Rubber Ring" that "the most impassionate song / To a lonely soul / Is so easily outgrown."[23] As we grow and change, an old song may no longer meet our needs.

Personalization highlights an important feature of one prominent mode of engagement with sad songs: it is best characterized as empathetic. As noted previously, we do not feel profound pity for the singer; we feel sad. Many sad songs are told in the first person, but this does not elicit pity. We do not just sympathize; we empathize. Strangely, we often suffer in a way akin to the narrator. We feel as she purports to feel. This likely marks a profound difference between the ways in which we engage with narrative fiction and song. Although contentious, it is far less clear that we empathetically engage with characters in most narrative fiction, but we clearly do with the singers of sad songs.[24] This is largely due to the way in which we listen to sad songs. We do not merely consider the singer, or the persona, we think of ourselves, our own problems, our own sorrows. In a way, we do not so much as empathize with the singer as feel sorry for ourselves, though we likely do both. To give it a label, we might call the prescribed mode of listening to sad songs the sullen teenager mode.

It is clear that people can form all sorts of associations with songs. Many couples have a song: "They're playing our song." And people often listen to songs that are not sad in a similar way, ruminating on personal associations. During a particularly difficult moment, one might listen to a familiar song repeatedly. Sometimes one might have emotions out of sync with the song one is listening to. An otherwise happy lyric might remind you of a moment of emotional distress in the past. Although this mode of engagement is somewhat similar to what I have described, it is not clear that in such cases this mode is prescribed. But in the case of sad songs, it is clear that they are intended for just such associative-emotive engagement. At least this seems to be how Morrissey thinks his own music will be used. "Rubber Ring" concludes, "I'm here with the cause / I'm holding the torch / In the corner of your room / Can you hear me?"

The Paradox of Painful Art

The preceding discussion raises a significant problem: Why in the world would anyone want to empathetically engage with the sad narrator of a sad song? Why would anyone want to wallow in despair? This is a species of a much larger problem, a problem widely known as the paradox of tragedy. The paradox of tragedy has often been framed as a question about pleasure: how is it that audiences can take pleasure in the portrayal of the suffering of others? I find this question too narrow and think that the paradox should take a more general form. The more important question concerns artworks that are putatively painful. I argue that the paradox of tragedy should be considered a subproblem of the *paradox of painful art*.[25] The fundamental question is this: why do audiences seek out artworks that they know will arouse negative feelings, when people generally avoid situations that elicit such reactions in their normal lives?[26]

The paradox of painful art is essentially a conflict between audience reports and a default assumption of motivational hedonism. If audiences really do find some artworks painful, why do they want to see them? Most theorists propose hedonic compensatory solutions to the problem, suggesting that audiences must find some pleasure to compensate for the pain. The problem with all hedonic solutions is that although there are surely many pleasures to be had from a well-crafted narrative, audiences do not always describe their experiences as on the whole pleasurable. In fact, there are many cases where people describe their experiences as genuinely painful. I take it that our experience with sad songs can be heart-wrenching. Often we find no clear hedonic compensation in our engagement with sad songs. The same goes for many works in other art forms.[27]

Consider Ingmar Bergman's horribly depressing six-hour series *Scenes from a Marriage* (1973). The third episode, "Paula," is one of the most excruciating stories ever told. Marianne (Liv Ullmann) is at the summer house for the week with the children. Her husband, Johan, is not expected home until the weekend. When he makes a surprise midweek visit, Marianne is overjoyed. A giddy child, she runs around the house merrily fixing Johan a snack, saying how happy she is that he came to the cottage earlier than expected. Her happiness makes Johan's news all that more crushing: he tells Marianne that he has fallen in love with another woman (Paula) and will be leaving that night with his mistress on a six-month trip. Their conversation lasts for an excruciating half hour of screen time, during which Johan proceeds to show Marianne, albeit at her request, a wallet picture of his lover! Only a sadist could take joy in this episode.

I would not describe my experience of this episode as in any way pleasurable, but I find it to be one of the most effective affair fictions ever created. Indeed, pardon my gushing, it contains some of the most powerful moments in cinematic history. I would recommend it to others, largely for the experience. But it is not pleasurable. No, it is nothing less than emotionally devastating. And to use terms that we might otherwise think are indicative of pleasure, I am "into it" and give it a big "thumbs up." But I am "into" the work because of the decidedly nonpleasurable experiences it affords. I desire the overall sad experience while it is occurring. I am not merely retrospectively glad to have undergone the emotional turmoil. At several moments along the way, if you stopped the movie and asked me what I thought, I would say, through a mist of tears, that it was terrific and absolutely crushing.

In the sense of "like" that simply means that I think it is excellent and would recommend it to others, I like it. I like the work (in part for the experiences it affords); however, I hesitate to say that I "like" the work, since it carries connotations of pleasure. If "to like" means something closer to being pleased that something is the case, I certainly did not like watching *Scenes from a Marriage*. But everyone should see it if they have not already.

One might reply that although pleasure might not be the source of motivation, audiences must be seeking out some other source of value. The painful experiences are perhaps instrumental to this value, but the pain is not intrinsically valuable. The problem with this suggestion is that it does not accord with the way we talk about painful art. Audiences do not talk about even the most painful experiences had in response to art as having mere instrumental value. Watching *Scenes from a Marriage* is not like going to the dentist. We do not endure the drilling to end a throbbing ache. Certainly we may find value in the insightful portrayal of suffering and marriage, but that does not exhaust our motivation. Although audiences may find various forms of value in experiencing the work, no compensation is necessary for the negative experiences it engenders. The negative experience is not the price we have to pay for some compensatory value; it seems that the negative experience is its own reward.

Although the painful emotions one feels in response to art are not clearly instrumentally valuable, perhaps they are constitutive of other types of value, such as the cognitive value of recognizing humanity's profoundly depressing proclivity to cruelty. Somehow, one might argue, fully understanding such insights necessarily involves painful emotional experiences. Clearly, this style of explanation is highly plausible. Indeed, I think that it is part of the complete motivational story. But what it would have to show, if it were to preclude the suggestion that we intrinsically desire painful affect, is that audiences only desire painful emotional responses as constitutive of other kinds of value, and never for themselves. I find this highly implausible, especially since the kinds of cognitive value one can take from art are typically banal. We know all too well that the universe is indifferent to our desires and that people are capable of beastly acts of violence, cruelty, and gross insensitivity. It is hard to imagine that the desire to be reminded of such depressing trivialities is the primary source of audience motivation, one to which all negative affect must be subsumed. Surely it accounts for some of our motivation, but it seems that audiences do in fact desire the ultimately unpleasant experiences for the sake of having the experiences. At least that is how we often talk about such works: we praise Bergman's powers of emotional devastation in addition to his humanity and depth of insight.

Although it is not the complete story, my claim is that audiences seek out painful artworks at least in part for the painful experiences they afford. Narratives provide long and varied experiences. Most provide at least some pleasures. But overall, some works are best described as painful. Although we seek out painful art for a variety of reasons, one reason is for the experiences themselves. When engaging with painful artworks, one sometimes intrinsically desires the nonpleasant experiences they afford. Perhaps this sounds odd, but there is good evidence for my claim: after the fact, we praise many works for their effectiveness at eliciting just such painful responses. We praise *Scenes from a Marriage* for its power to disturb—to elicit heart-wrenching, painfully felt sorrow. In part, this is what we intrinsically desire from the work. The perplexing question is why in the world would we want this?

I will forgo any further development of a general solution to the paradox of painful art; instead I will attempt to develop a more robust account of our desire for sad songs. Our question is this: Just what is it that motivates people to listen to sad songs, knowing full well that they will likely feel worse? Do they really want to feel worse, and if so, why? As a reply to the more general question of why we listen to sad music, Stephen Davies says that this is just the way we are (1994, 307–20). But we need not bottom out the explanation here; we can be more specific in regard to sad songs. We have good reasons, personal reasons.

Why Do We Listen to Sad Songs?

If we reflect on our experience with sad songs and discuss the phenomenon with others, it quickly becomes clear not only that sad songs frequently make us feel worse, but that we desire them precisely because they heighten our suffering. Sometimes a sad song might help us grieve; it might help purge our sorrow by "having a good cry." But, more often than not, we do not purge our sorrow; we enhance it. We seek not catharsis or purgation, but *anticatharsis*. Although this sounds odd, it has solid phenomenological support. Further, it is to be expected given the prescribed mode of engagement.

There is no doubt that priggish listening is largely the wrong way to listen to sad songs. One may of course listen for formal elements and delight in the arrangement of the piece, but one is typically also presented with poetry, sometimes a narrative that requires a much different kind of listening—what, in self-parody, I dubbed the sullen teenager mode. Skeletal narratives and vivid imagery provoke personal associations, thereby providing the catalyst for imaginative reflection. The musical accompaniment can enhance, refine, and contradict the lyrics, modifying the affect of the song while inviting us to engage in emotional-associative imagining. The end result is intensely felt emotions directed at thoughts of the personalized narrative content.

Sad songs present us with brief, often merely suggestive narratives that we personalize with private thoughts. As noted above, our engagement with the singer-persona of a sad song is often one best characterized as empathetic. We do not feel pity for the singer, so much as we feel the singer's pain. We use the attenuated narratives as the seeds for imagining episodes from our own lives. Of course, this is not the only way to listen to sad songs, but it is far from abnormal. Hence, it is no surprise that engaging with sad songs can elicit viscerally felt sorrow. And given that many people turn to sad songs during moments of emotional distress, we should expect to find that people are made to feel much worse through listening to sad songs. The question is not whether people do this, for they surely do, but why?

My answer is that we listen to sad songs as a way to intensify negative emotions; we do this partly as a means of focusing our reflection on situations of great importance. Emotions have a searchlight ability to enhance focus. The object of focus can be internal or external. Fear rivets our attention to a dangerous object. Strong emotions can also help us achieve profound levels of concentration that can afford rich reflective, imaginative experiences. Sad songs, particularly those with suggestive narrative structures, aid in reflective processes of tremendous import. Backed by mood-inducing instrumentation and vocalization, the narrative content of sad songs seeds our reflection on personal events. This is not always therapeutic. Dwelling on a loss, a misstep, an unfortunate circumstance does not always lead to acceptance or atonement. It can lead to frustration and suffering. But profound loss deserves profound grief.

Sad songs can help us see what we have had as well as what we have lost. It is clear that reflection does not always make us feel better. Indeed, sometimes it makes things worse. We know this. But we also want to understand what we have lost and to feel the significance. The value of such emotionally charged reflection is not merely cognitive, but it does serve to deepen our understanding, in some sense of the term. We listen partly for the experiences themselves, but the experiences are also constitutive of our enhanced understanding. Partly, what it is to appreciate the significance of some event is to feel it—to feel the significance. We assume that those who feel nothing have yet to accept their loss. They certainly do not understand the significance, not yet, at least.

This might sound a bit obscure, but we frequently make use of this notion of understanding. It is not know-that and it is not know-how, it is something different—a matter of understanding the felt significance, a form of nonpropositional awareness of value. Imagine asking someone if they understood the enormity of some genocide, battle, bombing, or other horrific event. In reply they say sure, and spin off a few statistics. We ask: "Isn't it just awful to think about? It's incomprehensible." A reply that "No, it is perfectly comprehensible: x number of people died" misses the point. Similarly, consider someone who is completely unmoved at the death of a friend's child. It is incoherent to say, "I understand how horrible it is to lose a child, but it just doesn't sadden me one bit." Either the person does not care or simply does not understand. This is not merely a matter of knowing how it feels to lose a child. It is a matter of understanding the significance, of being fully aware of the loss of value. Sometimes one may be overwhelmed, moved into a nearly affectless state, but before this extreme, one cannot even approximately understand the loss of a child without feeling pity or grief. The same goes for things that happen to us. Understanding the significance of things that matter to us sometimes requires feeling profound sadness.[28]

I have only offered a vague sketch of the kind of understanding at issue. Ultimately, such a conception might not be entirely defensible. For instance, one might object that I have not offered good reason to think that the role of the emotions is anything but instrumental to our understanding the significance of important events. Rather than appeal to a fuzzy notion of nonpropositional understanding, we would be on more secure ground if we thought of the emotional experiences as conducive to the realization of some insights, not as constitutive of the understanding. If so, then what I offer will turn out to be a nonhedonic compensatory solution to the paradox. The painful experiences will find compensation in the cognitive value to which they are instrumental. This would not jeopardize much of my explanation for why we listen to sad songs. But I suspect that the emotional responses play a more significant role—that they are constitutive of our understanding.[29]

Although I think that the notion of nonpropositional understanding involving an emotional awareness of the loss of value is likely defensible, I cannot develop the idea further here. I will rest my defense on the thought that there is something incoherent in the suggestion that we could care deeply about something and feel no sadness in response to its loss. It is not simply that an affectless state would be atypical, but that the unmoved either do not care or do not understand. To value is not merely to think valuable, or even to desire to promote and preserve, but to feel.[30] One cannot unambiguously be said to value something if one feels nothing when it is threatened or lost.

Either way, if painful emotional responses are constitutive of our understanding the significance of the loss of value or if they are merely instrumental, they are extremely cognitively valuable. Hence, our engagement with sad songs is not irrational, nor is it a case of pathetic wallowing in self-pity. One should not just buck up. Only someone who is incapable of caring about anything could fail to see the importance of reflective turmoil. It is not irrational. It is perfectly human. We need to feel in order to understand what we care about.

Conclusion

Kivy complains that "Narcissus-like, we listen to music and hear only ourselves" (2005, 13). This is close to the truth, but it is not always a bad thing. Many sad songs are designed for just that—to let us hear ourselves. The short, skeletal narratives that we find in a large number of sad songs allow us to personalize the content. The prescribed mode of engagement is radically at odds with that of priggish listening. Yes, to us "clever swine" this mode of listening may strike us as adolescent, but adolescents feel things more intensely. Sad songs can elicit and intensify strong personally directed emotions. In this way, we might say that sad songs are not only typically accompanied by instrumental music, sad songs accompany you. As Morrissey notes, when playing our records, our disks, our rubber rings, we are not alone.

So, why do we listen to sad songs? It is undeniable that listening to sad songs often makes us feel worse. The experience is typically anticathartic.

Many people seek out the intensifying effect, simply because some situations warrant profound emotional distress. It seems that the experience is at least partly intrinsically valuable. But more importantly, the experience has constitutive value. One comes to understand the significance of loss through reflective, emotional episodes. The enhanced understanding is not so much the result of the episode; it is not that the listening experience is merely instrumentally valuable, but that the experience is part of the understanding. Feeling sadness is constitutive of what it is to understand the significance of our lives.

NOTES

I thank Heidi Bollich, John Gibson, and Matthew Gerrig for feedback on previous versions of this essay. I also thank Tony Alterman, my commentator at the American Society for Aesthetics, Eastern Division, meeting (April 2010). I thank the audience at the ASA for their questions and criticisms. Anthony Aumann rightly pressed me to defend my notion of understanding.

1. Some of these issues are taken on by John Fisher in his provocative essay "The Concept of a Song" (n.d.).

2. For an account of a wide variety of the uses of music, see Alperson and Carroll (2008).

3. Whether the painful affect should be classified as an emotion, a mood, or simply a feeling is irrelevant to the paradox of painful art. This is why the paradox should not be called the "paradox of negative emotion." The painful affect encompasses more than emotions proper. You cannot avoid the paradox through mere classification. You still have to account for the phenomenology.

4. Kivy (1991). This label suggests that music is instrumentation and words are something else. It suggests that song is a hybrid artform.

5. See Grackyck (1996) for foundational work on rock. His "Popular Music" entry in the *Internet Encyclopedia of Philosophy* is also very useful: http://www.iep.utm.edu/music-po/.

6. This is the exemplification view of musical expression.

7. For a critical evaluation of the cognitive theory, see Robinson (2005).

8. Most of the literature concerns musical expression. How can absolute music express anything? What does it mean to say that a song is sad or that it expresses sadness? The same underlying considerations give rise to the related problem concerning the content of the putative emotions aroused by absolute music.

9. Kivy notes this in Kivy (2005, 5).

10. Kania defends the focus on music alone for similar reasons (2007).

11. Levinson (1996b, 43). This essay contains several other complicating examples: *Sprechstimme,* recitative, chant, and vocalize.

12. Bicknell (2005, 266). If so, the difference between a failed performance and a radical interpretation will be difficult to specify.

13. Fisher claims that singing is one of the core, or basic, features of song.

14. I'm lumping together appearance and hearability theories. There are important distinctions between the two, but I merely want to contrast arousal and nonarousal theories. For a recent defense of hearability theory, see Levinson (2006).

15. Of course it will be difficult to noncircularly explain what makes a listener appropriately receptive. This theory of sad songs suffers from the same kinds of problems as response-dependent of color.

16. Stephen Davies (2006) argues that we use "sad" in reference to music in a secondary, although nonmetaphorical, sense of the term, in the same way that we talk about hound dogs and willow trees.

17. I argue that this pattern can be found in *In the Company of Men* (Neil LaBute, 1997). See Smuts (2007a). Berys Gaut dubs it the "seduction strategy" (2007). It's hard to imagine a song adopting a similar strategy, but I take it that it could be done.

18. Not everyone agrees that friendship can be promiscuous. Montaigne, for instance, disagrees.

19. Kivy is often saddled with this model, but he claims to be an emoter. However, his model comes dangerously close. He claims that the emotions he feels are directed at the beauty of the work. He does not feel sadness, but some nameless emotion in response to the beautiful sadness of the work. I do not doubt that we can also be moved by the beauty of the work, but to deny that we feel sadness strikes me as an ad hoc move motivated by a rigid adherence to the cognitive theory of the emotions, a theory which has far less support than the common phenomenology of musical experience.

20. Many songs meet the minimal conditions for narratives as defended by Carroll (2001o.

21. A similar but slightly more complicated example in the same genre would be Richard Buckner's "Lil' Wallet Picture."

22. Fisher notes that most songs are "memorable," partly because they are short enough to remember (n.d., sec. 5).

23. Of course, in some sense Morrissey is making fun of the emotional excesses of teenagers, and perhaps the exaggerated significance given to his own work. "Rubber Ring" is not a sad song. It's about sad songs.

24. For an excellent overview of the way in which we engage with narrative fictions, see Carroll (2008, chap. 6).

25. For an overview of the various positions, see Smuts (2009).

26. There are a variety of answers on the table to the paradox of painful art. Control theorists argue that the putative painfulness of some artworks is mitigated by our ability to stop experiencing them at will. Compensation theorists argue that any painful reactions must be compensated for by other pleasures, either in the craft of the narrative (Hume) or in the awareness that we are sympathetic creatures responsive to the suffering of others (Feagin 1983). Conversion theorists argue that the overall experience of painful artworks is not one of pain but of pleasure, as the pain is converted into a larger, more pleasurable experience (Hume). Power theorists argue that we enjoy the feeling of power that arises from either the realization of the endurance of humanity (Price 1998), or through the overcoming of our fear (Shaw 2001). Rich experience theorists argue that there are many reasons why people do things other than to feel pleasure. The overall experience of painful art may be one of pain, but the experience can still be seen as valuable, and, as such, motivating (Smuts 2007b).

27. Jerrold Levinson also defends a similar criticism of the hedonic solutions (1996a, 18–19).

28. My suggestion has precedence in the work of Martha Nussbaum. But I add that in addition to expanding our experiential range, narrative fiction can also help us focus on our own lives, on our own experiences. Here I am not endorsing Nussbaum's Aristotelian account of practical reason. I am merely gesturing towards a notion of nonpropositional understanding.

29. An alternative, but related, suggestion might be that the painful emotional experiences let us "work through" traumatic events. As Freud thought, the truth must be accepted emotionally before we can fully recover. In some sense, this seems right. But I am not so sure that we are typically trying to recover when we listen to sad songs. We are trying to understand what we lost, and what it means to us. This might eventually lead to recovery, but that is secondary and not required.

30. I do not have a fully worked out theory of what it is "to value," but I am not satisfied with either belief or desire accounts. Although a depressive may believe her child's education is valuable, she may lack any desire to drive her child to school. Yes, but I am uncomfortable saying that she values her child's education, at least not fully. If she feels nothing when it is threatened, she does not value it, not completely. This sounds right: from the perspective of the depressive, the world seems to lack value. For a critical account of desire theories of valuing, see Smith (1995, chap. 5).

REFERENCES

Alperson, Philip, and Noël Carroll. 2008. "Music, Mind, and Morality: Arousing the Body Politic." *Journal of Aesthetic Education* 42 (1): 1–15.

Bicknell, Jeanette. 2005. "Just a Song? Exploring the Aesthetics of Popular Song Performance." *Journal of Aesthetics and Art Criticism* 63 (3): 261–70.

Booth, Mark W. 1981. *The Experience of Songs*. New Haven: Yale University Press.

Bouwsma, O. K. 1969. "The Expression Theory of Art." In *Philosophical Essays,* 21–50. Lincoln: University of Nebraska Press.

Carroll, Noël. 2001. "On the Narrative Connection." In *New Perspectives on Narrative Perspective,* edited by Willie van Peer and Seymour Chatman, 21–42. Albany: SUNY Press.

———. 2008. *The Philosophy of Motion Pictures*. Oxford: Basil Blackwell.

Davies, Stephen. 1994. *Musical Meaning and Expression*. Ithaca: Cornell University Press.

———. 2003. "Music." In *The Oxford Handbook of Aesthetics,* edited by Jerrold Levinson. Oxford: Oxford University Press.

———. 2006. "Artistic Expression and the Hard Case of Pure Music." In *Contemporary Debates in Aesthetics and the Philosophy of Art,* edited by Matthew Kieran, 179–91. Oxford: Basil Blackwell.

Feagin, Susan. 1983. "The Pleasures of Tragedy." *American Philosophical Quarterly* 20 (1): 95–104.

Fisher, John. n.d. "The Concept of a Song."

Gaut, Berys. 2007. *Art, Emotion, and Ethics*. Oxford University Press.

Grackyck, Theodore. 1996. *Rhythm and Noise: An Aesthetics of Rock*. Durham: Duke University Press, 1996.

Hume, David. 1985. *Essays Moral, Political, and Literary*. Indianapolis: Liberty Fund.

Kania, Andrew. 2007. "Philosophy of Music." In *Stanford Encyclopedia of Philosophy,* edited by Edward N. Zalta, http://plato.stanford.edu/entries/music/.

Kivy, Peter. 1991. *Music Alone: Philosophical Reflections on the Purely Musical Experience*. Ithaca: Cornell University Press.

———. 1999. *Osmin's Rage: Philosophical Reflections on Opera, Dance, and Text*. Ithaca: Cornell University Press.

———. 2003. "Another Go at Musical Profundity." *British Journal of Aesthetics* 43 (4): 401–11.

———. 2005. "Feeling the Music." *British Journal of Aesthetics* 39 (1): 1–13.

Levinson, Jerrold. 1996a. "Pleasure and the Value of Works of Art." In *The Pleasures of Aesthetics*, 11–26. Ithaca: Cornell University Press.

———. 1996b. "Song and Music Drama." In *The Pleasures of Aesthetics*, 42–59. Ithaca: Cornell University Press.

———. 2006. "Musical Expressiveness as Hearability-as-Expression." In *Contemporary Debates in Aesthetics and the Philosophy of Art*, edited by Matthew Kieran, 192–204. Oxford: Basil Blackwell.

Neil, Alex. 1992. "On a Paradox of the Heart." *Philosophical Studies* 65:53–65.

Nussbaum, Martha C. 1990. "The Discernment of Perception: An Aristotelian Conception of Private and Public Rationality." In *Love's Knowledge: Essays on Philosophy and Literature*, 54–105. Oxford: Oxford University Press.

Price, Amy. 1998. "Nietzsche and the Paradox of Tragedy." *British Journal of Aesthetics* 4:384–93.

Robinson, Jenefer. 2005. *Deeper than Reason: Emotion and Its Role in Literature, Music, and Art*. Oxford: Oxford University Press.

Shaw, Daniel. 2001. "Power, Horror, and Ambivalence." In "Horror," special issue of *Film and Philosophy*, 1–12.

Smith, Michael. 1995. *The Moral Problem*. Oxford: Basil Blackwell.

Smuts, Aaron. 2007a. "The Joke Is the Thing: 'In the Company of Men' and the Ethics of Humor." *Film and Philosophy* 11:49–66.

———. 2007b. "The Paradox of Painful Art." *Journal of Aesthetic Education* 41 (3): 59–77.

———. 2009. "Art and Negative Affect." *Philosophy Compass* 4 (1): 39–55.

Discovery Plots in Tragedy

Susan L. Feagin

Arthur Miller wrote that the difference between tragedy and pathos is that in tragedy there is enlightenment but in pathos there is not (1996, 9). It is ironic, then, that debates over the possibility of tragedy in the twentieth century tended to focus on his play *Death of a Salesman,* in which the protagonist, Willy Loman, remains clueless to the end, never figuring out that what he steadfastly believes is the key to financial success will never get him there, and never realizing that financial success does not guarantee a happy life. Taking a cue from Miller's comment on the centrality of enlightenment to tragedy, I argue here that what I call "discovery" is central to tragedy in the sense that it is the fulcrum of *one* important type of tragic plot, which I call the "discovery plot."[1] I begin with an explanation of the notion of discovery and make some rough comparisons with Aristotle's notion of *anagnorisis*. In section II, I highlight two salient features of tragedies with discovery plots: first, that unusual sets of circumstances are crucial for the plot and hence for generating the tragedy; and second, that the protagonist is key to the discovery plot, which is nevertheless, as Aristotle claimed, the most important element of tragedy.

One reason tragedies are of special interest is that they deal with some of the most fundamental questions about how to live in an uncertain world, and it bears asking why tragedy as a genre seems less important during some particular periods of time than it does in others. During the twentieth century in the West, for example, it was widely debated whether tragedy as a living genre was possible, given the social and political realities of the era, and whether related ideas could surface instead only as a "tragic view of life" (see, e.g., Krutch 1929, chap. 5; Unamuno 1972). While I am not interested in the empirical particulars of such debates here, I do propose that particular sorts of beliefs may undermine the possibilities for the two salient features of discovery plots described above, and could help to explain the limited viability of tragedy as a genre in a culture at a given time. Regardless of one's views about tragedy in the twentieth century, there does appear to be a resurgence of the genre in the twenty-first. In section III, I examine one such tragedy, Wajdi Mouawad's *Scorched* (*Incendies*, 2003), as an exemplar of how a discovery plot may draw on elements of contemporary life that manifest not only its relevance as a genre for its time, but also its adaptability to many times. It is an especially compelling example, overtly a modern version of Greek tragedy, but resonant with Hegelian ideas as well.

In what follows, I am concerned with tragedy as a genre of drama, presented in the manner of dramatic action, which Aristotle distinguishes from narrative. Aristotle identifies tragedy as a genre of drama in which the characters carry out or present the action themselves, and he contrasts it with narrative, where one "remains oneself" (1448a3, chap. 3).[2] This distinction can also be described in terms of different ways of presenting a story, that is, on the one hand, through acting the story out, or, on the other hand, through telling it. As Aristotle writes, it is because the characters in drama carry out the action themselves that the Dorians lay claim to originating tragic drama to an extent on linguistic grounds, given that *drân* is their word for action, and the drama is an imitation of action (1448b1, chap. 3).

The distinction between dramatic action and narration is important to Aristotle in part because he is concerned with the differences in effects on those watching a play as opposed to those listening to someone tell a story. Today, however, due to advanced technologies and differences in social context, other distinctions have assumed greater importance. With respect to dramatic action, we now *watch* dramatic action in both live theater and films. But we can also *read* plays and film scripts, options that Aristotle, for obvious reasons, never considered. With respect to narratives, we can *listen* to storytellers in person and to recorded narratives, and we can also *read* a narrative. In ancient Greek tragedy, the chorus would often provide the background narrative for the action of the play, but rarely as characters in the play. It is more common now to have plays or films with narrator-characters, that is, narrators who are also characters in the action. In film, the practice of voice-over narration by characters is widespread; an iconic example is Joe Gillis (William Holden) in *Sunset Boulevard* (Billy Wilder, 1950). A film may also contain written narration on the screen, the norm in silent films, though rarely that of a narrator-character and decidedly less common today than it used to be. In films where there is narration on the screen or delivered by a narrator who is not a narrator-character, the story is presented in the manner of both narration and dramatic action, as Aristotle says occurs in epics.

Films share other crucial features with live performance: they are presented in (generally) a relatively short period of time (roughly, one to three hours) and at a fixed rate of speed that is not under the control of the viewer.[3] Viewing films in theaters differs from reading scores or scripts in the latter respect, yet not from listening to narratives that are delivered orally.[4] In what follows, then, I group films with stage plays as presenting a story in the manner of dramatic action because the action is presented or "carried out" by the characters, while recognizing that both can also contain some narrative. In addition to Sophocles' Oedipus trilogy and *Scorched,* I discuss *The Manchurian Candidate* (John Frankenheimer, 1962), and, controversially, I propose that *Hamlet* can be considered to be an example of a tragedy with a discovery plot.

I. The Concept of Discovery

The notion of discovery I propose as central to discovery plots involves a cognitive achievement on the part of the tragedy's protagonist at a particular point in the action of the play. At such a point, the protagonist discovers some fact about him or herself, or about something he or she has done, is doing, or is about to do. Other characters may make similar discoveries about the protagonists or their actions, as may the audience. But it is the protagonists' discoveries about themselves that are the fulcrum of the plot, the central event around which the plot revolves, and not just another element in the unfolding of the action. For example, in Sophocles' *Oedipus Tyrannus,* Oedipus discovers that the person he has been searching for, the person who has brought pollution and catastrophe on the city of Thebes, is himself. The "core" discovery can be seen equally as about his own actions or as about himself—about the person for whom he has been searching— though what he discovers has implications involving facts about other people, most notably his mother and his children, and possibly about their actions. Upon making the discovery, Oedipus quickly realizes several of its implications: that when he married the queen of Thebes he married his own mother; that when he slept with the queen he slept with his own mother; that the mother of his children is his own mother; and that the children to whom Jocasta gave birth are both his children and his brothers and sisters.

A discovery about one's actions (rather than about oneself) is a discovery that one's actions have or had a certain inherent quality (which may include some relational qualities), rather than that they had or will have certain consequences or effects. For example, Creon issues the edict that anyone who buries the body of the traitor Polyneices be put to death, and, by an unanticipated chain of events, his edict results in the death of his wife and son. If the fact that one's actions can have horrible, unanticipated *consequences* were the central idea of tragedy, tragedy would be a much more mundane genre than it is, even if it is surprising or even shocking that one's own actions led to or caused a given sequence of calamities. It is always incumbent upon us, given adequate time, to consider not only the likely but also the somewhat improbable but possible consequences of our actions. But a discovery is of something more insidious: it is a revelation that some significant aspect or feature of the action itself (or of oneself) was different from what one thought, even though one was apparently in control of one's behavior at the time. Most of the time, we quite reasonably believe that we know, in relevant respects, what we are doing, even if the *rest* of the world is not under our control. Discoveries in discovery plots occur when it *seems* that protagonists know what they are doing, that is, when they have no (special) reason to think they do not know what they are doing. Indeed, that one's actions are *normally* taken to be perspicuous in this way, even under unusual circumstances, is crucial for discovery plots.

In addition, discovery plots do not trade on discovering mere logical implications of what one is doing. Creon could have figured out that, *if* his son's fiancée were to bury the traitor, in condemning to death whoever buries the traitor, he would be condemning his son's fiancée to death. Further, discovering or perceiving the relevant inherent quality of one's actions or of oneself must involve an evaluative shift in the concept of who one is or of what one is doing (has done, or is about to do), what is sometimes called its "normative valence." Even after Creon realizes that Antigone, his son's fiancée, buried the traitor, he does not come to doubt the wisdom of his edict, a sure sign that he has not made the appropriate discovery. Only after the deaths of his wife and son does he make the discovery, for only then does his concept of the edict as just and necessary shift to the concept of it as unjust and inappropriately harsh. That is, even though the consequences of his actions lead to his discovery, the content of his discovery concerns the edict itself, not its consequences.

It is often difficult to figure out how one should treat other people in the wake of discovering something profound about them—for example, that they have deceived you about something important or simply not revealed something important about themselves—something that, as Aristotle puts it, reveals them to be both enemies and friends. But discoveries about oneself and about one's own actions have a special significance with respect to how one is to behave in the future. "Avoidance behavior" may be possible, even if ultimately unsatisfactory, with respect to somebody else, but it is clearly not an option when the discovery is about oneself. There is no way to distance oneself from oneself, at least not without separating parts of one's own mind.[5] But to dismember one's mind is to go mad, and in Greek tragedy those who don't go mad end up committing suicide because they cannot live with themselves, knowing who they are and what they have done. Being both a friend and an enemy to some *other* person creates problems, for sure, but hardly the internal disruption to one's own identity that is created within one's own mind when one discovers that one is both a friend and an enemy to oneself.

Plato uses *anagnorisis* or recognition to describe the application of a concept one already possesses to something newly encountered in the world. Aristotle explicitly recognizes multiple uses of the term, though he specifies a technical sense for its use in chapter 11 of the *Poetics* as a particular type of change from ignorance to knowledge. Unfortunately, his explanation of *anagnorisis* in chapters 11 and 16 contains troubling inconsistencies. Most of what he says, especially the multiple examples of the phenomenon he provides in chapter 16, takes recognition to be an event where there is a change from ignorance to knowledge about *another person*. That is, the protagonist comes to realize that someone *else* is someone he had no idea she was, or is not the person he thought she was.

According to Aristotle, what makes recognition important is that it leads "either to friendship or to hostility on the part of those persons who are marked for good fortune or bad" (1982, 56 [*Poetics* 1452a]). Scholars have debated how to interpret the tricky phrase that is here rendered as "on the part of those persons who are marked for good fortune or bad." James Hutton, for example, takes the change to friendship or hostility to be felt by the person making the recognition, with the change in his or her attitude as due to the recognition (in Aristotle 1982, 94). But if this is the case, Aristotle's example from *Oedipus* is problematic, since it is not clear how

Oedipus's recognition that Jocasta is his mother changes his attitude towards *her* into the reverse of what it was, that is, from friendship to hostility. One thing it does do is change his attitude towards *himself*: he becomes both a friend and an enemy to *himself*.

The dramatic shift in attitude at the moment of tragic discovery, though of the utmost importance, can be triggered by something as apparently trivial as someone's name. Aristotle's disquisition on the importance of calling things by their right names has special import for tragedy, since names can reveal and name changes obscure facts about a person's identity. In tragedy, even proper names are anything but arbitrary and meaningless—one of its features that make it ripe for parody. For example, Oscar Wilde exploits the triviality of a proper name to great comic irony in *The Importance of Being Earnest*—where a character discovers that he actually is the person he has been pretending to be—as does Woody Allen in his near-tragic comedy *Mighty Aphrodite* (1995).

Because it is "natural" in the normative sense, as Aristotle says, to live in society with others, Aristotelian recognitions about other people will virtually inevitably issue from discoveries of protagonists about themselves. As in *Oedipus,* a barrage of emotionally and ontologically freighted recognitions is often precipitated by a core discovery. Both consequences and implications of who a protagonist is and of what he or she has done will extend to the protagonist's family, the community, and, if the protagonist is a powerful person, to the governance of the state as well. The *tragedy* associated with protagonists' discoveries about themselves, about who they are or what they have done, is necessarily connected with its noncausal implications (and possibly with its causal consequences), which deepen its significance. In *The Manchurian Candidate,* for example, Raymond Shaw's realization of the implications of what he has done is revealed in his brief but powerful expression of utter abjection just before he kills himself at the end of the movie.

For at least these reasons, discoveries as they occur in discovery plots have special dramatic potential, a potential that carries over to plots that might be seen as not paradigmatically discovery plots but whose analysis as such brings out something important about them. I describe here three types of cases. First, the *absence* of a discovery at a particular moment could be a crucial component of a discovery plot, just as much as a discovery would be. The moment where a discovery is appropriate but still not achieved might be revelatory and constitute the fulcrum of the plot, accounting for why the action of the plot takes the form it does, in virtue of its absence. At a minimum, it reveals to the audience something about the nature of the protagonist's character. Where a protagonist does not make an evaluative gestalt shift, there is no dialectic between character and events. Since what happens in the world makes no (relevant) difference to the protagonist, it feeds into an explanation for why each generation may be condemned to fight the same battles that have been fought before. When Creon is told of the series of self-inflicted deaths of his son's fiancé, his son, and his wife, if he *still* didn't think his edict was too harsh he would be more of a monster than a man, more sociopathic than (merely) stubborn, and the play would be invested with a very different worldview. *Medea* and *Death of a Salesman* both have plots that highlight the interpretive task of explaining why the protagonists do *not* see the light, and they exemplify the pathos, as Miller might say, of such benightedness. In *The Manchurian Candidate,* Mrs. Iselin (Angela Lansbury) has the potential to be the protagonist, but she knows that it was her own son who would be sacrificed in the plan to overthrow the American government. Instead of taking this as an indication that something is wrong with the plan, she allows her son to be sacrificed in the pursuit of power, vowing revenge on those who were responsible.

The second type of case is discussed by Aristotle. According to Aristotle, a recognition *prior to* carrying out an action may enable one to avoid the irreparable harm that would be produced by that action. So also, a discovery prior to performing an action one contemplates or intends to perform might enable one to avoid a particular type of irreparable harm, though it does not follow that tragedy will not eventually ensue in spite of it. It only follows that a particular tragic event or situation is avoided. Consider *Hamlet,* albeit controversially, as an illustration of the point. In what is widely recognized to be *a,* and perhaps *the,* pivotal scene of the play, Hamlet has what seems to be the perfect opportunity to kill Claudius while he is praying in the chapel. Hamlet checks himself, however, since it would hardly be a fitting revenge if Claudius were in the process of repenting his sins, for if he were, Hamlet's killing him would ensure that Claudius would go to heaven. Hamlet, being of a self-reflective nature, recognizes the possibility that he is deceiving himself as to his motive: Is he merely being cowardly, or does he not have the courage to carry out the act? Will he ever have another chance? Yet he knows that he is exceedingly ambitious and is acutely aware that he was next in line for the throne before his mother's marriage to Claudius, which took the throne away from him. His desire to kill Claudius might be motivated more by ambition than by revenge for his father's murder, in addition to worries that he will never have as good a chance to kill Claudius, whatever his motives, as he does in the chapel. Thus, he cannot convince himself that (what he sees as) a justified desire for revenge would be his motive.[6] In Aristotelian terms, Hamlet fears that the act would turn him into a friend of Claudius, rather than an enemy. The scene acquires additional poignancy when we learn from Claudius that he was trying to repent but was unable to do so.

Hamlet's *discovery* about the action he comes so close to performing leaves him deeply frustrated, and it can be seen as a turning point in the play. The adrenaline rush, its original object denied, "searches" for another target. Having been summoned to his mother's chamber, he vents his frustration on her, lecturing her on how she ought to behave—perhaps, after the failure of his own efforts—attempting indirectly to get Claudius out of the picture. Already in a kind of frenzy, when Hamlet sees movement in the curtain, and likely instinctively fearing for his life, he *impulsively* stabs and kills whoever is there. It turns out to be poor old Polonius, who is doing a little sleuthing to determine whether Hamlet's "madness" is real or feigned. When Hamlet sees that he has killed Polonius, he devotes only one line to the pity of it and expresses no remorse. He must see his mission as extremely important for it to justify such a heinous act; he is becoming ruthless and starts grasping at straws to resolve the cognitive dissonance between his behavior and what he would like to see as his motivation. The "unfortunate" incident with Polonius does not lead Hamlet to doubt or even rethink the wisdom of his desire to do away with Claudius, but steadies his resolve to pursue it with greater single-mindedness. There is potential for deep irony in this moment, in that his madness, which has been feigned until this point, may begin to be more real.

The third type of case includes some tragedies that fit a Hegelian rather than an Aristotelian paradigm. On Hegel's view, tragedy is essentially a struggle or conflict between two competing goods, such that acting in accord with one requires destroying the other. There may *be* discoveries in Hegelian tragedy; for example, the moment one realizes one is faced with such a dilemma might be part of the action of the plot, but on Hegel's view the essence of tragedy lies in the struggle. Protagonists might also discover that they should have given more credence to the importance of a value that conflicts with what they chose to pursue, but again such a recognition will not have a salient role in the action of the play *as tragedy*. For this, one needs the struggle, as in *Antigone,* which Hegel describes as the most perfect tragedy. It is essentially a dramatization of a struggle between two defenders of something good—Antigone of filial piety and Creon of loyalty to the state—where each one claims greater dominion than is justified and refuses to recognize the merits of the other. Creon eventually has his moment of enlightenment, when he discovers that his edict that whoever buries the traitor Polyneices be put to death is too harsh, but it would be a tragedy on the Hegelian account even if he never achieved this realization. Antigone, it should be noted, never comes to believe that she has overreached. Because Antigone and Creon individually advocate competing goods, the question arises whether the one or the other is *the* protagonist or "tragic hero" of the play. If the play is seen as a tragedy of the discovery plot type, the weight shifts to Creon, since he eventually realizes the error of his edict. *Antigone* then possesses a richer resonance with *Oedipus Tyrannus,* in that Oedipus and Creon manifest the same type of intransigence and resistance to taking advice, exemplifying the continuing cycle of revenge that can engulf a community, since they see the light only after it is too late.

II. Implications

In discovery plots, protagonists acquire a level of importance in the story in part because they make discoveries about themselves and their own actions and in part because this discovery involves an evaluative or normative shift in how they think about themselves. Nevertheless, discoveries also highlight the importance of plot and plot construction. The plot needs to be constructed so that a discovery of such significance was plausible at a particular point in the action and that it plausibly remained hidden for so long. I explore some aspects of both these implications in this section, beginning with the dependence of discoveries on unusual sets of circumstances and then progressing to the importance of the protagonist in the plot.

I. TRAGEDIES ARISE IN UNUSUAL CIRCUMSTANCES

Ruby Meager argues that tragedies do not present us with a "tragic view of life," or instructions on "how to live," but rather with "climactic moments of unfortunate conjunctions of circumstances" that have the power to throw the ordinary circumstances of life into relief precisely because they are unusual (Meager 1960, 185). Building on this idea, we can observe that the unfortunate conjunctions of circumstances in "climactic moments" may be of at least two varieties.

First, there may be a peculiar combination of events that is instrumental in generating the tragic plot. These events may or may not be dramatized on stage in the actions of the characters. For example, what happens as backstory for the action of the play is generally narrated or alluded to rather than dramatized by the characters. Oedipus happens upon his father at a crossroads, but this coincidence occurred prior to the time when the action begins and is only related or narrated in the play. In *The Manchurian Candidate,* it is a coincidence that the Communists have the opportunity to use the son of their "mole" as the agent to carry out the planned assassination. That Hamlet's best opportunity to kill Claudius occurs while Claudius is praying is coincidental, and on the interpretation of the play proffered above, it is a climactic moment in the play since it precipitates the cataclysmic set of actions that make the plot tragic.

It is possible for there to be widespread beliefs in a society or culture that could undermine the status of the alleged coincidences as *unusual* conjunctions of circumstances and hence subvert the tragic implications of a discovery. Such beliefs may well have been a barrier to taking tragedy as a genre relevant to the twentieth century. For example, there are theories of history that take historical change not to be under the control of any single individual. If this were the case, no single individual (an Oedipus, or a Hamlet) would be powerful enough to bring about or prevent the relevant calamity. Under such a view, the protagonist lacks the relevant type of agency to be the protagonist of a tragedy. If such a belief is widespread—that we are all victims of historical forces beyond our control; that institutional racism, sexism, and hierarchies of class will persist despite the efforts of individuals to change them; that deeply rooted conspiracies prevent any single person from "changing the world" for good *or* ill—it may well stifle the development of genres that depend on believing that individuals can be the relevant force for social and political continuity or change.

A second variety of coincidence is the particular combination of circumstances that prevents someone from *knowing* the relevant and important aspects of what one is doing. For example, one would ordinarily know whether it is one's father one is killing or one's mother one is marrying (Oedipus), whether one is attempting to and whether one succeeded in killing someone (Raymond Shaw), or whether one is motivated by revenge or ambition (Hamlet). Special circumstances are needed to explain how and why one would *not* know such things about oneself or one's actions.

The possibility for peculiar coincidences of circumstances that prevent one from having crucial information about oneself and one's actions might also be undermined, in this case by beliefs that take such ignorance to be the norm rather than in need of some special explanation. As I indicated in section I, it is a requirement for discovery that it does not merely *seem* as though we know what we are doing, but that for the most part we *do* know what we are doing. Suppose, for example, that one subscribes to the quasi-Freudian view that the reasons we give to ourselves for why we do what we do are always rationalizations or confabulations, always a cover for the socially unacceptable desires of the Id, whose actual role eludes our attempts at self-knowledge. On this view, despite the fact that it normally *seems* as though we know what we are doing, we would always be the victims of our own repression and denial. Protagonists would then be unable to achieve the discovery required by discovery plots, and protagonists would be depicted as, to use Arthur Miller's term, pathetic, rather than tragic.

There is another significant connection between discovery and the unusual or coincidental status of the sets of circumstances that make it possible. Discovery facilitates irony, which is historically an important component of tragedy. Doing precisely what one was trying to avoid, or undoing precisely what one was trying to achieve, has ironic impact only if knowledge is the norm and ignorance not a pathetic continuant in the life of humanity. Its unusualness helps to make it remarkable, which contributes to its effectiveness as a component of the dramatic moment of discovery.[7]

II. THE CENTRALITY OF THE PROTAGONIST TO THE PLOT

Discovery, arising out of unfortunate conjunctions of circumstances, is the plot's fulcrum, a balancing point between the protagonist's ignorance and subsequent knowledge that represents the tragic calamity of the plot. Hence, the presentation and development of the protagonist's character will be intertwined with the plot in important ways, raising questions about which is the more important. As Ruby Meager writes, "Aristotle himself is at great pains to insist that the principle or 'soul' of a tragedy, that which the poet-maker is the maker of, is not the character of the hero but the plot."[8] One factor that increases the centrality of plot, not merely in spite of but because of the focus on a protagonist, is if the action of a tragedy is driven not solely by a protagonist's *fixed* character traits, but by the ways the character responds to and is shaped by objects and events that take place in the world of the work. Protagonists may think and act in light of their own plans and purposes, in relation to their own character traits and settled dispositions, but they may also act in light of and in response to events that occur in the world of the work.[9] If the protagonist never changes, no matter what happens, the relationship between plot and character becomes correspondingly less important, for it will focus on who the character *is* rather than on what he or she is to become. Events may change a person, and when they do, the "action" itself, the character of the sequence of events, assumes a greater significance. One way to take Aristotle's point would be to say that plots that depend solely on the particular, unchanging character traits of the protagonist, rather than an evolving pattern of actions and events, are less successful as tragedies than those that do not.

If the protagonists change in response to events that occur in the work, their actions will not be understandable atomistically, that is, independently of other things the character has experienced, thought, or done. The embeddedness of actions in past experience as well as a network of plans and purposes is characteristic of human agency in general, and also part of what keeps a character in a play from being a mere cipher. As Meager puts the point, an individual action, within itself, comprises a "pattern of aim, action and achievement" whose components are conceptually closely related but also "factually independent of each other" (1960, 176). A plot, then, "is not merely a sequence of events but a series of responsible actions and counteractions" (176). Plots involve a combination of events that occur in relation to the explicit and implied agency of the protagonist and of other characters in the play. Part of the skill of tragic plot construction is to make it plausible for protagonists to act as they do, with the normal degree of reflection and forethought, but without knowing the horrific descriptions that apply to them. In addition, the protagonists' discoveries must be believable and plausible at that particular moment in the story.

Though I have described discovery as the fulcrum of the plot, it does not follow that it occurs somewhere around the middle of the play. Indeed, it typically occurs near the end of ancient Greek plays, since, not to put too fine a point on it, once the discovery is made, there is rarely much left for protagonists to do except kill themselves. The discovery thus needs to be sufficiently important that the impasse that confronts the protagonist balances the weight of the rest of the play. That balance, of course, is established by the way the action or plot of the play is constructed. Sophocles' version of the Oedipus myth is exceptional in finding a plausible action for Oedipus other than suicide. Oedipus's discovery occurs near the end of *Oedipus Tyrannus,* at which point he blinds and ostracizes himself, and returns in the subsequent play of the trilogy to learn what transpired in the city after he left. For a writer, having the protagonist commit suicide may be the easy option. In terms of plot and genre, it can be more difficult to motivate how protagonists might *live* in light of their discoveries, taking responsibility for their actions, while avoiding cliché. An actual person, after drunkenly causing a lethal car accident, may resolve to campaign on behalf of Mothers Against Drunk Driving, and whether one is able to live up to such resolutions is a significant test of a person's character. For a character in a play, simply making a commitment is too easy and too obvious; yet incorporating the difficulties of living up to it as a significant part of the plot risks making the play the story of *those* trials and tribulations rather than a tragedy.

III. Contemporary Tragedy

Classically, tragic plots have been grounded in political and, more recently, social conflict, and they reveal ways that such conflicts can tear individuals and families apart. But wars and the ways that wars impact the family also give rise to tragic situations. They are filled with "unfortunate conjunctions of circumstances," flukes that lead to survival or, equally absurdly, death. In the twentieth century, the coincidences of wartime were appropriated by existentialists and absurdists who stressed the irrational, meaningless contingencies of life and death, and their literature typically casts a rather jaundiced eye on human agency and its possibilities. Jean-Paul Sartre's notion of "absurd freedom," for example, is not associated with heroic action. But war's contingencies, as much as political intrigue and social repression, can create a fertile ground for discoveries of the sort that I have proposed lie at the center of a certain type of tragic plot, and hence for the relevance of the genre in eras when war is a salient feature of life. I illustrate the point with Wajdi Mouawad's *Scorched*, the second play of a tetralogy, the components of which explore various questions about personal identity and origins.

Nawal, the protagonist, was born in a country plagued by persistent civil war, where neighboring communities and even members of the same family are hostile toward each other. She bears a son, the product of a forbidden romance with a young man who is from a family that is an enemy to her own. But her family is no friend to her. Her own mother offers her a bitter choice: either give up the baby or, if she chooses to keep it, suffer public humiliation and ostracism from the community. Nawal chooses reluctantly to give up the baby, and as he is taken away, she promises that she will always love him. As one might expect, she lives to regret the choice. Her grandmother has more sympathy for her situation and more respect for her than her mother does, and makes her promise to "learn to read, to speak, to write, to count, learn to think" (*Scorched,* 64). Nawal does learn, and she returns to perform what in her community is the exceptional task of carving her grandmother's name on her tombstone, in accord with her grandmother's request. She then begins searching for her son in her country, which is still torn apart by war. Along the way, she publishes a newspaper that flourishes until its staff is gruesomely slaughtered by one of the warring factions. Nawal is captured, imprisoned, and repeatedly and brutally raped by a sadistic guard, Abou Tarek, who has become notorious as a torturer of prisoners. Once again she becomes pregnant and bears a child, which is taken to the river, like all the other children Abou Tarek has fathered, to be drowned.

This backstory to the plot is sometimes revealed in dialogue among the characters, but mostly acted out on stage in flashbacks, in an intricate dance of plot construction. The play itself begins with a scene that takes place shortly after Nawal dies. Her two twenty-something children, the twins Simon and Janine, are at her solicitor's office to hear the reading of her will. The discovery that drives the plot occurs about five years before the action of the play begins but is dramatized in flashback, as in traditional tragedy, toward the end of the play. What Nawal saw and heard when she made her discovery is presented in the actions of a character, not narrated, and the audience learns what Nawal discovered in the same way that she discovered it, at the same time she is represented as discovering it. (All descriptions of Nawal's discovery occur in the endnotes to this essay, so that one can avoid the "spoilers" if one chooses.)

Nawal was a difficult woman, not the least because, for the last five years of her life, she refused to speak. Her silence haunts the action of the play and cries out for explanation. It is easy to read it as the passive-aggressive behavior of a petulant child, as the expression of a kind of powerlessness rather than the considered action of a rational adult. Simon and Janine, as children will—and they have more reason than most—see it as just one more way that their mother had of making their lives hell. But passive-aggressive behavior for her would be out of character, especially given the importance of words in her life. The possibility of madness is considered, naturally, but madness explains too little. The reason for her silence is also the reason for the instructions in her will for the peculiar way she wanted to be buried, for requiring Janine to find her father and give him a letter she wrote, and for requiring Simon to find his brother and give him another letter she wrote.

And the reason for her silence is also the reason for the one time she was known to break it, on her children's birthday, to utter the enigmatic sentence that she uttered when they were born, "Now that we're together, everything feels better," which runs like a mantra through the play. Hamlet has nothing on Nawal when it comes to injecting method into apparent madness.

The play explores a dialectic between her silence, on the one hand, and words, on the other—learning to read and returning to her grandmother's village to inscribe her name on her tombstone, the instructions for inscribing Nawal's name on her own tombstone, running a newspaper, the letters to be delivered by her children to their father and their brother. Nawal's writing and speaking play the same role as Oedipus's eyes. His eyes are the vehicle of his curiosity and desire to know, and when he obtains the horrific knowledge that he unwittingly sought, he plucks them out. Nawal's words are the vehicle of her agency, and writing and speaking out were central to her identity as a free person for all but the final five years of her adult life. What discovery, what contingency of circumstances, could make silence, instead of speech, a tragically fitting response to her discovery?

Structurally, Nawal's choice appears to be a Hegelian synthesis of two antithetical duties, even without our knowing what the discovery is or why silence is an appropriate response. She is faced with a Hegelian tragic dilemma, where she cannot speak without doing something wrong, where she cannot pursue one duty without failing in the other.[10] But her response is neither death nor madness; indeed, remaining silent while conscious and sane requires an extraordinary act of will and psychological strength.[11] Perhaps it deserves to be called by Miller's favored term, "enlightenment." Her behavior constitutes a kind of Hegelian synthesis of her antithetical duties, not mere redescriptions of individual bits of behavior but a globally different way of conceiving of and engaging with the world, one that was first misunderstood and resisted by her children, but eventually shared by them. Both her instructions to her children and the flashback structure of the play encourage an interpretation that points towards possibilities for the future rather than to eternal pollution caused by the sins of the past. The final scene of the play is not Nawal's discovery or the announcement of her decision to henceforth remain silent. The play ends with what her children do when they find out what her discovery was. They join with their mother in silence, revealing the meaning of the enigmatic sentence "Now that we're together, everything feels better."

Both how Nawal could have acquired conflicting duties and how she could have remained ignorant of the fact that they conflicted are due to unusual combinations of circumstances, made plausible by the virtually endless series of wars in the country of her birth, fueled by continuing cycles of revenge, where friends become enemies and enemies become friends. The tragedy in *Scorched* arises out of war, yet also feeds on there being strong bonds of family. Though the role of the individual within the family has changed in many respects since Aristotle's time, especially in the Western world, the family's potential for generating conflict and discovery, in the main, has not. Consider, for example, how a *non*traditional attitude towards family can prevent the uptake of a tragic plot. Bertolt Brecht's *Caucasian Chalk Circle* has the ingredients for a tragedy: a child's mother, in the confusion of a sudden invasion, flees to safety without her child, and the child ends up in the hands of someone who, though reluctantly at first, lovingly nurtures him for several years. *Circle*'s central dramatic moment, the courtroom decision about whether the birth mother or the woman who raised the child should henceforth be legally considered the child's mother, has the potential for a tragic denouement. But Brecht favored the rights of those people "who do the work," so to speak, over those who benefit from mere inheritance, and the play depicts it as right and fitting that the woman who nurtured him rather than the woman who bore him be considered the child's mother. For Brecht, it's not ultimately about families—except to the extent that they are the problem, not part of the solution.[12]

The importance of family is compounded by the importance of place and its relation to a person's sense of identity. Oedipus survives in spite of his ostracism, and his story is notably one of displacement: belonging in Thebes but growing up in Corinth, returning to Thebes as king, ostracism, and then returning to a specific site where the rituals surrounding his death are to be performed. Oedipus's children-siblings are trapped in the cycle of revenge, battling over their power and status within the city. Nawal, in contrast, takes her children with her to Canada. "The old country" is clearly identified as hers, not theirs, even though they were born there. In sending them back, Nawal clearly intends that her silence is not to be an erasure. Simon and Janine grew up away from the site of revenge; the problems they face in their lives are drift, a lack of grounding in history, but not the problem of being mired in a cycle of revenge.

Janine and Simon can live with the discovery they eventually share with their mother, but avoid the cycle of self-hatred and suicide that entraps those living in the "old country" and that threatened to entrap Nawal. *Scorched* is, in this sense, a play about how to live, about Nawal's silence as a way of transcending her conflicting duties and of sparing her children at least one tragic possibility of their aftermath. But the question about how to live is a personal question, one that is explored by the protagonist in his or her unique situation, not a general formula for the audience to live by. As a general formula, justice, as administered by a court, might help. We are told that Nawal, just before her silence, spent days in a courtroom, observing the trials being conducted by an international war tribunal, including the trial of the notorious Abou Tarek, at which she feels compelled to testify. She states that "to remain silent about your acts would make me an accomplice to your crimes" (64), and she recalls her promise to her grandmother to speak out. But *justice* goes only so far, and what can actually stop the cycle, if anything can, involves the special types of feelings that members of a family have for one another. The institutional reconciliation is not enough; it requires personal involvement in one's own situation. Sets of circumstances that are *not* the norm can destroy the emotional bonds that are expected to unite members of a family.[13] Indeed, Creon discovers, belatedly, the malignancy of his own edict because of its effects on his own family. Nawal is eventually able to say to Simon and Janine's father, about his children, "if you are capable of recognizing the invigorating beauty inside them, then there will be hope" (63).

It is a feature of modern drama, beginning with the so-called bourgeois tragedy of the seventeenth century, that tragic plots do not depend on the protagonist's having an important political position or social status or role. Arthur Miller insisted that the protagonist of a tragedy could be the "common" man or woman, and that the importance of enlightenment—for our purposes, discovery—is just as deep for persons with no special status in a society as for its leaders. Unlike *Death of a Salesman,* Miller's slightly later play *All My Sons* (1947) qualifies as a tragedy with a discovery plot and meets his "enlightenment" condition for tragedy, even though its protagonist, Joe Keller, is a deeply morally reprehensible man. Yet Keller does something (that Antigone, for example, does not) in eventually realizing that his war profiteering (selling defective cylinder heads for airplanes to the government) has resulted in the death of his own son, a pilot, and that he was therefore responsible for destroying one person—and, as it turns out, pretty much also the rest of his family and his closest friendships—whom his actions were intended to benefit. War in *All My Sons,* as in *Scorched,* provides for the unfortunate and unusual circumstances that lead to the action of the play. They do not lead to the senseless, meaningless "radical contingency" of human choice that finds its home in existentialism and theater of the absurd, but culminate in the meaningfulness of tragic discovery.

NOTES

1. My notion of discovery is quite different from Miller's notion of enlightenment, which is "in the largest sense, . . . knowledge pertaining to the right way of living in the world," or "the illumination of the ethical" (1996, 9). The two are not incompatible, however, and viewing tragedies with discovery plots may lead to enlightenment in Miller's sense.

2. Deborah Knight describes tragedy as "a narrative form of the sort originally described by Aristotle" (2009, 536) and contrasts it with a way of thinking about the "artistic vision" of an author or filmmaker. However, Aristotle does not see tragedy as a form of narrative, but contrasts it as drama with narrative.

3. Once again, technology threatens to displace this assumption about the canonical mode of presentation of a film. The DVD of *Memento* (Christopher Nolan, 2000), for example, provides the opportunity to view scenes of the film in chronological order, whereas the film as shown in theaters presented them in reverse chronological order.

4. Thus, it is not clear that externally imposed time constraints should be appealed to when examining why drama might have been thought by Aristotle have greater emotional impact than narrative. For a contrary view, see Meager (1960).

5. Storm (1998) argues that *sparagmos,* the ritual dismemberment of the self, is central to tragedy.

6. For the tradition of revenge tragedy, which may be used as a context for appreciating *Hamlet,* see Rist (2008).

7. The general subject of tragedy and irony is too large and complicated to explore here. See, however, Menke (2009).

8. Meager (1960, 170–71). Interestingly, Meager does not discuss the concept of *anagnorisis* in her analysis. She concentrates more on Aristotle's requirement that a tragedy be dramatic rather than narrative in form, and on its relation to the emotive power of tragedy, points to which I turn below.

9. For argument that in tragedy actions are represented as independent of character and that character is not embedded within one's actions, see Belfiore (1992, 91–92).

10. In *Antigone,* it is clear that Creon's edict is responsible for the tragedy and for tragic irony. In his penetrating analysis of Sophocles' Oedipus trilogy, Christoph Menke argues that the tragedy in *Oedipus Tyrannus* is generated by Oedipus's edict that the person responsible for the plague on the city must suffer, and the edict is tragically ironic. One might take a similar line with *Scorched,* seeing the tragedy as generated by Nawal's making unconditional promises to her son and to her grandmother. However, one might argue that in the case of her promise to her son, it merely makes explicit what is a moral duty, to love one's children, whether or not one promises to do so. Further, the same point cannot be made with respect to her promise to her grandmother. Nevertheless, it is her *choice* to give up her son that Nawal regrets, not the *promises* she makes to her son or her grandmother.

11. This "mere" exercise of reason takes on the dimensions of Nietzschean fortitude. There are other Nietzschean elements in the play, such as the mythic role of "the woman who sings," but there is not space to explore them here.

12. Janine and Simon were cared for by a family that rescued them from the river. But the family laid no claim to keeping them as their own, and were eager to turn them over to Nawal. If they had sued for custody, the tragedy of the story would have been entirely different.

13. Abou Tarek testifies at his own trial, and during his unrepentant grandstanding in front of the court he takes out a little red clown's nose that was given to him by his mother—the clown's nose that Nawal gave to her son before he was taken away from her. Abou Tarek turns out to be her torturer and both father and brother to her children. As with Oedipus, there was unintentional incest. This is the son whom she promised always to love, and the torturer about whose acts she has promised to speak out.

REFERENCES

Aristotle. 1982. *Aristotle's Poetics.* Translated by James Hutton. New York: W. W. Norton.
Belfiore, Elizabeth S. 1992. *Tragic Pleasures: Aristotle on Plot and Emotion.* Princeton: Princeton University Press.
Knight, Deborah. 2009. "Tragedy and Comedy." In *The Routledge Companion to Philosophy and Film,* edited by Paisley Livingston and Carl Plantinga, 536–45. London: Routledge.
Krutch, Joseph Wood. 1929. *The Modern Temper: A Study and a Confession.* New York: Harcourt, Brace.
Meager, Ruby. 1960. "Tragedy." *Proceedings of the Aristotelian Society Proceedings,* supp. vol. 34: 165–86.
Menke, Christoph. 2009. *Tragic Play: Irony and Theater from Sophocles to Beckett.* Translated by James Phillips. New York: Columbia University Press.
Miller, Arthur. 1996. "Tragedy and the Common Man." In *The Theater Essays of Arthur Miller,* edited by Robert A. Martin and Steven R. Centola, 3–7. New York: Da Capo Press.
Mouawad, Wajdi. 2005. *Scorched.* Translated by Linda Gaboriau. Toronto: Playwrights Canada Press.
Rist, Thomas. 2008. *Revenge Tragedy and the Drama of Commemoration in Reforming England.* Aldershot: Ashgate.
Storm, William. 1998. *After Dionysus: A Theory of the Tragic.* Ithaca: Cornell University Press.
Unamuno, Miguel de. 1972. *The Tragic Sense of Life in Men and Nations.* Translated by Anthony Kerrigan. Princeton: Princeton University Press.

Imagination, Fiction, and Documentary

Derek Matravers

It is my contention in this essay that work on narrative fiction has been vitiated by a confusion between two distinctions, both marked using the concept of the imagination.[1] Once this is clarified, the fog lifts and the lie of the land can be seen not to be as it was thought to be.

Particularly clear statements of the confusion can be found in two of the seminal contributions to the modern debate. The first is from Colin Radford, who is considering the view that our psychological engagement with fictions can be explained by our forgetting we are watching a play, and treating the fictional characters as real persons: "If we really did think someone was being slain, either a person called Mercutio or the actor playing that role, we would try to do something or think we should" (2002, 242). The second is from Kendall Walton, who is raising the question of the best way of characterizing our psychological attitudes to fictional characters, given that we are unable to interact with them: "To allow that mere fictions are the objects of our psychological attitudes while disallowing the possibility of physical interaction severs the normal links between the physical and the psychological. What is pity or anger which is never to be acted on? What is love that cannot be expressed to its object and it logically or metaphysically incapable of consummation? We cannot even try to rescue Robinson Crusoe from his island, not matter how deep our concern for him."[2]

The confusion, however, is still rife. Here is a more recent example. Aaron Meskin and Jonathan Weinberg are presenting "a theory of the cognitive imagination as it functions in our engagement with fiction" (2006,

222): "Yet we do not (generally) find audience members behaving fully as they do when they have emotional responses in ordinary (i.e., nonfictive) life. Horror movie viewers do not typically flee the cinema screaming" (224).

The basic argumentative strategy common to all three is to argue that, prima facie, the situation demands action and yet action is not forthcoming. The explanation that is given in each case is that the situation with which we are confronted is fictional. The structure of the argument is as follows. Were the situation nonfictional, we would be in the kind of mental state that would motivate us to act. As we are not motivated to act, we can infer that we are not in that kind of mental state. Hence, we must be in some different kind of mental state (that is, one characteristic of fiction) that does not carry a motivation to act. In short, we read back from the absence of motivation to the nature of the mental state characteristic of fiction. In the first example, the absence of motivation is given as a reason for the claim that the mental state we are in is not belief. In the second case, the absence of motivation is given as a reason for the claim that our apparent psychological attitudes, such as pity and anger, cannot really be those attitudes. In the third case, our absence of motivation is given as a reason for the claim that our "affective responses to fiction" share some but not all of "its non-fictive analogue" (Meskin and Weinberg 2006, 224).

This argumentative structure, however, is flawed, as it is clearly not the case that were the situation nonfictional, we would be in the kind of mental state that would motivate us to act. One can see this if quite easily if one changes each example such that the situation with which the audience is faced is nonfictional. Imagine, in the first instance, one is watching a dramatic reenactment of (for example) Darnley's assassination of David Rizzio. The assassins burst in and Rizzio is run through with a sword. The audience (rightly) do not believe they are watching a fiction, and yet clearly they do not try to do something or think they should. In the second case, one can simply change the example from the fictional Robinson Crusoe to the non-fictional Alexander Selkirk, an actual marooned sailor on whose experiences Defoe drew in writing his novel. Once again, it makes no difference for the motivation to action: there is still no possibility of physical interaction. It makes no difference to the final example whether the object being watched is a horror movie or a documentary about the First World War. In neither case would it make any sense at all of the audience to "flee the cinema screaming," as in neither case would fleeing the cinema alter the risk the audience faces from what is depicted on the screen.

Special cases aside, what is going on is this. Representations depict events happening in some other place and (generally) at some other time.[3] It is the content of the representation that is the object of our psychological attitudes, and any motivations we would have would be directed to that: that is, to something happening in some other place and (generally) at some other time. Hence, there is no reason at all—not even any prima facie reason—to think that some explanation is needed as to why we are not motivated to act either towards or away from the representation itself. The absence of motivation follows trivially from the fact that what we are confronted with is a representation. Whether the content of the representation is fictional or not is irrelevant: motivation is absent whether the representation is fiction or nonfiction (I shall refer to a nonfictional representation as "a documentary"). Put generally, the difference between the two scenarios is this. In what I shall call "a confrontation-relation," the object of our perception would also be the object of our action were we to choose to act. In what I shall call "a representation-relation," the object of our perception would not be the object of our action were we to choose to act.[4] To make the point intuitively with an example, I obstruct the person who is trying to hit an acquaintance, I do not obstruct the representation of someone trying to hit an acquaintance. As the usual case is that we have confrontation relations with things in our immediate environment, and representation relations with things not in our immediate environment, I will also use this way of making the distinction.

There is a problem with this distinction that stems from a discussion by Walton of a different topic: his claim that photographs are "transparent" (see Walton 2008). This is the claim that if I look at a photograph of an X, then the object of my perception is the X. This would make all relations in which I was looking at a documentary photograph confrontation relations, as in all cases the object of our perception would also be the object of our action were we to choose to act. However, as numerous of Walton's critics have pointed out, a photograph of X does not spatially locate X with respect to the observer. Hence, someone who chose to act on the object of their perception would not be able to as he or she would not know where to find it. The easiest way to deal with this problem is to include cases in which we are in perceptual contact with the object but cannot spatially locate it with respect to ourselves, as representation relations.[5]

The two distinctions mentioned in my opening paragraph can now be stated clearly. Imagination has been used to mark the distinction between a confrontation relation and a representation relation, the latter requiring imagination in the way the former does not. It has also been used to mark the distinction between documentary and fiction, with, again, the latter requiring the imagination in the way the former does not. Imagination is needed for the first distinction, but not for the second. Furthermore, the distinctions are completely independent of each other.

It would make for a neat world if full motivations were always engaged in confrontation relations and never engaged in representation relationships. However, confrontation relations might not engage our motivations; I might just not care that the person in front of me is crying. Representation relations might engage our motivations; I might donate money to charity upon seeing a representation of poverty. There is a temptation to think that the fiction/nonfiction divide comes back in the latter case; that is, that it is only representation relations with documentaries that are able to engage our motivations. However, that is simply not the case. A representation relation with a fiction such as Harriet Beecher Stowe's *Uncle Tom's Cabin* or George Orwell's *1984* have had at least as great an effect on motivation as any documentary. One might try to refine this to the claim that only representation relations to documentaries can generate a motivation where the object of the motivation is part of the content of the documentary. Intuitively, a program about poverty could motivate me to help that particular child, yet Orwell's *1984* could not motivate me to help Winston Smith. However, this confuses the fiction/documentary distinction with the unreal/real distinction. There are plenty of fictions about real people and events that could generate a motivation towards those people and events. Furthermore, even the refined distinction could provide at most a sufficient condition for being a documentary. There are plenty of documentaries which have contents that could not be the object of our motivations: all documentaries whose content is sufficiently removed from us in time or space, for example.

Let us return to the main thread. The confusion I have identified is in an argumentative strategy that uses the absence of motivation to support some claim about our relation to fiction; my claim is that is that it would only support some claim about our relation to representations more generally. This confusion can, I will argue, be traced to Walton's discussion in *Mimesis as Make-Believe*. Walton argues that we engage with fictions via imagining their contents: "a fictional truth consists in there being a prescription or mandate in some context to imagine something" (1990, 39). In chapter 2 of the book "Fiction and Non-fiction," there is a nest of claims that do not sit happily together.

One role Walton has for the imagination is explicitly psychological: "Some histories are written in such a vivid, novelistic style that they almost inevitably induce the reader to imagine what is said, regardless of whether or not he believes it. (Indeed this may be true of Prescott's *History of the Conquest of Peru*.) If we think of the work as prescribing such a reaction, it serves as a prop in a game of make-believe" (71). In general, no special explanation is needed as to why I am engaged with events with which I am in a confrontation relation; I am aware of, and engaged with, my immediate environment. By contrast, some explanation is needed as to why I am engaged with events with which I am in a representation relation. Some representations engage us, and other representations do not. The explanation, as Walton says, is going to be a matter of the vivacity and interest with which the representation presents its content. What is it to be engaged with a representation? Again, as Walton argues, it is to "imagine what is said." Notoriously, Walton does not have an account of the imagination regarding the term "as a placeholder for a notion that has yet to be fully clarified" (21). Yet one function of the imagination is clear: it is to make the content of a representation alive for us, so that it engages us and provokes our sympathies and other psychological relations.

However, as is clear from the above quotation, imagination needs to play this role for a much larger class of representations than what we traditionally count as fictions. This much is evident from Walton's own words, where he explicitly includes Prescott's *History of the Conquest of Peru*—clearly a documentary representation. Walton is open about his claims being revisionary, that "the classifications need refining" and that "there are differences of degree along several dimensions" (72). His considered view is that "Works of fiction are simply representations in our special sense, works whose function is to serve as props in games of make-believe" (71). The problem, however, is that the "mandate to imagine" test is completely independent of our traditional distinction between fiction and nonfiction. Walton is too cautious with his inclusion of only "some histories," of which *History of the Conquest of Peru* is his exemplar (one publisher describes it as "filled with drama[;] every page captures the cruelty and pride of the conquistadors"). Any narrative that needs to engage us, including histories, biographies, and many newspaper reports, will require imagination to play this role. Hence, this role of the imagination does not tell us anything in particular about the traditional category of fiction—rather, it is needed to play this role in our engagement to narrative representations generally.

For which representations does the imagination not have this role to play? In his list of exemplars of nonfictions, Walton includes "philosophical treatises, mathematics textbooks, instruction manuals, recipes, legal documents and requests to pass the salt" (70). Many of these will not be narratives and hence not need us to psychologically engage with them in the right sense (many will, incidentally, such as philosophical treatises in dialogue form or instruction manuals in the form of animations). Walton's other examples are Darwin's *Origin of Species,* Prescott's *History of the Conquest of Peru,* and Sandburg's biography of Lincoln. Sandburg's biography notoriously subordinates historical detail to broader imaginative sweep, hence that too must join Prescott in Walton's extended category of fiction. What of Darwin's book? This is, I think, an interesting critical question. To what extent does Darwin employ the techniques of narrative, and to what extent does that undermine his book as pure science (the same question arises for those other two great unmaskers of human life, Marx and Freud)? To the extent that it is presented as a narrative, it will require that imagination have the role we are discussing.

The confusion comes in that Walton wants to preserve something of the traditional distinction between fiction and nonfiction: "The notion of fiction is a natural descendant of the one used by booksellers and librarians in separating fairy tales, short stories, novels, and Superman comic books from newspaper articles, instruction manuals, geography textbooks, biographies, and histories" (72). As the "mandated to imagine" test is not going to give us this distinction, Walton adverts to a different argument in order to preserve something like the traditional distinction (once again, the example is *The Origin of Species*): "In writing his book Darwin no doubt intended to get readers believe certain things. But there is no understanding to the effect that readers are to believe whatever the book says just because it says it. If we are to believe the theory of evolution, it is because that theory is true, or because there is good evidence for it, not because it is expressed in *The Origin of Species*—though of course *The Origin of Species* might convince us of the theory's truth or inform us of evidence for it" (70). In order to reconstruct Walton's thought here, we need to make use of his notion of "entertaining a proposition." For Walton, this is a weak notion, similar to considering or having in mind a proposition (20). The thought then might be this. In engaging with a representation, we entertain what is expressed in that representation. For some representations, including all of what we traditionally think of as fiction but a lot more besides, we also imagine what is expressed in that representation: "imagining . . . is doing something with a proposition one has in mind" (20). This stage, the imagining stage, is the point and purpose of many of those representations we think of as fictions. However, for some representations there is an additional question which is independent of all this: namely, should we believe the content of the representation? If we should, the question of which of the propositions that we imagine we also believe is settled by whether those propositions are true: that is, by the way the world is. It is those propositions, namely those for which this question arises and is settled in this manner, that are a large part of the traditional class of nonfictional representations. The rest of the class is made up of many of those representations whose content we merely entertain and do not imagine, but which (again) we believe only if we think their content is true.

Notice that it is part of the structure of the distinction Walton is drawing here that there is a stage of our engaging with representations (where we imagine their content) which is common to those for which the question of belief arises and those for which the question of belief does not arise. In other words, the story of our engaging with narratives is independent of whether we take them to be fictional or nonfictional. That is, as Walton says, "imagining something is entirely compatible with knowing it to be true" (13). However, there is a tendency in the literature (as we can see from the three examples with which I started) to contrast our attitude to propositions true in fictions ("make-belief") with our attitudes to propositions true in the actual world ("belief"). We can see now that the situation is more complicated. Whether I believe the narrative I am reading to be documentary or fiction, I will imagine the propositions that form its content. A simple further thought would be that in the case of documentary, we not only imagine the propositions but also believe them, while in the case of fiction we imagine and yet do not believe.

This further thought, however, is too simple. There are many propositions (such as metaphors) in documentaries that we do not believe. It is also the case that we believe almost all the content of almost all fictions. While we might not believe that Mr. Darcy proposed to Elizabeth Bennet, we do believe that people breathe air, walk on the ground, wear clothes, seldom if ever spontaneously combust, and so on (all arguably part of the content of *Pride and Prejudice*). We can learn about the real world (even banal facts about the real world) through fiction; much of what I believe about the history of the East Anglian landscape I learned through Graham Swift's novel *Waterland* (see Friend 2008). The relation between engaging with a narrative—for which we need the imagination—and our subsequent beliefs is a complicated one, and fortunately one that is amenable to empirical study. In an article which summarizes their own and much other research, Prentice and Gerrig argue for two conclusions, both amenable to the line taken in this essay. First, that there is "nothing unique about the experience of fiction, and no need to invoke special mental processes to account for it."[6] Second, that the difference (or at least one difference) between fiction and nonfiction lies in the way the information is processed (that is, the route from imagination to belief).

The interesting consequence of this is that, given that we need the mental state of imagining that p to explain our engagement with narratives (whether fiction or documentary), it does not do any further work in explaining our mental attitude to propositions that are true in fictions. Once again, there seems a confusion in the literature. Consider the following argument.

> Suppose that I walk through the middle of a child's game of mud-pies, inadvertently stepping on little Johnny's carefully crafted glob of mud. Johnny bursts into floods of tears, and I realize (having in the past played games of this sort myself) that it is make-believedly the case that I have just ruined a beautiful pie. . . . Compare this to the case in which Johnny inadvertently steps on and flattens his own glob of mud. Again, he is likely to be distressed at this, and again we might say— following Walton's theory—that the cause of his distress is his belief that make-believedly he has ruined his pie. But, again, there is a better explanation available to us. Johnny is distressed not because he *believes* that it is make-believe that he has ruined his pie, but rather because he is *making-believe* that he has ruined it. The difference between Johnny and me is that his standpoint is *internal* to the game, mine is *external*. From the external standpoint, one has *beliefs* about what is make-believedly the case relative to the game. (Neill 1991, 51; cf. Currie 1990, 210)

What is right in this argument is that "believing it is make-believe the case" or "believing that it is imaginary that" will not distinguish between what Neill characterizes as the "external" and the "internal" standpoint. What is wrong is the implication that this has anything in particular to do with fiction. There is an external and an internal standpoint on Prescott's *History of the Conquest of Peru*. I might believe that it is part of the content of that book that the Inca commander, Quizquiz, was massacred by his own soldiers in cold blood—that would be an external standpoint. The internal standpoint—being gripped by the narrative—requires that not only do I believe it to be part of the content, I make-believe it (or imagine it) as well.

It is easy to see how this confusion arose. The natural reading of make-believe as an operator on propositions (it is make-believe the case that p) is that p is part of the content of a fiction rather than documentary. It is then easy to move to the thought that the contents of the propositional attitude of make-believe are propositions that have make-believe as an operator (that is, the contents of fiction). That is, it is easy to think that we make-believe only those propositions that are make-believe. However, as we have seen, the contents of the propositional attitude are the contents of both fictional and documentary representations: those which are make-believe the case, and those which are really the case. To repeat, it follows from what we have said so far that there is no distinctive mental state connected with engaging with fiction.

What consequences for philosophy are there for sorting out the confusion? Two distinct questions emerge. The first concerns the nature with our engagement with narrative. Once it is shorn of any reference to fiction (in the traditional sense), Walton's work on the imagination has done much to throw light on this issue. I shall simply assert here that there are two ways in which the literature since Walton has gone wrong. First, there is a tendency to focus on the propositional imagination: affective states get in, if at all, as a result of our propositional imaginings. This neglects nonpropositional engagement, through effects that alter mood, set up expectations, or operate through other priming effects.[7] Second, it has been thought that our engagement with narrative must conform to all features of the imagination, including it being impossible to imagine contradictory states of affairs. This seems to me an error; it is simply a datum that, in terms of our psychological engagement, there is no interesting distinction between possible and impossible fictions (although there are problems in this area; see Stock 2003). The second question concerns the distinction between fiction and nonfiction. This tends to get confused with a myriad of other distinctions: between that which we imagine and that which we believe, between that which is true and that which is make-believe, and between that which is real and that which is imaginary. Once again, Walton's discussion has advanced this issue with his talk of the grounds for our beliefs. The important point is not to confuse these two questions: our engagement with narrative is one issue, the distinction between fiction and nonfiction quite another.

NOTES

1. The main points of this essay can be found in Matravers (1998). However, it is only recently that I have realized their full significance.

2. Walton (1990, 196). Walton does fall prey to the confusion in this passage. However, in other passages he seems aware that there is a problem, even if (as I will argue later) he does not get the problem fully into focus.

3. The literature on this topic, as one can see from the examples, covers various different media including film and the written word. I shall restrict myself to the written word; it strikes me that our imaginative engagement with film might demand a different story (although I shall not argue for that here).

4. I am grateful to Cressida Gaukroger for suggesting this way of putting the point.

5. Walton's essay suggests other, more problematic cases. What if one is having a fight with someone in a hall of mirrors? One can see the person's image, but one cannot locate the person. Intuitively, this seems to me a confrontation relation. For the points I would like to make, I do not need the claim that the distinction between confrontation and representation relations will always and everywhere be clear.

6. Prentice and Gerrig (1999, 530). I am grateful to Stacie Friend for drawing my attention to this essay, which I have obviously not dealt with fully here. I hope to remedy this on some future occasion.

7. Amy Coplan has developed a research program on this, some of the results of which have been presented as conference papers.

REFERENCES

Currie, Gregory. 1990. *The Nature of Fiction.* Cambridge: Cambridge University Press.

Friend, Stacey. 2008. "Imagining Fact and Fiction." In *New Waves in Aesthetics,* edited by Kathleen Stock and Katherine Thomson-Jones, 150–69. Basingstoke: Palgrave Macmillan.

Matravers, Derek. 1998. *Art and Emotion.* Oxford: Oxford University Press.

Meskin, Aaron, and Jonathan Weinberg. 2006. "Imagine That!" In *Contemporary Discussions in Aesthetics and the Philosophy of Art,* edited by, Matthew Kieran, 222–35. Oxford: Basil Blackwell.

Neill, Alex. 1991. "Fear, Fiction and Make-Believe." *Journal of Aesthetics and Art Criticism* 49 (1): 47–56.

Prentice, Deborah A., and Richard J. Gerrig. 1999. "Exploring the Boundary Between Fiction and Reality." In *Dual-Process Theories in Social Psychology,* edited by Shelly Chaiken and Yaacov Trope, 529–46. New York: Guilford Press.

Radford, Colin. 2002. "How Can We Be Moved by the Fate of Anna Karenina?" In *Arguing About Art,* edited by Alex Neill and Aaron Ridley, 239–49. London: Routledge.

Stock, Kathleen. 2003. "The Tower of Goldbach and Other Impossible Tales." In *Imagination, Philosophy, and the Arts,* edited by Matthew Kieran and Dominic M. Lopes, 107–24. London: Routledge.

Walton, Kendal. 1990. *Mimesis as Make-Believe: On The Foundations of The Representational Arts*. Cambridge, Mass.: Harvard University Press.

———. 2008. "Transparent Pictures: On the Nature of Photographic Realism." In *Marvellous Images: On Values and the Arts*, 79–116. Oxford: Oxford University Press.

Contributors

Noël Carroll is a Distinguished Professor in the Philosophy Program at the Graduate Center of the City University of New York. His most recent books are *The Philosophy of Motion Pictures, On Criticism, A Very Short Introduction to Humour,* and *Art in Three Dimensions.*

Richard Eldridge is Charles and Harriett Cox McDowell Professor of Philosophy at Swarthmore College. He is the author of *Literature, Life, and Modernity* (Columbia University Press, 2008) and *The Persistence of Romanticism* (Cambridge University Press, 2001) and the editor of *The Oxford Handbook of Philosophy and Literature.*

Susan L. Feagin is Visiting Research Professor of Philosophy at Temple University and editor of the *Journal of Aesthetics and Art Criticism.* She is the author of *Reading with Feeling: The Aesthetics of Appreciation* (Cornell University Press, 1996), editor of *Global Theories of Aesthetics and the Arts* (Wiley-Blackwell, 2005), and coeditor of *Aesthetics* (Oxford University Press, 1997). She writes on issues that intersect philosophy of art and philosophy of mind, and on literature, the visual arts, and film.

Berys Gaut is Professor of Philosophy at the University of St. Andrews. He writes mainly on issues in aesthetics, the philosophy of film, creativity, and moral philosophy. Besides being the author of numerous articles, he is the author of *Art, Emotion and Ethics* (Oxford University Press, 2007) and *A Philosophy of Cinematic Art* (Cambridge University Press, 2010). He is also coeditor of *The Routledge Companion to Aesthetics* (Routledge, 2nd ed., 2005), *The Creation of Art* (Cambridge University Press, 2003), and *Ethics and Practical Reason* (Oxford University Press, 1997).

John Gibson is Associate Professor of Philosophy at the University of Louisville. He is the author of *Fiction and the Weave of Life* (Oxford University Press, 2007) and coeditor of *A Sense of the World: Essays on Fiction, Narrative, and Knowledge* (Routledge, 2007) and *The Literary Wittgenstein* (Routledge, 2004). He is currently writing an introduction to the philosophy of literature for Routledge and completing a manuscript on meaning in poetry and metaphor.

Peter Goldie is the Samuel Hall Chair at the University of Manchester. His main philosophical interests are in the philosophy of mind, ethics and aesthetics, and particularly in questions concerning value and how the mind engages with value. He is the author of *The Emotions: A Philosophical Exploration* (Clarendon Press, 2000) and *On Personality* (Routledge, 2004) and coauthor of *Who's Afraid of Conceptual Art?* (Routledge, 2009). He is editor of *Understanding Emotions: Mind and Morals* (Ashgate, 2002), coeditor of *Philosophy and Conceptual Art* (Oxford University Press, 2006), and editor of *The Oxford Handbook of Philosophy of Emotion* (Oxford University Press, 2009). He is writing a monograph on narrative for Oxford University Press.

Derek Matravers is a Senior Lecturer in Philosophy at the Open University and an Associate Lecturer at the University of Cambridge. His current interests lie in aesthetics, particularly with our engagement with various forms of art. To this end he is working on a book on value, and also researching mental states such as empathy and what role (if any) they play in our engagement with narratives. He is the author of *Art and Emotion* (Clarendon Press, 1998), as well as numerous articles in aesthetics, ethics, and the philosophy of mind.

Amy Mullin is Professor of Philosophy at the University of Toronto. She works primarily on topics in aesthetics and feminist theory.

Aaron Smuts is Assistant Professor in the Philosophy Department at Rhode Island College. Aaron's interests range across a wide variety of topics in ethics, the philosophy of art, metaphysics, and general value theory, such as: the nature of pleasure, well-being, love, the metaphysics of death, humor, the appeal of horror, and the nature of aesthetic value. He has published over two dozen articles in a variety of books and academic journals. His website is http://www.aaronsmuts.com.

Index